Intimate Exchanges

A Play

Alan Ayckbourn

Volume II

Samuel Fre
New York – Sya

INTIMATE EXCHANGES

First produced at the Stephen Joseph Theatre in the Round, Scarborough, on 3rd June 1982

with the following Cast

Celia **Rowena** **Sylvie** **Josephine,** Celia's mother **Irene Pridworthy**	Lavinia Bertram
Miles, Rowena's husband **Toby,** Celia's husband **Lionel** **Joe,** Lionel's father **Reg Schooner**	Robin Herford

Directed by Alan Ayckbourn

Designed by Edward Lipscomb

Subsequently produced at the Greenwich Theatre on 11th June 1984 and the Ambassador's Theatre on 13th August 1984, with the same cast, director and designer

INTIMATE EXCHANGES
A related series of plays

Volume I

Volume II

INTIMATE EXCHANGES

Volume II

Volume I of *Intimate Exchanges*, containing the four plays on the left-hand side of the plan, is available from Samuel French Ltd.

AUTHOR'S NOTE

These plays were written originally for a cast of two. They could of course be performed by a larger cast but the end result would, in my view, be infinitely less satisfying. Similarly with choice of alternatives; it's possible to do just one version but far less theatrically exciting. If, for some unavoidable reason, a decision is taken to mount only one alternative, or one alternative with a larger cast, or even several alternative versions with a larger cast, I would be grateful if the audience could be informed of my original preferences. This would serve (a) to explain why the plays are so idiosyncratically constructed and (b) to let people know what they've missed.

A.A.

INTIMATE EXCHANGES is a related series of plays totalling eight scripts

This is the Fifth

A CRICKET MATCH

CHARACTERS
APPEARING IN THIS SERIES OF SCENES

Celia
Miles
Sylvie
Josephine
Toby
Rowena
Lionel
Reg Schooner

HOW IT BEGAN

Toby and Celia's garden. Since this set will cover all possible seven scenes during the first half of the play, it will vary only in that occasionally we may wish to feature one area more prominently than another. In total, though, it is a well-kept garden which has been left, over the past few years, to go very much to seed. A garden which gives children great opportunities for play and most adults huge feelings of guilt that it isn't tidier. There is a small paved area at one side, the patio, bounded by a low wall which presumably leads directly off the lounge of the house. There is a garden table on this but no chairs. The table, it would appear, has been left out all winter. On it is an empty coffee cup, a packet of cigarettes and a lighter. A lumpy lawn, some of it may even have been flower beds at one time, leads to a garden shed at the bottom of the garden. Beyond that and unseen is a fence. And beyond that again playing fields. From this direction, throughout this scene, occasional shouts of children are heard

All the garden belongs of course to the house, although this is in fact a bungalow. Or sometimes, as it is more grandly known, the Headmaster's Cottage. It is modern, built by Toby's predecessor within the grounds of Bilbury Lodge, Preparatory School for Boys and Girls. It is a mild, sunny June day—in fact, Monday June 14th. The summer term is underway

In a moment, Celia, a rather worried-looking woman in her mid-thirties, comes out of the house. She has on her working-clothes with a scarf tied round her head. She is evidently involved in some heavy domestic cleaning work

Celia (*calling back into the house*) They must be in the shed. I'll have a look. . . . Listen, Sylvie, you carry on up in the loft. I'll join you, all right? (*She listens, then calls*) Sylvie . . .

There is no reply

Celia shrugs, then, stands for a moment on the patio to catch her breath. She's obviously been overdoing it more than she realizes. She squints into the sun and breathes the fresh air for a moment. She then looks at herself and cursorily brushes some of the dust off her clothes. She mops her brow with her forearm. Glad of the rest, she now goes to move off towards the shed. Her eyes light on the cigarette packet on the table. She hesitates, stopping in her tracks. She deliberates. Should she or shouldn't she weaken to temptation?

In fact, at this point, we reach the first of our alternatives. Throughout the play, the action will sub-divide as the characters are faced with alternative choices of action. Initially, the choices are smaller. Should she break her rule and have a cigarette before 6 p.m.?

A VISIT FROM A FRIEND

In this instance, Celia resists the temptation and virtuously goes off down the garden and into the shed. Although the inside of this is not much visible during this particular scene, we hear her from the inside and gather it is fairly cluttered with junk

Celia (*in the shed*) Oh, God. (*She clumps about looking for something*)

Sound of the front doorbell. Celia, not hearing it, carries on sorting

(*In the shed*) I mean, honestly. . . . How is anyone expected to . . . (*she grunts as she heaves something heavy down*) . . . find anything in this . . . uggh. (*She clumps and grunts some more*)

Sound of the front doorbell

The noises in the shed stop

Celia sticks her head out of the shed door and listens, uncertain if she heard anything or not. Hearing nothing more, she goes back into the shed. A moment later, she emerges with a step ladder. Closing the shed door, she lugs the ladder back towards the house. Again, she passes the cigarettes on the patio. Again she pauses, tempted. She stands, deliberating

Miles enters. He is a lean, rather sad man about the same age as Celia

Miles Celia.
Celia Oh, hallo, Miles.
Miles How are things?
Celia Super. Was that you?
Miles I'm sorry.
Celia Was that you ringing?
Miles No.
Celia The doorbell.
Miles No.
Celia Just now.
Miles No.
Celia I thought I heard somebody.
Miles I don't think it was me. No, it couldn't have been. Hang on, it could have very possibly been Hepplewick.
Celia Hepplewick.
Miles You know, Lionel Hepplewick. I thought I saw him stomping away a minute ago.
Celia Oh. Really. Wonder what he wanted.
Miles You're looking busy.

Celia Yes. I'm taking down the sitting-room curtains.
Miles Ah. Yes.
Celia Sylvie and I are just having a clear out.
Miles Spring cleaning.
Celia In June, yes. Better late than never.
Miles Er—Celia. Have you a minute to spare?
Celia Not really, no.
Miles (*stymied*) Oh. All right, then.

Pause

Celia If you don't mind, Miles, we're frightfully busy.
Miles Yes.
Celia I mean, I'm absolutely . . . we're absolutely . . . well, we're completely.
. . . (*Irritably*) You can see we are, surely?
Miles Oh, yes, yes, yes. No, no, no. Doesn't matter. No, no.

A silence. Miles continues to stand there

Celia It's obviously important.
Miles Yes, well . . .
Celia Oh, Lord. OK. (*She stands, still holding the steps*)
Miles Do you want to put those down?
Celia (*ignoring this suggestion*) It's not something you could possibly talk to
Toby about, is it?
Miles Not really, no.
Celia Oh.
Miles It's really about Toby, you see.
Celia Oh, why talk to me, Miles? Why me?
Miles You're his wife, Celia, for one thing.
Celia Yes, I know but . . . there's nothing I can say. What Toby does is his
own concern. Talk to him.
Miles It's more than just Toby. It's the school as well, Celia, I'm talking
about the school.
Celia Then talk to the Headmaster. I'm only his wife. I don't have any
influence. I'm just an honorary non-voting, non-participating . . . thing in
the background. There's no point in talking to me, Miles. Honestly there
isn't.
Miles That isn't true, Celia, you know it. (*After a pause*) You're certainly
not a thing. (*After a pause*) Look. Look, I'm taking the gloves off now,
Celia, and I'm going to put all the cards on the table and I'm going to be
absolutely frank. Now, I'm wearing my Chairman of the Board of
Governors hat at the moment, all right?
Celia Hat, no gloves.
Miles Sorry?
Celia Look, I've left Sylvie in the loft.
Miles You're the absolute hub of this place, you know that, Celia. The rack
and pinion of this establishment. The whole institution would cave in
without you.
Celia Rubbish.

Miles Everyone comes to you with their troubles. . . .
Celia Well, they do that, yes. Because I'm stupid enough to listen.
Miles The staff come to you. The kids come to you. The parents.
Celia The parents certainly do.
Miles Well, then. You're marvellous. Not a non-participating thing at all.
Very much the reverse. If Toby only had one quarter of that.
Celia I'm sorry. I'm not prepared to start talking about Toby.
Miles Yes, that shows great loyalty. Great loyalty.
Celia Nothing to do with loyalty. I'm just sick to death talking about him.
Let's talk about me.
Miles Just one micro-second, I promise you.
Celia (*reluctantly*) Well, wait there a minute. I'll have to go and sort Sylvie
out first. She's straddled up there in the rafters.
Miles Do you want me to . . .?
Celia No, for heaven's sake don't come in here, it's frightful. I'll be back.
(*Then, as an afterthought*) Oh, could you fish a couple of chairs out of the
shed?
Miles Yup.

Celia goes into the house with the stepladder

(*After she's gone, rather lamely*) Don't be too long, will you? I've got a
meeting in a few . . . oh. (*His voice tails away and he mutters to himself*)
Got to talk to the Board.

*Miles wanders towards the shed, still muttering to himself. At first, these
mutterings seem fairly incomprehensible but then it transpires he's running
over his speech*

Meeuurrr . . . meeuurrr . . . nah- nah-nah-nah . . . meeuurrr . . . nah, ladies
and gentlemen of the Board . . . here is a . . . meeuurrr who over the
meeuurrr has been nah-meeuurrr and meeuurrr. Hair-hore . . . therefore
. . . (*He opens the door of the shed and pauses*) . . . therefore, before we rush
into this . . . no, before we leap into this . . . before we jump to—jump to
hasty judgements—conclusions. Rush into any hasty conclusions, let us be
quite certain, let's be perfectly certain . . . (*He finds two fold-up chairs just
inside the shed and pulls them out*) no, let us be sure that we're not
attempting to lay the blame for something at the door of a man . . . at the
feet of a man . . . on the head of a man . . . heap the blame on a man's feet
. . . no, on his head. Can't heap blame on his feet . . . on a man who is
himself limbless . . . no, blameless . . . oh, hell. (*He stands in the doorway of
the shed, having reached an impasse with his speech*)

Celia comes out of the house

Celia I've put the kettle on. Like a cup of something, would you?
Miles Oh, thanks. I think I've just got time. Here. (*He proffers the chairs*)
Celia Oh, well.

They assemble the chairs and sit

I'll say this for Sylvie, she's not very bright but once you've told her what to do and pointed her in the right direction, she's off like a dose of salts.

Miles That's the Bell girl, is it?

Celia Yes, the older one. Mrs Bell's eldest. She comes round twice a week. The best I've ever had. She won't last. She'll get married or something.

Miles Really? Who's she marrying?

Celia Oh, not yet. Not yet. She's a baby. I think Hepplewick's lurking somewhere.

Miles Lionel Hepplewick? Good heavens. Wouldn't want to marry him.

Celia So she tells me. She's playing it very cool, though, sensible girl.

Miles Well, look, anyway, I've got this meeting in a minute or two, Celia, so let me just . . .

Celia Don't let me forget the kettle.

Miles No, right. You see, the point is that things . . .

Celia I think I ought to say something, Miles, before you go any further. I really think I ought.

Miles Oh, are you sure you need to?

Celia You must have been aware that recently, Toby and I, we've—well, we've been barely rubbing along, to be quite honest. We've both been getting on each other's nerves most frightfully. Now, I realize he's having a very rough time at work. . . .

Miles He's having one hell of a time.

Celia Yes, I know. I can see what it's doing to him. I mean, most nights he's drinking himself senseless.

Miles Is he, is he?

Celia And most days. God, you must have noticed. Everyone's noticed.

Miles Well, now and then. I mean, I don't think I can say honestly and truly that I've ever seen Toby drunk on the job, not on the job. Off the job, yes. Yes, I'll concede that. Quite often. Off the job. But then what a chap does in his own time . . .

Celia Is my concern.

Miles Oh, yes. Put that way. . . . He gets very drunk, does he?

Celia Unbearably.

Toby Oh, dear. Poor old you. I didn't know. Of course, Rowena and I haven't seen much of you both lately. She's been so . . . with other things. We must sometime. Get together. One evening. Now it's summer and all that.

Celia The point is, I don't know how much longer we're going to be able to stay together. Toby and me.

Miles Oh, I see. (*After a pause*) I see.

Celia So.

Miles Yes.

Celia You're not surprised?

Miles No. Well, yes. I don't know. I don't think it's a very good idea, is it, Celia?

Celia It may not be to you. I don't think I can take much more of it, I really can't. He's violent. He's unpleasant. He's rude. He's unpredictable. And he never considers me for a minute. I don't think I can take much more of it. (*She seems very near tears*)

Miles (*embarrassed*) Oh, dear.
Celia I really don't.
Miles Yes, well, that's not really something I can. . . . You see, bluntly, Celia, Toby's no longer doing a very good job as Headmaster.
Celia I'm not surprised. He can hardly see where he's going most of the time.

Miles laughs rather feebly

No, honestly, Miles. He sets off some mornings for assembly, across that field there. I watch him from the bedroom window. He wanders round and round in circles looking for the gate.
Miles He may be thinking. He may be thinking, you know. People do walk in circles, Celia, when they're thinking.
Celia He gave up thinking a long time ago.
Miles Anyway, it's undoubtedly true that standards are slipping. Good staff are leaving and parents are now starting to complain.
Celia Don't tell me. Who do you think they complain to?
Miles Now the Governors themselves are involved. And my attention as Chairman has been drawn. Which puts me in a very nasty position as you can imagine. I'm going to see if I can hold them off. Colonel Malton is definitely out for blood, I can sense it. So is Irene Pridworthy who never liked Toby from the off, let's face it.
Celia Oh, well.
Miles As Chairman I am supposed to be impartial but of course everyone knows I'm not. Toby and I are—God, I put him up for the job, didn't I? Anyway, what I'm saying is I'll do what I can.
Celia I'm sure he'll appreciate it.
Miles The point is, do you think there's any guarantee, Celia, that he's going to try and pull his socks up in the future?
Celia Absolutely none, I should imagine.
Miles So I can't even tell them that? That he's making an effort.
Celia It would be very unwise of you.
Miles So what do I tell the Board?
Celia Don't ask me. Tell them they've employed a drunk. That's what he is.
Miles I'd hate to see you both go down the drain, Celia, I really would.
Celia Well. (*She reflects*) Oh, God, the kettle. Just a sec.

Celia nips back into the house

Miles Oh, dear. (*He gets up and paces about*) I don't know what I'm going to tell them. I can hardly say he's a drunk. Meeuurrr-nah . . . meeuurrr . . . meeuurrr . . . or let us contemplate, or even consider, yes, let us consider, rather, the record of this remarkable teacher. Five years, six years, five years ago, this school of only—of less than two hundred pupils, many of them girls at that, managed to produce a cricket team second to none. And I quote, although I'm sure Colonel Malton has these figures engraved in his hat. In his heart: played twelve, won nine, drawn three, lost none. I repeat, lost none. Or let us turn to squash. Out of nine matches . . . (*he breaks off as something in the field catches his attention. He* *calls*) Oh, good afternoon, Lionel. How are you . . .? Good. How's your father . . .? What? No, I said how's Mr Hepplewick . . .? Oh, good. Splendid. (*He watches Hepplewick depart*) He's a very odd cove, he is. Why are those kids playing soccer, it's the cricket season . . . Or squash. An unbeaten record, members of the Board. Let us not forget this when we . . .

Sylvie enters. She is a fresh faced, rather lumpen, awkward girl of around twenty. She is carrying a load of cardboard boxes, obviously part of the clearing out routine

Oh, hallo, Sylvie.
Sylvie (*shyly*) Afternoon, Mr Coombes.
Miles I was just—er——

Sylvie patters past him and round the back of the shed

Miles watches her

Sound of dustbin lids clattering

Sylvie (*off*) You go away. Go on. You just get away.

Sylvie appears in view. She is talking to someone in the field

Go on. Off you go. No, you buzz off. Go on. (*After a pause she turns satisfied, sees Miles and smiles shyly*) Some of 'em won't give up, will they?

Sylvie goes back into the house

Miles seems a little perplexed by this exchange

Miles (*resuming*) All this excellence surely points to a thriving headmaster. Ship. Headmastership. And surely, as we all know, and you'll be the first to know this, Colonel Malton, leadership only comes from the top.
Celia (*off*) Do you take sugar, Miles?
Miles Sorry?
Celia (*off*) No, put them with the others, Sylvie. Be sensible now. (*To Miles*) I said, do you like sugar?
Miles No, thank you, no. (*Continuing*) I'm going to be perfectly honest and say to you, yes, Mrs Pridworthy I do have an interested vested here, vested interest here. If you can call friendship an interest. Toby Teasdale is a friend. Celia Teasdale is a friend. Toby and I were at school together. A school, Reverend Fognorth, not unlike the one we're sat in today. As I look out of these windows . . . I better make sure I'm sitting the right way. Otherwise it'll have to be as I look out of this door. Not quite so good. At these grounds—at this hallway—steeped in tradition, I may be excused a small lump in my throat. For surely . . .

Celia appears with two mugs

Celia Here you are.
Miles Oh, thank you very much.

They sit with their coffee

Toby's going to fall apart, you know, if you leave him.

Celia I was under the impression he already had, actually.

Miles Well. If it is all over bar the shouting, I'll say this. He never deserved you.

Celia (*quite touched*) Oh, Miles.

Miles No, he didn't. Toby always takes everything just as it comes. Never a "thank you". Never a "good heavens, aren't I lucky"?

Celia True.

Miles I bet he's never said thank you to you, has he? Not in, what is it, ten years?

Celia (*thinking*) No. I can't remember him saying thank you. No. Still, you don't expect that, do you? People don't much. Husbands and wives. Go around saying thank you very much all the time, do they?

Miles I would have done. I'd have said thank you to you. Every day.

Celia Oh, that's lovely. Do you say that to Rowena a lot?

Miles I certainly don't. I've nothing to thank her for. Nothing at all. Quite the reverse. The way she behaves. I'm still waiting for a thank you from her.

Celia Oh. (*She doesn't want to get involved in this conversation*) I think Toby said "Well done" once or twice early on. Which was quite encouraging while it lasted. But then that sort of died out.

Miles Well done? What, do you mean in bed?

Celia Good Lord, no. He never said that in bed. Well done. Terribly offputting. No, I meant if I'd made a good pie or something. Got something cheap.

Miles (*mystified*) Cheap.

Celia When we were hard-up. Toothpaste or loo rolls or something. "Well done", he'd say.

Miles Not very romantic.

Celia Not romantic, no. I'm not saying that. I said it was quite encouraging. I can do without romance but I do need encouragement. Anyway.

Miles Perhaps I should have said that to Rowena more often. Well done.

Celia No, I don't think so. Not to Rowena. She's a different sort. She's not the well done sort. She's not a well done sort of person.

Miles winces

Oh, I'm sorry, Miles.

Miles That's all right.

Celia No, I didn't mean to say that.

Miles Just a rather unfortunate phrase, that's all.

Celia Yes, I'm dreadfully sorry. Really.

Miles So you're actually thinking of splitting up?

Celia Yes.

Miles What about the kids? Lucy and James? What's going to happen to them?

Celia They'll come with me, presumably. Wherever I end up.

Miles You'll take them away from the school? From here?

Celia I'll have to. It's a shame but—anyway, they're not that happy here, anyway.

Miles What nonsense.

Celia They're not.

Miles I've never seen two more happy children.

Celia Look, do you mind, they're my children. Don't start trying to tell me about my own kids.

Miles It's rubbish.

Celia I know when my children are happy and when they're not, thank you very much. I'll probably move back to London.

Miles Where to?

Celia Somewhere. I don't know.

Miles Seems a bit vague.

Celia Not at all. Maybe to my mother. Just temporarily.

Miles No, I don't believe this is going to happen. You won't split up. Anyway, people who are splitting up don't rush around spring cleaning, do they?

Celia They do if they want to sell the house. (*She rises*)

Miles And what about Toby?

Celia To hell with Toby.

Miles What am I going to tell the Board? That his wife's leaving him as well? I tell them that, that's virtually certain curtains on his career. You realize that, don't you?

Celia I don't care.

Miles Well, I'm telling you, it will be. There was just a chance, just a slim wafer of a chance—whisker of a chance, that if I played all the right cards, I could have given the Board pause for thought.

Celia Well, that's terribly noble of you, Miles, but to be quite honest, I think you're flogging a dead horse. Toby ought to go anyway. He's a liability, he really is.

Miles What are you saying?

Celia I'm saying that I don't consider he's a fit person to be Headmaster of a school any more. And if I wasn't leaving, I'd take the kids away anyway.

Miles What a terrible thing to say.

Celia Miles, it's true.

Miles You can't say that. Not about Toby, not about your own husband.

Celia Miles, he's an incoherent, ill-tempered, irrational, unpredictable slob. You know it and I know it. (*After a pause, she speaks more quietly*) And the kids are beginning to see it too, which is more to the point. I want to get them out before they get hurt. I don't care about me. . . . Now, I must get on. I'm sorry, Miles. I can see you're very shocked by what you consider my disloyalty to Toby but I've lived with the man now for twelve years and I can tell you the last four or five have been no joke, Miles, they really haven't.

Miles (*unhappily*) You can't expect it to be all fun all the time, Celia, you really can't.

Celia It has to be better than this. I deserve a little bit of fun. Sometimes. Surely. Before it's too late.

Miles He needs help badly, you know, Celia. You can't walk out on a man who's flat on his back.
Celia You're his friend, Miles, you pick him up. You're so fond of him apparently.
Miles So were you once.
Celia (*angrily*) Oh, go away, Miles. Just go right away. Go on, clear off.

Celia stamps into the house

Miles Look, Celia . . . oh. (*He stands still in frustration*)
Celia (*off, angrily*) Look, don't put that on there, Sylvie. Use a tiny bit of nous, girl. That is clean washing, Sylvie, isn't it?
Sylvie (*off*) Yes, Mrs Teasdale.
Celia You know the word clean, do you?
Sylvie Yes, Mrs Teasdale.
Celia You can be so stupid, stupid, stupid, Sylvie. Now look at them. Look at this.
Sylvie (*off*) Yes, Mrs Teasdale.

Miles moves away from all this, unhappily. He pauses in the middle of the garden, reaches in his pocket and takes out his diary. He consults it

Celia (*off*) Thank you so much. That's better. Now, will you put that out the back in the dustbins, not on the washing. That will be much more helpful. Off you go.

Sylvie comes out of the house. She is carrying an armload of old paint tins, very dusty and congealed

Sylvie (*speaking, as she comes*) Yes, Mrs Teasdale. (*She sees Miles, smiles and jerks her head to indicate Celia*) Done it again, haven't I?

Sylvie goes off to the dustbins

Miles moves towards the house

Miles (*calling tentatively*) Celia, Celia, could I. . . . (*He listens*) Celia?

Silence

Sound of a crash of tins from the dustbin area

Oh, hell.

Sylvie returns from the dustbins.

Sylvie I think she went up to the loft. She's in one of her moods.
Miles Ah.

Sylvie moves towards the house

Sylvie?
Sylvie Yes, Mr Coombes.
Miles Would you—could you tell Mrs Teasdale that—er——
Sylvie Go in, if you like, she's only just in the loft.
Miles No, it's all right. Could you tell her—er——

EITHER he says:

Miles Tell her I don't believe her and to prove it this Friday—have you got that—this Friday. . . .
Sylvie This Friday.
Miles No, it can't be Friday, that's the County Game—this Saturday, are you getting this. . . .
Sylvie You don't believe her and this Saturday—she's only just up the ladder . . .
Miles No, this Saturday we are all four of us having dinner together.
Sylvie Having dinner together.
Miles Like old times.
Sylvie Like old times.
Miles Right.
Sylvie Right.
Miles You tell her that.
Sylvie I will, Mr Coombes, I will. (*She begins to move inside*)
Miles This Saturday.
Sylvie Saturday, yes.

Sylvie goes inside

Miles (*pleased*) So there. (*He slams shut his diary and starts off down the garden*) Meeuurrr—nah . . . we've always, I think . . . I know, recognized Toby Teasdale as a man of strong quirks . . . quirky strength . . . strong quirkiness . . . in fact, it is his very quirkiness which first attached him to us . . . attracted him to us . . . us to him . . . oh, hell.

He disappears from view behind the shed and can be heard muttering into the distance as the Lights fade to a Black-out

To: DINNER ON THE PATIO (page 17)

OR he says:

Miles (*slamming his diary shut irritably*) You tell her I'm—I'm extremely disappointed in her.
Sylvie You're disappointed in her, right. (*She turns to go into the house*)
Miles No, hang on, I haven't finished. Also tell her——
Sylvie She's only just up the ladder in the loft. . . .
Miles No, no. Also tell her that I intend to stand by—she knows who—and to blazes with her. You tell her that.
Sylvie She knows who, to blazes with her. Yes, Mr Coombes.

Sylvie goes into the house

Miles (*pleased*) So there. (*He stuffs his diary back in his pocket and starts off down the garden*) Meeuurrr—nah . . . we've always, I think . . . I know, recognized Toby Teasdale as a man of strong quirks . . . quirky strength . . . strong quirkiness . . . in fact, it is his very quirkiness which first attached him to us . . . attracted him to us . . . us to him . . . oh, hell.

He disappears from view behind the shed and can be heard into the distance as the Lights fade to a Black-out

To: CONFESSIONS IN A GARDEN SHED (page 115)

DINNER ON THE PATIO

The same, with perhaps a little more of the patio area now in view. It is Saturday evening, June 19th, just before eight o'clock. It is a pleasant, mellow evening

The patio table now has four dining-room chairs round it and is laid for four people for a small informal dinner party. In the centre of the table is a candle in a glass bowl

There is the sound of shouts from children on the playing field

In a moment, Miles comes out from the house, a glass of sherry in his hand

Miles Oh, we're out here, are we?

Celia (*off*) Yes, I hope it will be all right.

Miles Lovely. Super. (*He consults the sky*) Yes, we should be OK anyway.

Celia enters carrying a glass of sherry, wine bottle and corkscrew

Celia Yes. When it rained this afternoon I thought, well, that's that.

Miles Only a shower though, wasn't it?

Celia Yes. (*She hands him the bottle*) There you are. Open, please.

Miles OK.

Celia I always finish up with the cork inside the bottle for some reason. (*She hands him the corkscrew*)

Miles Ah well, there's a trick to it, you see. You have to pull and not push.

Celia Oh, is that what it is?

Miles Easy mistake to make. (*He starts to open the bottle*)

Celia stands puzzled for a moment, then laughs at the joke rather belatedly

Celia Oh, I see. Yes. I've got one open already. Toby opened it. But I think we'll need more than the one, won't we?

Miles Yes, I think we might, yes.

Celia With him here.

Miles With the four of us, anyway.

Celia Thank you for bringing that.

Miles Least we could do.

Celia I don't think it'll rain again, will it?

Miles Not a chance.

Celia It'll be just my luck. You know, we've lived here six years and when we moved in, we said, "Oh, how lovely. A patio." And, you know, we've never had a single meal out here. Not even tea. It's either snowing or the kids have got colds. Just a second, I'm going to check.

Celia exits

Miles I know what you mean. We've got a breakfast room in our place, you
know. I've certainly never had breakfast in it in my life. Well, I couldn't.
It's full of cardboard boxes. All Rowena's Oxfam stuff. She'll be here in a
sec. She obviously got held up at this meeting. She told me to come on
alone if she wasn't back and to send her apologies. Hope we haven't upset
your timing. (*He sniffs the now opened bottle*) I think this is OK. I hope so.

Celia returns

I'm saying I hope we haven't spoiled the meal. With Rowena being late.
Celia Oh, no. I never bother with things that spoil. Not in this household.
Everything I cook is either cooked to death or not at all. Raw or stewed,
take your pick.
Miles Ah. (*He smiles a little apprehensively*)
Celia None of them bother with mealtimes, they're all as bad as each other.

Pause

Actually, to be perfectly honest, I don't quite know where Toby is at the
moment. He went to get some cigarettes half an hour ago, in case we felt
like one. Though I really shouldn't smoke.
Miles Where on earth did he go to get them?
Celia Only down the road to the pub.
Miles Ah.

Pause

Celia Cheers.
Miles Good health.

They drink

Celia Look, I'm afraid I was rather rude to you the other day, wasn't I?
Miles Were you? Oh, you mean with. . . . Well. Understood.
Celia We'd had a rather rough patch, Toby and me.
Miles Yes, well. . . . Never mind. You've made up now, I take it?
Celia No.
Miles Oh. I rather gathered . . .
Celia Not at all.
Miles You're still going ahead with—with——
Celia We're separating, yes. We're waiting till the school holidays.
Miles Oh, I see. I rather hoped you might both have . . .
Celia No. Still, what I wanted to say to you was, thank you for whatever
you did that obviously saved Toby his job.
Miles Oh, well.
Celia Whatever you said to the Board seems to have done the trick.
Miles I think they all went a bit glazed really. I don't think Colonel Malton
was very impressed, but I banged the table a couple of times and used
words like "integrity" and "passionately" and so on. (*After a slight pause*)
It's not too good to hear he's in the pub, though, is it?
Celia He only went for some cigarettes.
Miles Yes, I know but half an hour for a packet of fags. . . . He's obviously
driving a pretty hard bargain.

Celia How's Rowena?
Miles Oh, she's terribly well.
Celia Good.
Miles Well, you'll see for yourself.
Celia Yes.
Miles Looking forward to seeing you.
Celia Is she?
Miles Oh yes. You bet. Rather. No, she's blooming. Absolutely blooming. (*After a slight pause*) I think I may have been pretty rude the other day, too, you know.
Celia No, you weren't.
Miles I think I may have been.
Celia No.
Miles Well, if I was——
Celia You weren't.

Pause

Miles So where will you be going? Still London, is it?
Celia Probably.
Miles Not much of a place to live, is it?
Celia I'll need a job. There's nothing round here.
Miles What did you used to do before you were married? Organize things, didn't you?
Celia Conferences. We organized conferences.
Miles Packing them off to Eastbourne, eh?
Celia That sort of thing. More sherry?
Miles Oh, well. What the hell.

Celia goes in, taking their glasses with her

Well, there's always plenty of those, you know. Conferences. We've got a whole department now, our firm, which deals exclusively in micro-circuitry, micro-electronic stuff. Only eighty-five per cent of what they produce is totally invisible to the human eye. You can't see it at all. So there we are. We've got a whole load of chaps on absolutely fantastic salaries producing something we can only take their word for. I mean, if they stopped producing them we'd be none the wiser. We'd carry on posting off empty boxes to Kuwait. Anyway, these chaps are always going to conferences. They spend their lives meeting over large free Scotches paid for by us and talking about literally nothing at all. Literally.

Celia returns with refilled glasses

Celia Well, it's the thing of the future, isn't it?
Miles Well, yes. Mind you, it's really rather left to those sort of chaps whether we've got a future at all. Still, it's very profitable. A step up from lawnmowers. Do you know, we started out making lawnmowers? Before my time. But that's how we started out fifty years ago. Thereabouts. Then we went to tractors. Then these things. I prefer the tractors. You can count them. Check if they're in the boxes.

Celia mm's and ah's throughout this without apparently hearing a word
You know, I owe you a further apology.
Celia You're not going to spend the whole evening apologizing are you?
Miles I hope not. But, you see, when I said let's have dinner, I really meant, come round to our place for dinner.
Celia Oh, did you? You didn't say that.
Miles Well, that's what I meant originally. Only I didn't push it. It seemed Rowena wasn't geared for cooking. Not this week. She's got something on the kitchen table she can't move.
Celia What?
Miles Mud, I think.
Celia Mud?
Miles Well, probably clay. She's doing a project with the kids. Only now we have to wait for it to dry. So in the meantime food is a bit scarce.
Celia How awful.
Miles Well.

From the direction of the field, a hand bell rings
Celia (*glancing at her watch*) Eight o'clock bedtime.
Miles Yes. Your two in bed?
Celia I don't think they're asleep. They read till they're cross-eyed. They're being very grown-up about all this, they really are.
Miles They know?
Celia Oh, yes. I had to tell them. Lucy's nearly nine.
Miles They're very hard-boiled, aren't they, kids? I remember when I broke my foot. My three just stood round laughing.
Celia I think they'll just be so relieved to live somewhere where it's a little quieter. They're very quiet children, both of them.
Miles Wish to God mine were.
Celia You never know they're there. And I mean Toby and I have had some of the most appalling. . . . (*She shudders*) Really appalling.
Miles Dear.
Celia You don't have rows, you and Rowena?
Miles Not a lot. She's not there much. Except when she's making mud pies.
Celia She always seems very jolly. I'll say that about her. She's a very jolly woman. And you're—er—well, you're fairly easy going, aren't you?
Miles Sometimes. I don't think I'd remember Rowena for her jolliness.
Celia What then?
Miles I don't know. She's just bloody infuriating most of the time. No, that's unfair. I'm quite fond of her really. But she does drive me up the wall.
Celia (*after a pause*) I'm going to give them another three minutes and then I think we'll start without them, don't you?
Miles Suits me.
Celia I mean, it's ridiculous. The whole idea was to eat out here. In another half hour, it's going to be too cold.
Miles I could help shift this inside.
Celia No, that's not the point. I want to eat out here.

Miles Yes, of course.
Celia More sherry?
Miles Oh, no, no. My limit.
Celia Then let's have some of this. (*She picks up the wine bottle*) We'll try ours, it's slightly suspect.
Miles Right. (*He holds out his hand*) May I?
Celia Yes, do, thank you.

Celia hands Miles the bottle. He pours two glasses of wine

(*Watching him as he pours*) I take it, you don't see a lot of Rowena?
Miles Well, a bit. I am married to her.
Celia That doesn't necessarily follow. Does it? I know couples who don't meet for weeks.
Miles Well, we see something of each other. Not an awful lot. I suppose I see slightly less of her than I see of the au pair and slightly more of her than I see of the cleaning woman. But that's only average. Occasionally Rowena leaves notes for the cleaning woman forbidding her to clean anything so then the poor old soul comes and talks to me. And that bumps the average up.
Celia What I'm saying is, you don't keep very close track of her, do you?
Miles No. Why? Why do you ask?
Celia Nothing. I was just curious.
Miles I usually have a vague idea where she is. In case of emergencies.
Celia Where is she tonight, then?
Miles No idea. This meeting thing, wherever it is. Somewhere. I don't know. I don't quite see your point.
Celia I was just curious.
Miles (*tetchily*) I mean, I don't have her rigged up with a homing device or something.
Celia (*softly*) Maybe you should.
Miles What?
Celia I said, maybe you should, Miles.
Miles (*tasting the wine*) This isn't bad, is it, where did you get it?
Celia Oh, you know. That place.
Miles What, you mean——?
Celia Yes. That place.
Miles Oh, there. Not bad, not bad. (*Suddenly*) Look, I might as well tell you because you've obviously guessed anyway. She's not coming. Rowena's not coming tonight, I'm sorry.
Celia Not——?
Miles No.
Celia Oh, for God's sake.
Miles Sorry.
Celia Why didn't you say so before?
Miles Because I—I couldn't think of an excuse why she wasn't coming. That's really why. You know, headache, flu, fallen out of the kitchen window. They all sound so phoney, don't they?
Celia But I mean why isn't she coming? I mean, the real reason.

Miles The real reason she isn't coming is—because she doesn't want to come. That's the real reason. But you can't just say that to your hostess, can you? Sorry, my wife doesn't want to come. It's so bloody rude.

Celia Oh.

Miles There you are, I've said it now.

Celia I still don't see why she doesn't want to come.

Miles She just doesn't. She didn't offer an excuse. She just said about ten minutes before we were coming, I'm not going. That's all she said. I'm not going. I can't face them tonight.

Celia Us.

Miles Yes.

Celia Meaning me and Toby.

Miles Yes.

Celia I see. Well, bugger her.

Miles Right you are.

Celia So it's just you, is it?

Miles I'm afraid so. Sorry, I would've said something earlier only I was frightened you'd just decide to cancel the whole meal. When you heard it was just me. I was rather looking forward to it.

Celia I didn't know she disliked me quite so much.

Miles Oh, she doesn't.

Celia I mean, I realized she wasn't that fond of me. She found me bossy and over-organized and over-bearing, I'm sure.

Miles (*rather too emphatically*) No, no, no, no.

Celia I suppose if I were to be honest, I do find her one of the most transparent and stupid women I've ever met but we've always sort of got along. Reasonably well. I sorted out all those bloody refugee clothes for her. I never got a word of thanks. Or a card. Or anything.

Miles (*mumbling*) Well, I'm sure she. . . . I'm sure . . .

Celia I think that's what it is about her. She's rather graceless, isn't she? Or maybe it's thoughtless. Maybe that's it, she just doesn't think. Doesn't use her tiny brain, does she? Still, why bother? She'll survive on her charm. Men falling over themselves. Good luck to her. Cheers.

Miles It was really my fault, Celia. For not thinking up a decent excuse.

Celia Don't start apologizing again, Miles. For God's sake.

Miles Sorry.

Celia Because you're married to a very boorish woman isn't necesarily your fault. In retrospect, it was possibly a very stupid choice but then people who live in glass houses. . . . Who am I?

Miles (*unhappily*) Stupid of me really. I didn't realize you would be quite so upset.

Celia You deserve someone better than Rowena, Miles, you really do. You're too nice a man for what she's doing to you.

Silence

I'm sorry.

Miles (*gently carving at the table with a knife*) Yes, well . . .

Celia Well, shall I get us some food? Before you start eating the table.

Miles I'm sorry, I didn't realize I was . . .
Celia It doesn't look as if we're going to get Toby either. So——(*she makes to go*)
Miles I think if it is hometruths time and it seems to be, you're worth a damn sight more than Toby.
Celia Food?
Miles Did you hear what I said?
Celia (*briskly*) Yes, I did. Thank you, Miles. I'm asking you if you'd like to eat.
Miles Yes, I damn well do.
Celia All right, wait there.
Miles (*indicating the table*) I'll clear us a bit more room, shall I?
Celia No, leave it. It'll serve to remind us of our absentee loved ones. Pour me some more of that, will you?
Miles OK. Right you are.

Celia exits

Miles pours the wine and sets both glasses on the table. He seems quite cheerful all of a sudden. He lights the candle

Celia returns with four glass dishes on a tray

Celia Here we are. Try this.
Miles Aha, marvellous.
Celia Oh, you lit the candle. Good for you. I hope you enjoy this meal because there are seconds and thirds of everything. You sit here. And I'll sit next to you there. We'll put Rowena over there. In the draught. And dear old Toby here.

Miles laughs a little nervously

I will confess to you I had a couple of sherries before you came.
Miles Lord.
Celia I couldn't face Rowena without them. So be warned. Right, eat up.

They eat

Miles (*approvingly*) Mmm . . . mmm . . . mmm . . . mmm . . . mmmm.
Celia All right.
Miles Mmm.
Celia Do you like it?
Miles Very much. What is it?
Celia Grapefruit and prawns.
Miles Ah-ha.
Celia (*as they eat*) Bit of onion . . .
Miles (*chewing*) Mm-mm . . .
Celia Parsley . . . lemon juice . . . white wine . . .
Miles Um . . .
Celia (*with her mouth full*) Ooool-oll.
Miles Sorry?
Celia (*swallowing*) Sorry. Olive oil.

Miles Olive oil, yes.
Celia Mayonnaise.
Miles Mm.
Celia Tabasco.
Miles Ah.
Celia Olives.
Miles Oh.
Celia And lettuce.
Miles Golly.
Celia (*as an afterthought*) Oh, and paprika.
Miles Well, it's excellent. Excellent.
Celia Is Rowena a good cook? I seem to remember she's not bad.
Miles Oh, yes. When she puts her mind to it.
Celia Must be small portions, then. (*She laughs*)
Miles (*frowning*) Sorry?

Pause

Celia Jolly good wine, isn't it?
Miles Yes, it is. Excellent. (*He notices her glass is empty*) Oh, sorry.
Celia I married the most awful bastard, you know. Really. What a bastard.
Miles Oh, no. He's OK. Toby.
Celia He's not OK.
Miles No, he's OK, Celia.
Celia (*furiously*) Don't tell me he's OK. There's nothing OK about him.
He's a bastard.
Miles Well. He certainly isn't worthy of you.
Celia He certainly isn't. (*After a pause*) We're sitting here looking absolute
fools, aren't we? While they're out doing whatever they're both doing,
we're sitting here like two nanas.
Miles I don't know.
Celia While they're out gallivanting.
Miles I'm perfectly happy here. With you. Not at all nana-like. Very
pleasant.
Celia Thank you.
Miles (*finishing his first course*) That was wonderful. Absolutely wonderful.
Celia More?
Miles Er—no, thank you.
Celia I'll get the rest in a minute. It can carry on stewing a bit longer. Good
health.
Miles And to you.
Celia And to hell with those two.
Miles (*cheerfully*) Rather.
Celia Do you know, Miles, I think there's something rather special about
you.
Miles Thank you. And you.
Celia Thank you.
Miles Look, I have to own up.
Celia What?

Miles You won't get angry again, will you?
Celia No.
Miles Promise?
Celia Of course. What is it?
Miles Well, it's just that—Rowena didn't say any of that.
Celia Any of what?
Miles She didn't say she didn't want to come and all that. I made it all up.
Celia Did you?
Miles Yes.
Celia What did she say then?
Miles She didn't say anything actually. I never told her she was invited in the first place.
Celia You didn't?
Miles No.
Celia You didn't ask her?
Miles No.
Celia What a peculiar thing to do.
Miles Not really. You see ... well, I——
Celia (*smiling*) I don't think I want to know why, Miles.
Miles Righty-ho.

Pause

Celia Although. No, I don't think I do see. I mean, why did you want it to be just you and me and Toby?
Miles Ah, well. You see, I knew it wasn't going to be that.
Celia Did you?
Miles Yes.
Celia How? How did you know?
Miles Because Toby had a word with me.
Celia Toby?
Miles Yes. He told me he intended to make himself scarce tonight.
Celia He did?
Miles A couple of days ago.
Celia Why?
Miles Well, you see he ——
Celia No, forget it, I don't think I want to know.
Miles Righty-ho.

Pause

Celia Yes, I do. Why?
Miles Well.
Celia He wasn't trying to pair us off, was he?
Miles Good Lord, no, what a grisly thought.
Celia Well, thank you very much.
Miles No, I meant grisly that he should try and pair us off. No, not grisly being paired to you. Far from grisly. I should imagine.
Celia So why?

Miles He wanted me to talk to you. About, well—you and him really. Getting back together.

Celia So all along you knew Toby wasn't coming and Rowena wasn't coming?

Miles Yes.

Celia (*icily*) Miles, I'm afraid I am beginning to get very angry indeed.

Miles Oh, don't do that. (*After a slight pause*) Please.

Celia All right. Toby wanted you to talk to me, did he?

Miles Yes.

Celia Then you'd better say what you have to say, then you can go away.

Miles Oh, now.

Celia Quickly, quickly.

Miles Come on.

Celia Miles, you've just made a complete fool of me, you realize that? Now that may be something that Rowena enjoys and in fact probably doesn't even notice but it's something I'm none too fond of.

Miles All right, all right. I'll say what I came to say.

Celia Please do.

Miles Here it comes. Celia, will you please reconsider your decision to leave your husband? Toby would like you back. Will you please go back to him?

Celia Is that it?

Miles Yes.

Celia Certainly not.

Miles (*cheerfully*) Fine, right. I've done my duty. Now where's the next course, then?

Celia What are you talking about?

Miles Well, that's it. I asked you. You said no. Now, let's get on and enjoy the dinner.

Celia I wish I knew what was going on.

Miles Nothing. Let's carry on as we were five minutes ago.

Celia Five minutes ago we were both sitting here victims of fate, drawn together through mutual feelings of persecution. Now I appear to be eating with Machiavelli. This whole thing is most sinister.

Miles It's not sinister.

Celia You were a lovely, shallow, sunny man a moment ago, Miles. Now you've got awful depths.

Miles I enjoy being here with you. Alone. I suppose that's pretty deep. If you must know, I also think you're very beautiful.

Celia Oh, don't talk rubbish.

Miles I do.

Celia I'll get the next course.

Miles It's an amazing face. Quite wonderful.

Celia Mediterranean Chicken Casserole.

Miles Full of life, everything about it.

Celia Have you ever had it, chicken casserole? It's sweet peppers ...

Miles   'Tis not a lip or eye we beauty call
                  But the joint force and full result of all.

Celia Yes, peppers, olive oil yet again . . .
Miles Yet again. Stendhal said, "Beauty is nothing other than the promise
of happiness."
Celia Cooked ham, shallots . . .
Miles Beauty hath no true glass except it be
In the sweet privacy of loving eyes . . .
Celia Onions, tomatoes, parsley . . .
Miles The point is, actually, Celia, I'm in love with you.
Celia Yes, I know that, Miles.
Miles You knew?
Celia Well, I rather feared as much, anyway. You've been giving me odd
looks for ages.
Miles No, I haven't.
Celia You have.
Miles When?
Celia All the time. For months and months. Whenever you thought I
wasn't looking. I kept catching sight of you out of the corner of my eye.
Miles I can't help it. I've tried. I mean, while Toby was around I——— Has
Toby noticed, do you think?
Celia Of course Toby hasn't noticed.
Miles I deliberately forced my feelings down . . .
Celia The coast's clear, get in quick, eh?
Miles Oh come on, Celia, don't be so damned aloof.
Celia Miles, I'm clinging on to the side of a mineshaft here. What are you
playing at? There are my two children along there, there is me, there is
you, there is Toby, there is your wife, Rowena. There are your three kids,
Hubert and Wilfred, or whoever they are . . .
Miles Colin, Sandra—and what's-his-name.
Celia So. The point is it is not practical, Miles.
Miles Timothy, that's his name.
Celia Regardless of anything else, it's not practical. So we concentrate on
the food.
Miles You feel absolutely nothing then? In return?
Celia I didn't say that.
Miles That was my greatest fear. That you'd feel nothing.
Celia I'm not saying anything, Miles.
Miles You do. A little. Don't you?
Celia Maybe.

Slight pause

Miles "A very small degree of hope is sufficient to cause the birth of
love . . ."
Celia What is this you keep quoting? Is that this Stendhal man again?
Miles That's right.
Celia Well, I do wish you'd keep him out of it. He's an absolute menace.
Let's stick to Robert Carrier. *Cooking for You*—page one four something
or other. Mediterranean Chicken Casserole. (*After a pause*) All I'm saying

is, I'm sorry, I can't cope. Not at the moment. I really can't. Let me get
over all this and then. . . . Life's just too complicated, isn't it?
Miles (*grimly*) Yes.
Celia You do agree?
Miles Right. Fair enough.
Celia Oh, God. Please, Miles . . .
Miles I should never have come here tonight, should I?

They sit unhappily for a moment, in silence

The doorbell rings

Celia Front door.
Miles Toby?
Celia Not Toby. He wouldn't ring. He uses his key. Unless he's incapable of
getting his hand in his pocket. Then he yells the place down. Rowena,
possibly?
Miles Never.
Celia All right. Sit tight. I'll go and see. I'll see. We're doing nothing to be
ashamed of, are we?
Miles (*gloomily*) No. No, we're not.

Celia exits, taking their first course dishes with her

Celia (*off*) Yes, all right, Lucy, I heard it. Now get back into bed. Shoo.

*Miles pours himself some more wine. As an afterthought he pours some into
Celia's glass as well. He wanders a little way along the patio*

*From the house Josephine's voice is heard, at first just a murmur, then more
distinctly and quite clearly an older Celia*

Josephine (*off*) I'll just pop and see them, Celia.
Celia (*off*) Yes, you do that.

Celia reappears. She is holding her mother's coat

You're not going to credit this.
Miles What?
Celia It's my mother.
Miles Oh God, shall I——? (*He moves to leave*)
Celia No, sit down. Finish your meal. She doesn't even want to join us.
She's eaten.
Miles Did you know she was coming?
Celia Well, yes. But I thought it was going to be rather later.
Miles You'll want to talk to her.
Celia I've got plenty of time. Sit down.
Miles Yes, but what's she going to think? Us two sitting out here having a
meal on our own.
Celia She's not that sort of person, she really isn't. She's gone along to see
the children, she'll be with them for hours. She's not the nosey type, thank
God. She minds her own business and what I do is entirely my own
concern. She'll keep well out of the way, I promise.

Miles Really?
Celia She's not interested. She's marvellous like that. Always has been. Have you never met?
Miles No.
Celia Oh, you must. You'll love her. Sit down. Anyway, we haven't finished talking, had we?
Miles I rather thought we had.
Celia I haven't.

Celia goes into the house

Miles (*confused*) Oh.
Josephine (*off*) Well, who is it? Let me have a peep?
Celia (*off*) Mother, will you please go away.
Josephine (*off*) No, I want to see.
Celia (*off*) Mother.
Josephine (*off*) I'm bursting to see.
Celia (*off*) Mother, he's just out there. He'll hear you. Now, mind your own business.
Josephine (*off, fainter*) It's all very secretive. (*Her voice fades away*)

In a second, Celia returns. She smiles at Miles

He smiles at her

Celia (*laughing*) It's coming.
Miles Great.
Celia I turned it down, the gas blew out and now it's cold. I'm just heating it up again.
Miles Ah.
Celia (*as she sits*) I take it then, things between you and Rowena aren't that rosy either?
Miles I think I ought to go.
Celia You leave now and I shall come and pour Mediterranean Chicken Casserole through your letter box, Miles. There's masses of it out there. The kids won't touch it. They only eat baked beans and Smarties. Both at once. And Mother's on a diet. So it's all down to you and me. It's your fault there's nobody here so you can damn well eat it. Now tell me about you and Rowena.
Miles Why?
Celia Because I want to know.
Miles There's nothing. Nothing I can tell you that you don't know already, I'm sure.
Celia Well, she's having an affair. I knew that.
Miles Oh, yes.
Celia With Terry Hogg, is that right?
Miles Yes.
Celia He's an odd choice. He's got a very long body and extremely short legs.
Miles Yes.
Celia Have you noticed?

Miles Yes, I used to play squash with him occasionally.

Celia Oh. Was it a disadvantage? Short legs? Playing squash?

Miles It didn't seem to be. He always used to win.

Celia Terribly corny of her, though, isn't it? With the school P.E. instructor. Honestly.

Miles I understood he was quite attractive.

Celia He doesn't do much for me. He jogs around the field there every morning. He's got this extraordinary little bottom. Well, actually, he's hardly got any bottom at all. It's very strange. Goes straight down practically.

Miles Does he?

Celia I like men with a bit of bottom. Not too much. But a bit. Otherwise they look like clothes pegs. Perhaps that's why people go to bed with him. To find out what happens. Where his back meets his legs.

Miles Look, Celia, do you mind, please.

Celia I'm sorry. I was just trying to cheer things up.

Miles Well, you're not going to cheer things up by talking about Hogg's bottom, are you? They're probably in bed together at this very minute.

Celia Does that upset you terribly?

Miles No. Yes. I don't know . . .

Celia Poor Miles. Anyway. That's why I'm not taking you too seriously because I think I might just be catching a rebound.

Miles Not at all. I love you. I always have loved you.

Celia Well. I expect Stendhal had a better phrase for it but hard cheese really.

Miles What an appalling thing to say to somebody.

Celia Sorry.

Miles I think I'm going to cry in a minute.

Celia Don't you dare.

Miles pours himself another glass of wine. He fills Celia's glass as well

Are you trying to get me drunk?

Miles Not particularly.

Celia It won't work. I don't get drunk. I've never been known to. Total waste of time. (*After a pause*) Now here's something interesting, said she, filling in gamely for her morose, brooding dinner partner. This is interesting. Did you know that Sylvie Bell is now getting very serious indeed, capital S, capital I, over a certain Lionel Hepplewick? Surprise, surprise. (*After a slight pause*) Oh, really? cried Miles. You amaze me. His good-natured face split into a boyish grin. What do you know. . . .

Miles (*shouting*) Look, shut up, Celia, will you? For God's sake, shut up.

Silence

Celia (*coolly*) I'll get the next course.

Miles I'm sorry.

Celia Don't be sorry. I can be the most awful bitch sometimes, Miles. You'll find that out. (*She walks into a chair*) Why do you think Toby drinks? Because I drive him to it. That's why. Excuse me.

Celia goes into the house a little awkwardly

(*Angrily, off*) Mother, what are you doing there? If you want to be useful, go in the kitchen.

Josephine (*off, growing fainter*) I only wanted to know, darling, if you wanted me to air the bed.

Miles Oh, hell. (*He stands uncertainly*)

The curtains at the window twitch as though tugged by a child's hand

Celia (*off*) No. No, you may not.

The curtains stop twitching

No, don't be so nosey. Lucy, will you please get back into bed this instant.

Miles comes to a decision and moves towards the garden

Miles Right. Goodnight. (*He drains his wine glass with great resolution, strides off the patio and into the now comparative darkness of the garden intent upon making his exit this way. After one pace on the grass, though, he turns his ankle on something*) Aaah! (*He hops about in some pain*) Ooo. Hoo. (*He hops back on to the patio*)

Josephine (*off*) You get into bed, Lucy. You do as your mummy tells you, you naughty girl.

Miles, anxious not to meet her, draws back into one corner of the patio and stands there in the shadows, flattened against the wall and balancing on one leg

(*Off, more loudly*) Or Grandma will be along. Then there'll be trouble. Trouble . . .

Josephine, in her late fifties, comes out on to the patio

Oh. There's nobody here. He's gone. (*She turns to go back in and catches sight of Miles*) Oh. Hallo.

Miles Hallo.

Josephine What are you doing there?

Miles OK, it's only me. I was just looking at some things over here.

Josephine Things?

Miles Hallo. Miles Coombes, hallo. You'll be Mrs—er——

Josephine Josephine Hamilton, how do you do?

Miles Hallo. I've just been having dinner with your daughter. Me and a couple of others. We were all just leaving.

Josephine What others?

Miles Oh, they've gone. I was just going only this damned ankle's gone on me.

Josephine Why are you all going? I think she's just serving up the main course.

Miles Is she now? Is she? Splendid. You mean, there's more to come? I think we'd all got the impression it had finished. Hang on, I'd better try and call them all back. (*He limps towards the door in an attempt to make a* *hurried exit, but a painful twinge from his ankle forces him to stop and lean against a chair)* Aaah!

Josephine Is that the ankle?

Miles Yes, yes.

Josephine You'd better sit down and rest it.

Miles *(reluctantly)* Yes. Stupid, isn't it? Not the sort of thing you'd expect to happen during dinner.

Josephine *(pulling out another chair)* Here. Put it on here.

Miles Thank you.

Josephine Would you like me to look?

Miles No, no, please. Honestly.

Josephine *(sitting in a chair, facing him)* Do you mind if I join you for a second?

Miles Not at all.

Josephine There's plenty of room now everyone's left.

Miles Yes.

Josephine *(smiling)* Yes.

Miles Pity they shot off really.

Josephine Yes. Still, it's sometimes nicer with two, isn't it?

Miles Two what?

Josephine People.

Miles Oh, yes. Sorry, I thought you meant two courses.

Josephine I think she's just popping Lucy back into bed. She'll be here in a minute.

Miles Good-oh.

Josephine Are you fond of children?

Miles No, I absolutely loathe them. Can't stand the sight of them, really.

Josephine *(smiling and speaking confidentially)* Listen, you don't need to pretend to me. I'm absolutely thrilled to bits, I don't mind telling you.

Miles Sorry?

Josephine That you're here. She should have done this years ago. Absolutely serve that P.I.G. right.

Miles P.I.G.?

Josephine This'll teach him. It's about time he saw she can have a life of her own.

Miles Oh, pig.

Josephine Do you know what she needs? My daughter? Do you know what she needs more than anything else in this world?

Miles Er—no.

Josephine She needs a damn good, thumping, no-holds-barred, get-in-between-the-sheets love affair.

Miles Ah.

Josephine There. That's her mother saying that. Her mother.

Miles Yes.

Josephine You agree with me?

Miles I don't think she would.

Josephine She owes that man nothing at all. Anything she ever owed to him she has paid back a thousand times.

Miles Really? Really?

Josephine (*warming up*) She phoned me up the other day. Absolute floods of tears.

Miles Oh, dear.

Josephine "Mummy," she said. "Mummy, mummy, I'm going to have to leave him. I don't know what I'm going to do, Mummy." I said, "Leave him, darling." She said, "How can I, Mummy, how can I?" I said, "Darling, for heaven's sake, while you can, please, while you can."—I mean, she's still young, isn't she?

Miles Oh, yes.

Josephine She could still start again. Give those children a fresh start. Give them all a fresh start. I mean, she's still attractive, isn't she?

Miles Oh, yes.

Josephine I mean, you're a man. Be honest with me, do you think she's attractive?

Miles Yes, yes, I do. Yes.

Josephine Have you slept with her yet?

Miles No, no.

Josephine Aphrodite, believe me.

Miles Oh, yes.

Josephine Last time I saw her. Silk. Skin like silk.

Miles Yes, I can imagine.

Josephine Wasted on that man.

Miles Quite.

Josephine Little tinpot schoolmaster. Little tinpot school. Drinking himself to death.

Miles Well, I think the thing with Toby is, really . . .

Josephine (*a little suspiciously*) Do you know Toby?

Miles Yes, yes, I do.

Josephine Oh, I see. I didn't realize that. I thought you were someone she'd just brought in.

Miles No, I've known Toby quite a long time actually.

Josephine Then you can see what he's doing to her.

Miles Very clearly.

Josephine Are you a friend of his?

Miles Yes.

Josephine I see.

Miles I suppose I'm his best friend, really.

Josephine I see. I've never met you.

Miles No. We nearly met actually at their wedding. I was due to be best man only I was abroad. Selling things.

Josephine What sort of things?

Miles Tractors.

Josephine You don't look like a farmer.

Miles I'm not.

Josephine Very peculiar. Not a very nice way for his best friend to behave, is it? Spending evenings alone with his friend's wife.

Miles No, it doesn't look so good, does it?

Josephine It certainly doesn't.

Miles I thought you approved of all this, though. Celia and me.

Josephine I approve of Celia trying to make a new life for herself certainly. Even having a little fun. With someone who truly appreciates her. I'm not altogether sure it should be with her husband's best friend. That sounds hole-in-corner to me. How's your foot?

Miles Fine. Time I was off.

Josephine Before your best friend gets back.

Miles Rather.

Josephine Don't want him to catch you here, do you?

Miles Oh, he knows. Don't worry.

Josephine He knows?

Miles Yes. He asked me to come.

Josephine While he was away?

Miles No, he's keeping away specially.

Josephine He is?

Miles Leave the old gate open occasionally, you know. Let another bull have a sniff round the field.

Josephine I don't think I like the sound of this at all.

Miles It's my night for her, you see.

Josephine Your night?

Miles Yes, Toby has her Tuesdays and Thursdays. I have her at weekends. Wednesdays, she gets laid by dear old Colonel Malton. And Fridays, it's a few physical jerks with our good old P.E. teacher, bottomless Terry Hogg. Then she gets Mondays off to do her hair.

Josephine I'm not sitting listening to this.

Miles Suit yourself.

Josephine You're drunk. You're like your friend. You're worse than your friend.

Miles You betcha.

Josephine moves to the door

Tell old Aphrodite to pop along for a quickie when she's finished, would you? Tell her old randy-socks here is on the rampage for a touch of the silk.

Josephine You're utterly disgusting.

Josephine goes indoors

Miles (*sinking his head in his hands*) Oh, God. (*In a second, he gets up and winces as he puts his weight on his foot. In a moment, when he's recoverd his equilibrium slightly, he starts to move across the lawn*) Aaaah. Ooooh. (*He mutters*) It's so damned dark here now. I can't see where I am. How am I expected to be able to see where I am? I don't know where I am. Where am I? (*He walks into the door of the shed*) Who's this? What's this? My God, it's a door. I didn't know there was a door here. How long have they had a door in their hedge? Bloody stupid thing to do. Put a door in a hedge. Typical Teasdale sort of thing to do.

Miles goes into the shed. A crash is heard

Where the hell am I? It's our breakfast room. How the hell did I get here? No, it isn't. It's a shed. Has she always had this shed? I don't remember there being a shed.

He walks into something. Another crash is heard

Oh, damn, bugger it. I think I'm going to sit down in this shed. (*He sits in the doorway*)

Celia comes out on to the patio with her casserole

Celia What have you been saying to my—? Miles? Miles, where are you? Have you gone home?
Miles No, I'm over here.
Celia Miles?
Miles It's all right, Celia, I'm over here.
Celia What are you doing?
Miles I'm sitting in your shed.
Celia Are you all right?
Miles Fine. I'm just having a sit in your shed.
Celia Well, come on, Miles. Are you going to eat?
Miles No, thank you very much.
Celia (*putting down her casserole and peering into the darkness*) Where are you? What are you doing? Are you drunk?
Miles Yes, definitely.
Celia Oh, Lord alive. Why does it always—Miles, come on. Come on, please. Come on.
Miles No.
Celia I'm not blundering around out there so you can come here.
Miles Not until I get some hope. I need a bit of hope.
Celia Miles.
Miles I'm a man in need of hope. Desperately.
Celia Oh, God, it's that bloody Stendhal again, isn't it? (*She moves a little way into the garden*) Miles, come on now.
Miles I love you.
Celia Yes, yes, all right. Quietly. I don't know what you said to Mother. She's had to go and lie down. Now listen, I can't see where you are but listen. I want you to know that it's not that I don't appreciate what you've said to me tonight about your feelings for me. I'm very grateful and I'm very touched. I needed someone to say that to me, I really did. It's just that—I wish to hell I could see. It's just that I can't necessarily—(*She treads on something*)—ouch—Miles, I wish you'd come where I can see you—I can't reciprocate at the moment——

Miles groans

Look, I'm not even sure of my own feelings at the moment. I'm really not. Miles, are you there?

Miles kicks the door to with a bang

Celia tries the handle, at last locating where he is

Miles, open the door.

EITHER she says:

Celia Miles, at least let me in. Please. Don't force me to say things before I'm ready to say them—that's all. It's not fair on me.

Pause. No reply. Celia sits by the shed door

Yes, all right, I do. I do like you very much. (*After a pause*) I do find you attractive, Miles. Very attractive. This is not fair, you're blackmailing me. I won't have it. Yes, I would love to sleep with you. Of course I would. You're very attractive. And I think Rowena's an idiot. And that sweaty Hogg's all she deserves. (*After a pause*) And maybe on day, perhaps, if things work out. . . . God, this is very one-sided, Miles, you've got to help me a little. All right, I want you, too. I've wanted you a very long time. That's not the reason I split up with Toby. I'm not that sort of person. But now that we have—Miles, please say something, for God's sake.

The shed door swings open

Where are you? (*She looks inside*) I can't even see you.

Celia goes in the shed, crouching low

Look, I hate these sort of games, Miles. If you're hiding somewhere, you'll—oh, you—oh, no, that really is . . . No, this is terribly sneaky. No, no, no really, I'm not. I'm—no. Miles. (*She giggles*) No.

The shed door is kicked shut. Almost immediately from the house, the sound of Toby's voice is heard

Toby (*off*) Hallo. Out here, did you say? Sorry, Jo, didn't realize you were here. Hope I didn't frighten you.

Toby comes out on to the patio. He is in his forties, crumpled, and at present very hot and flushed due to the good few drinks he's got under his belt

You go to sleep, Lucy, my girl or Daddy'll be through there and tan you black and blue. Do as your Gran tells you. (*He looks about*) Nobody out here. What do you mean, they're out here? Nobody out here at all. (*He looks at the table*) Bloody odd. (*He pours himself some wine. He opens the casserole*) Yuck. (*He puts the lid back on it*)

A clatter is heard from the shed, then a muffled cry from Celia

Who is that there? Who is that out there? Who's in there? Come on, come out at once. Do you hear me? This is the Headmaster. Come along. Whoever you are come out of that shed at once. You'll get double the punishment if you don't come out of there this minute. You should be in bed, anyway. I don't—ah.

Celia emerges rather rumpled

Celia (*brightly*) Hallo. (*She closes the shed door behind her*)

Toby What are you doing in there?

Celia Tidying up. What do you think?

Toby Tidying up?

Celia Want something to eat?

Toby You're looking very dirty.

Celia Food?

Toby Where are the guests?

Celia Gone home.

Toby Already?

A clatter is heard from the shed

Is there somebody in there?

Celia No. Mediterranean Chicken Casserole. Would you like some?

Toby There is. There's someone in there.

Celia It's nothing whatever to do with you, Toby. Now, mind your own business. Come on, sit down.

Toby (*stumbling across the lawn*) No, I want to know who the hell that is in my shed.

Celia Toby, will you please come and sit down.

Toby Come out of there, you.

Celia Toby, this will only be embarrassing. Please——

Toby (Open up. Who's in here? (*rattling the door handle*) Open

(*together*) this door, do you hear?

Celia This is really lovely. Chicken, cooked ham, shallots, peppers, olive oil. . . .

Toby Come out of there. (*He moves round and looks through the window*) Who are you? My God, there's someone in here trying to put his trousers on.

Celia I don't know what you're talking about.

Toby Miles? Is that you, Miles? It's Miles. There's Miles in here putting his trousers on.

Celia Toby, please. Come and sit down. Please.

Toby (*returning dazed*) What's he doing?

Another clatter from the shed

What's my best friend doing in my shed with his trousers off?

Celia (*handing him as plateful of food*) There you are.

Toby I don't want it.

Celia Sit down and eat.

Toby (*sitting, still greatly perplexed*) What's going on, Celia?

Celia We're having an affair, Toby, that's all. Miles and I, we're having an affair.

Toby You are?

Celia Yes.

Toby For how long?

Celia For as long as we both enjoy it, I suppose.

Toby No, I mean, how long has it been going on for?

Celia Oh, less than an hour.
Toby An hour?
Celia If that.
Toby I don't understand this at all. I really don't.
Celia A very small degree of hope is sufficient to cause the birth of love.
Toby I beg your pardon?
Celia Eat your chicken.

Another crash from the shed

The Lights fade to a Black-out

To: A CRICKET MATCH (page 43)

OR she says:

Celia Listen, I'm sorry about Mother. That wasn't planned, I promise.
Look, why don't you just go home now, Miles. Go home to Rowena.
There's nothing I can suggest. There's nothing I can offer you. There's
nothing I can give you at the moment, I'm sorry. I need to get my own
feelings sorted out, let alone. . . . All I can suggest is go home and sort out
your life. And leave me to sort out mine. And for God's sake stop reading
this Stendhal. Well, anyway, temporarily. Maybe sometime, we'll——
(*She gets up*) I'm sorry, that's it. Goodbye. (*After a pause*) Miles?

There is no reply

Miles?

Silence

Well, if you want to stay in there, that's fine by me. But please do not
make any noise. The children are trying to sleep. Do you hear me? All
right, goodnight. (*She picks her way back to the patio and says to herself*)
Honestly, what am I supposed to do?

From within the house, Toby's voice is heard

Toby (*off*) Hallo. Out here, did you say? Sorry, Jo, didn't realize you were
here. Hope I didn't frighten you.

Celia, somewhat panicked, runs back down the garden and locks the shed

*Toby comes out on to the patio. He is in his forties, crumpled, and at present
very hot and flushed due to the good few drinks he's got under his belt*

You go to sleep, Lucy, my girl or Daddy'll be through there and tan you
black and blue. Do as your Gran tells you. (*To Celia*) Oh, you still out
here?
Celia Yes.
Toby Bit cold, isn't it?
Celia Not really.

Toby Where are they, anyway?

Celia Who?

Toby Miles and Rowena. Where have they gone?

Celia They went home.

Toby (*glancing at his watch*) Really? Nobody seems to have eaten very much.

Celia Have you?

Toby No. Sorry, I got a bit—er—held up.

Celia In the pub.

Toby No, not in the pub. Well, yes, in the pub. Of course I was in the pub. But I wasn't drinking in the pub. I mean, I was sitting in the pub having the odd glass, obviously, but I wasn't seriously drinking. Not seriously.

Celia You were drinking jokingly.

Toby Now come on, Celia, I had very few. Very few indeed. You get with a lot of people who are having a few, you can't just sit back. I mean, can you? I mean, you're always telling me to be sociable. I'm trying to be sociable. Some of those people were possibly parents. I don't think any of them were, not in that place, but they could have been. I see your mother's here.

Celia Yes. Here. (*She serves him with food*)

Toby What's this?

Celia Mediterranean Chicken Casserole.

Toby (*examining it suspiciously*) Did any of them actually eat this?

Celia No.

Toby I'm not sure I will.

Celia Come on. (*She tastes it*) Oh, it's cold.

Toby Isn't it meant to be?

Celia No, of course it's not.

Toby Mediterranean, I thought that meant cold.

Celia Don't be so silly.

They eat

Toby (*making a great effort*) It's very nice cold, anyway. Absolutely first rate. Listen, I don't know if Miles said anything to you tonight . . . if he managed a quiet word?

Celia Yes, he managed a quiet word.

Toby He did?

Celia Oh, yes.

Toby You see—I—well, I realize I've been pretty unbearable lately—it's not all my fault. But a lot of it is, I admit it, I admit it. Some of it anyway. And I think, well, the kids, bless them and that . . . it would be a hell of a waste, Celia. We've got our life. And the whole of us . . . around together. For a hell of a long time. And. That's all. It would be a bloody shame. . . . Wouldn't it? Quite honestly? You see it happening all around you. People never find it anyway. . . . Even if they do. So. I think we really ought to give it a second. . . . Just a bit of breathing space. (*After a slight pause*) That's all I'm saying.

Celia (*after a pause*) All right.

Toby All right?

Celia We'll give it another try then.

Toby (*deeply moved*) Oh, my God. That's wonderful news. That is really wonderful news.

Celia We might as well. I'm not sure that the alternatives are any——

Toby Say no more, Celia. If you're prepared to give it a try, I'm prepared to make it work.

Celia (*not that impressed by this*) Good.

Pause

Toby You know something, Celia. It occurred to me tonight and it's now struck me again quite forcibly, one's very inclined to forget to say thank you to people, isn't one?

Celia Well . . .

Toby I mean, here we are, both of us perhaps guilty on occasions of not saying "thanks very much".

Celia I suppose sometimes it can be unspoken.

Toby No, it really can't, Celia. The trouble with things that are unspoken is that they're never said. And if they're not said, then the other person tends not to hear them. That's the trouble with the unspoken. Got to be said occasionally.

Celia Well, all right. I don't mind. Say it if you like.

Toby I intend to.

Celia OK.

Toby First thing tomorrow morning.

Celia Why are you waiting till tomorrow?

Toby Well, I can hardly say it now.

Celia Why not?

Toby There'd be no point.

Celia Why?

Toby Well, he's not here now, is he?

Celia Who isn't here?

Toby Miles isn't here.

Celia Miles?

Toby Yes.

Celia You're thanking Miles?

Toby I will when I see him. I'm not saying it now, it's a complete waste of breath. I want to say thank you for saving my job. Thank you for saving my marriage. I mean, I consider those two rather major reasons for wanting to say thank you. Wouldn't you?

Celia And what about me?

Toby Well, yes. I think you should say thank you to him as well.

Celia Who is going to say thank you to me?

Toby To you?

Celia (*very testily*) Yes.

Toby I don't know. Depends what you've done. (*Seeing he is upsetting her somehow, indicating the casserole*) Oh, you mean for this? Oh, it looks jolly good. Well done.

Celia Oh, God.

Toby No, the point is, Celia, let's face it. We're damn lucky to have friends like Miles, like Rowena, prepared to care about us in the way they do.

Celia (*dully*) Yes.

Toby So let's not be mealy-mouthed. Let's reciprocate. Let's show we can care about them. I intend to do that. I hope you intend to do that. Here's to them. (*He raises his glass*)

Celia Yes.

Toby (*rising unsteadily to his feet*) Here's to the two friends we're so incredibly lucky to have. People—oh, for God's sake, stand up, Celia, I'm toasting, I'm toasting——

Celia gets slowly to her feet with a sigh

People who have shown love. People who have shown that life is about care and understanding. People who above all have been prepared to say when the chips are down, yes, indeed, I am prepared to stand up and be counted.

The sound of a crash from the shed

Celia (*softly*) One.

Toby What the hell was that?

Celia Nothing. Eat your chicken.

As they sit, the Lights fade to a Black-out

To: A GAME OF GOLF (page 81)

A CRICKET MATCH

The corner of a cricket field. Five weeks later. It is the afternoon of Saturday, July 24th

A small hut serves as a pavilion and outside it there is a bench and a canvas chair. There are some tin numbers by the bench to hang on nails, hammered into the hut wall to serve as a scoreboard

There are sounds from the field of boys and men practising cricket

In a moment, Miles, not yet changed for the game, enters carrying his cricket bag

Miles (*to someone on the field*) Afternoon. Yes. . . . Well, just a bit rusty, yes. . . . We'll still give them a game, eh? Yes. (*He walks to the pavilion*)

As Miles reaches the pavilion, Rowena, an attractive, lively woman, a year or so younger than Miles and who it appears has been following him round the boundary, now comes into view

Rowena Isn't this just a super day? If it wasn't for all these awful people playing cricket, it would be just perfect.

Miles Rowena, don't let Timothy run on the field, darling. Those are hard balls they're playing with, they'll hurt him.

Miles goes into the pavilion

Rowena (*calling*) Timmy. Off the field. Timmy, off, off. Sandy, take him off, darling. Take him round to see the cows. Go and see the cows, Timmy. Round to the mooks.

Miles comes out of the pavilion without his bag

Miles I suppose this is where we're changing. There's a lot of kit in here, anyway.

Rowena Everybody else seems to have changed.

Miles Yes, that's because I'm late, darling.

Rowena Don't blame me.

Miles I do blame you. I blame you entirely.

Rowena I couldn't find Timmy's trousers. You don't want your son wandering round with no trousers on, do you?

Miles You could have sorted Timmy's trousers out this morning. You had plenty of time this morning. I don't know why the hell you—(*He breaks off as someone passes them*)—Afternoon—the hell you don't organize yourself just a little, Rowena, I really don't.

Rowena (*not really hearing him*) Who's that?

Miles Who?

Rowena The man you just said hallo to, who is it?

Miles That's old Raymond Grout. You know Ray Grout.

Rowena I've never seen him before. What a sweet old man.

Miles You must have seen him before. He used to teach here. French. Retired now.

Rowena Oh, look, he's got a little table. Isn't that nice? All to himself.

Miles He's scoring, darling, he's scoring.

Rowena He looks so cosy, all tucked up.

Miles Oh, do shut up about it. He's not a dear old man. He's an appalling bloke.

Rowena Don't be so mean.

Miles Well. Any time you see anything over the age of forty-seven, you go into these phoney geriatric raptures. Old people are no nicer and no nastier than anybody else. They're just older.

Rowena You'd better get changed, hadn't you?

Miles (*taking off his watch and handing it to her*) Here.

Rowena What's that?

Miles My watch.

Rowena What do you want me to do with it?

Miles Look after it. I don't want to leave it in here while I'm on the field. Can't risk that.

Rowena takes the watch from him. Miles goes into the pavilion

Rowena Well, I must say, that's a terrific spirit, isn't it? The great comradeship of cricket. Nobody trusts anybody. Is that why they all rush off the field at the end of Test matches? To see if anyone's stolen their watches?

Miles (*from within*) What are you prattling about?

Rowena Is this gold?

Miles Yes.

Rowena I didn't know it was gold.

Miles My twenty-first birthday present from my father. Never stopped once.

Rowena Is there much room in here? It doesn't look—(*She pushes the door open*)

Miles (*alarmed, from within*) Careful, darling, careful. Shut the door, for God's sake.

Rowena All right, all right. There's nothing very novel about seeing you jumping around in your jock strap, is there?

Miles Look, just close the door, will you? There's people out there.

Rowena (*still staring in through a crack in the door*) What's that thing?

Miles What thing?

Rowena That thing.

Miles Oh, that thing. That's a box. Now shut the door.

Rowena Oh, *that's* a box. I always wondered what a box was. I wonder why they call it a box? Box of tricks? Box of goodies? Box and cox, perhaps?

Pause

Are you frightened in case Celia sees you?

Miles (*after a pause*) Oh, do shut up.

Rowena You won't talk about it, will you?

Miles I prefer not to.

Rowena I don't mind talking about it. The fact that you are having an affair is, in my view, the best news for years. I am delighted. And I say that as a wife and mother. It's perked you up no end. In a little more than a month you are a changed man. Though how on earth an affair with Celia could possibly perk anyone up is beyond me. But it's done the trick.

Miles (*from within*) I don't think we want to talk too much about me, do we?

Rowena I've never hidden anything I do from you, Miles.

Miles I sometimes wish to God you did.

Rowena Oh, come on. Anything we had going fizzled out about four and a half minutes after I'd conceived our third child. You went off me. I went off you. Too bad. One of those things. If it hadn't been for the fact that I looked elsewhere and you weren't particularly interested in it anyway, we'd have split up years ago. No, my only worry was you. Living like a monk all this time. I was terrified you'd start developing things. You know. Something weird and repressed. Start jumping around the lawn in my nighties.

Miles Rowena, for goodness sake. Will you not scream all over the place?

Rowena Nobody's listening.

Miles You've got a voice like a ship-to-shore system.

Rowena I'm delighted, that's all. I won't talk to you any more. You obviously don't like talking to me so I'm off. I'll leave you to good old Ceel.

Miles, now changed, comes out of the pavilion.

Miles And please don't shout that out, either.

Rowena Everybody knows, Miles. Everybody knows.

Miles All the same. (*He reflects*) It's just my luck, isn't it? I mean, you go round with every man in the village and nobody seems to mind. I have one small, infinitesimal affair with my best friend's wife and that's the end of the friendship.

Rowena I think it was the shed that really did it, darling. I mean, rolling her in his own shed. That was a bit tactless.

Miles I didn't roll her in the shed.

Rowena You had a jolly good try. So legend has it. Oh, Miles, cheer up. Have a good time.

A cricket ball rolls near

You must enjoy your affair, Miles. Otherwise there's no point in having it. (*She picks up the ball*) I say, you're right. They are dreadfully hard, aren't they? Hup, catch, mind your slips——(*She tosses the ball to Miles who is unprepared for it. He makes a reflex grab and drops it. And stands nursing his finger*)

Miles Ow. (*He dances round*) Oh, hell.

Rowena Oh, Miles. That's pathetic.

Miles Ah. I think you've chipped the bone. Oh.

Rowena Let me see.

Miles No, no, no.

Rowena You'll have to do better than that. You don't see Geoffrey Botham hopping around, do you?

Miles I hate to bring this up but last year, in this same match, I scored an unbeaten sixty-eight which also happened to be the highest innings of the game.

Rowena Oh, yes, you won, didn't you?

Miles No, we didn't. But that wasn't my fault.

Rowena You won, even if they didn't.

Miles (*examining his fingers*) Oh well, I've still got nine of them left.

Rowena I think they're an awful idea. These Headmaster's Elevens, you know. All these middle-aged wrecks rolling around on the field being crippled by small boys. Is Toby playing?

Miles No, he's umpiring.

Rowena Thank heavens.

Miles He's captaining our side and umpiring. I don't know how he justifies that. I don't think I stand much of a chance of making a score. I'll be batting number eleven and out first ball. (*He moves off*) Ah well, better chuck a ball around for a bit. Till we're ready to start. You stopping?

Rowena Well, possibly. It always gets awfully boring in the middle, doesn't it? I'll see.

Miles Don't let the kids get lost.

Rowena No.

Miles Well, I know you.

Rowena Got your box on safely, darling?

Miles Rowena.

Rowena Well, do take care. For Celia's sake.

Miles Oh, my God.

Miles exits

Rowena (*giggling and then attempting conversation with Mr Grout*) Hallo, good afternoon. Is it very hard work, scoring? I said, is it very complicated work, scoring?

The reply she gets seems less than social

(*In a low voice*) Yes, Miles is right. You are a surly old sod, aren't you? (*In a louder voice, smiling*) Super.

Another cricket ball rolls to her. She picks it up

Whoops. Hallo, this yours? How old are you, then? (*After a pause*) Thirteen. Good heavens, you're huge for thirteen, aren't you. Whopping. (*She tosses him the ball*) Here you are. (*To herself*) He's gone all pink. What a stupid game, really. (*She calls*) Catch it, Miles. (*She watches*) And he's dropped it. Hooray. What a magnificent drop that was. And yes— (*She snatches up a couple of scoreboard numbers*)—look at that marking from the East Germans. It's a four five, that's got to be a winning score. (*She holds up the numbers*) Royaume Uni, nil points.

Toby comes out of the pavilion

Toby Hallo, Rowena, what are you playing at?

Rowena Sorry, Toby, I was just muddling up your numbers.

Toby (*calling to someone on the field*) Brian, phone call for you. Up at the school. Phone, yes. Why do doctors always get phone calls? I never get phone calls. (*To Rowena*) You going to do those?

Rowena What?

Toby The scoreboard.

Rowena Certainly not. No fear. How long have you been in there?

Toby In where?

Rowena In the shed.

Toby It's not a shed, it's a pavilion.

Rowena It looks very like a shed.

Toby Ah, it may look like a shed but it isn't. It has these nails here, you see. To hang those numbers on.

Rowena Oh, yes. They have a significance the numbers, do they?

Toby Oh, rather.

Rowena Something mystical?

Toby You bet. You see, it's a widely held belief among these primitive cricketers that providing you can hang the right combination of numbers up on these nails here, you can keep the enemy out there and afraid to come in and take over your hut.

Rowena Pavilion.

Toby Pavilion, beg your pardon.

Rowena This is absolutely fascinating, Headmaster. So if I put nine hundred here and an eight hundred here . . .

Toby Oh, that'd put the fear of God into them. They'd all be rushing away towards square leg waving their equipment. All ritual, you see. (*In a terrible voice to someone just out of our vision*) Don't do that with a cricket bat, Ruttling, you stupid boy! Now put it down. Put it down. That is an expensive piece of equipment. It is not a stone-age club. Now go on, clear off, you wretched anthropoid. Clear right off the field. Off, off, right off. (*He mutters*) Stupid lout. (*To Rowena*) Sorry.

Rowena Gosh. Such power, Toby, such power.

Toby Listen, just before we start—(*He calls*) You arrange the toss, Hogg. . . . Terry, get together with Cairns, will you? Sort out who's batting. Thank you. (*Confidentially*) Listen, Rowena, we obviously both know what's happening at present.

Rowena Sorry?

Toby With Miles and Celia.

Rowena Oh yes, rather, yes.

Toby I haven't—wanted to talk to you about it before—I haven't wanted to talk about it at all . . . it's been a hell of a blow to me. No doubt it has to you.

Rowena Well, actually . . .

Toby I mean, Miles was a very special friend, there's no denying it. Only a few months ago the man probably saved my job so it makes it all doubly . . . but it still doesn't excuse him. The fact is I'm not—I'm afraid it's not in my nature to forgive that sort of behaviour. In either of them.

Rowena That's awful for you.

Toby You seem reasonably sanguine.

Rowena Yes, I am. You see, I think I sort of rather approve really.

Toby You do?

Rowena Yes. Do you think that's terrible of me?

Toby I think it's fairly typically modern.

Rowena Oh, I don't know. It was very fashionable to overlook these sort of things years ago. The French did.

Toby Oh, the French. I'm not talking about the bloody French. I just don't think it's on. Either she's my wife or she isn't. Either he's your husband or he isn't.

Rowena Yes, put that way . . .

Toby What other way is there to put it?

Rowena Yes, you're right. The trouble with me is, Toby, the real trouble with me is that I don't think.

Toby I don't believe that for a minute.

Rowena What?

Toby You think all right when it suits you.

Rowena God, you've discovered my secret.

Toby (*hunting around in the grass*) S'right.

Rowena What are you doing?

Toby I'm looking for things. Six things to count with. Here we are, bottle tops. Those'll do.

Rowena Ah, you teach the new bottle top maths, do you, Headmaster? How fascinating.

Toby Yes, I can sort of see Miles's point of view after ten minutes of being with you. You could make any marriage, however brief, seem like a lifetime together.

Rowena Will this do? (*She hands him another bottle top*)

Toby Thank you.

Rowena I'm thirty-seven years old this year, Toby. Miles thinks I'm thirty-six but I'm thirty-seven and I'm going to get as much out of my life as I can while I can. I don't think that necessarily means that I have to be selfish. It just means I refuse to get solemn and boring and dragged down by the same dreary tiny preoccupations that seem to obsess most people. Miles is getting something from Celia which he didn't get and didn't even want from me. Presumably. And presumably Celia is getting something from Miles that she doesn't get from you. Now, if you want Celia to stop getting things from Miles that you think she ought to be getting from you, you'd better start giving Celia the things she's having to get from Miles because you're not giving them to her. And then perhaps she won't want them from him any more and she'll come to you for them. Which is what she should have done in the first place. And that's my advice to you, Toby. Toodle-oo. (*She begins to walk off round the field*) Play up, boys.

She disappears from view

Toby Complete mad woman. (*He calls*) Completely mad, that one, Raymond. Loopy, yes. (*He looks up as someone calls to him from across the field*) What's that? Ah, we're batting. Jolly good. You want the batting order, Mr Grout, for my lot? (*He takes a piece of paper from his pocket*) Now then. One, Schooner. Two, Hogg. Three, Coombes. Four, Burgess. (*He yells*) You all right to open, are you, Terry? Five, Hawker. Six, Wills. Seven, Bartlett. (*He breaks off as he sees somebody in the pavilion*) What are you doing in there? Are you a cricketer? I said, are you a cricketer? No, you are not a cricketer, are you? Then get out. That is for cricketers only. Now, go away. I don't care. You're old enough to control yourself. That toilet is for cricketers only. Now, go away. Shoo. Seven, Bartlett. Eight, Colonel Malton—although he should be ten. Nine, Tobitt. Ten, Halliwell. And that blasted Hepplewick man, number eleven. Beggars can't be choosers.

Celia comes along round the edge of the field. She has a cardigan in a bag

(*Continuing to talk to Grout and ignoring Celia*) I don't know what Hepplewick's done to this pitch, I'm sure. His father spent twenty years of his life making that one of the best strips in the county. Hepplewick's destroyed it in three days. It now has all the fine texture of the inside of a rowing boat. (*To Celia, coolly*) Afternoon to you.
Celia (*likewise*) Good afternoon.

Pause

Toby Very noble of you to turn out.
Celia I usually do, don't I?
Toby You haven't been much in evidence at school functions of late, have you?
Celia I'm amazed you missed me. I imagined you must have forgotten all about me.
Toby Ah, now that is difficult, Celia. It really is. What with the floods of enquiries I receive about your progress and welfare, the phone ringing constantly, it's been awfully hard to put you entirely out of my mind. May I enquire, Headmaster, how is your wife's affair these days? Oh, not so bad, thank you, Colonel Malton. She had another good night last night. And I think things are beginning to take a turn for the better.
Celia What nonsense.
Toby Celia, there is nobody left in the county that doesn't know about it. I can't make out whether I'm angrier with you for your infidelity or your sheer bloody ineptitude. They're practically posting bulletins about you on the school noticeboard. Oh,yes, they're both fine. They had a good meal at *The Swan* last night. He had fillet steak and she had a jolly nice sole off the bone. That was a couple of the school Governors sitting at the next table. And then you just happened to stay at *The Wheatsheaf* at Chittling which just happens to be where every parent takes their wretched child out for tea. So I get a full report from the fourth form.

Celia I think you've just been having us followed.

Toby There's no question of having you followed. I don't need to. You're both following everybody else.

Celia Well, if that's all you're worried about. Your reputation.

Toby Well, a Headmaster needs the odd shred or two. To try and maintain some sort of credibility.

Celia Yours went out of the window with the empties.

Toby Yes, well, thank you very much for helping to screw the lid down on me as well.

Celia That is a vile thing to say. I've stood by you for years, Toby. Absolute years. I've covered up for you. . . . Now, I'm having a little tiny bit of fun.

Toby Everybody seems to be in search of fun this afternoon.

Celia Why not?

Toby Well, I wish to God at least you looked as if you were having some. I could just about put up with it if you looked a little radiant or fulfilled. . . . You look like a lemur with mange.

Celia moves away a little

All right, I'm going out there now. I've got to umpire. You sit here and chat to your boyfriend. You can do the numbers.

Celia I'm not doing the numbers.

Toby Oh, come on, Celia. Do something.

Celia Ask the boys. It's the boys' job.

Toby The boys aren't allowed here. I've put it out of bounds to everyone except the teams.

Celia What an extraordinary thing to do.

Toby Not after what they were up to in the middle of the night, it wasn't. Hawker caught them at it.

Celia Caught them at what?

Toby (*rattling a handful of bottle tops from his pocket*) God knows. Playing Headmaster's Wives probably. Right.

Celia What are those? Bottle tops?

Toby Right.

Celia What are you doing with pockets full of bottle tops?

Toby You should see where I've got the bottles. (*He shouts*) It's twenty-five to. Are we starting? Well, I've been waiting for you lot. (*He starts to move*) Come on then, Thompson, get your hands out of your pockets. Very few good bowlers bowl with their hands in their pockets, I can tell you.

Toby exits

Celia sits on the bench, looking far from happy

We hear the sound of men shouting on the field and the general clatter from people in the cricket pavilion

A cricket ball rolls near Celia. Abstractedly, she doesn't notice

Celia (*her attention brought to the ball*) What? Oh, yes, all right. (*She picks it up and throws it, rather feebly, back*) Try not to let it over here, William.

Thank you. Good afternoon, Mr Grout. (*She sits and lights a cigarette, her eyes darting hither and thither*)

Miles runs towards Celia

Miles Heads! (*He intercepts a cricket ball which apparently was heading for Celia and throws it back with a flourish causing Celia to duck as he does so*)
Celia Oh.
Miles Hallo, then.
Celia Hallo.
Miles Get everything done?
Celia What?
Miles You said you had a lot to get done this morning.
Celia Oh, yes. Well, Cubs and things. I had to sort out his uniform.
Miles Ah. (*He surveys the ground*) Extraordinary pitch this year. Don't know what's happened to it.
Celia Apparently the groundsman's ruined it.
Miles Lionel Hepplewick? He's certainly done something very strange. It's sort of corrugated. I don't fancy batting on it. You OK?
Celia Yes.
Miles You look a bit low.
Celia Like a lemur with mange apparently.
Miles Pardon?
Celia That's what Toby told me I looked like.
Miles What a terrible thing to say to you. He's an appalling man occasionally, isn't he? Absolutely appalling. When I think I used to be a friend of his. A close friend. But the more I hear about the way he's treated you. . . . Well, it makes be absolutely boil.
Celia Oh, I shouldn't have told you.
Miles No wonder you look flattened.
Celia Do I?
Miles I'd better get my pads on. I'm first wicket down. (*He goes into the pavilion*)
Celia (*talking to him through the door*) Toby's always called me things. He doesn't really mean them. I think it's just part of our relationship. Me standing there and him calling me names. I think originally they were intended to show affection. At one time. Only the meaning's been lost over the years. Even in his speech at our wedding day he referred to me as looking like an oven-ready chicken wrapped in butter muslin. Which was only a joke. I think. Mother didn't think so. But I'm sort of used to it really.
Miles (*from within*) You don't want me to start calling you names, do you?
Celia No. I think I have quite enough to be going on with, thank you.

A figure runs out of the pavilion wearing pads and carrying a bat

Oh, good luck, Mr Schooner.
Schooner Thank you, Mrs Teasdale.

Schooner exits

Celia I didn't know he was in there. Miles, why didn't you tell me Reg Schooner was in there? Miles?

Sound of a toilet flushing

Oh.

Celia claps the opening batsman rather limply along with some other applause

What was that, Mr Grout? Bowler's name. (*In a shrill voice*) Could we have the bowler's name, please. The name of the bowler. The bowler—oh, God. Thompson, I think he said, Mr Grout. Thompson G. Yes, it is. It's Thompson G. Thompson H. is tiny.

Miles comes out of the pavilion

OK?

Miles Yes, I always forget to go before I put my pads on.

Celia Oh, is that tricky?

Miles Not really tricky. Just adds to the general hazard. Now who've we got bowling? Ah.

Celia Thompson G.

Toby Oh, yes. He's fairly quick. I remember him from last year. Caught me on the elbow.

They watch

Ah, we're away. Nice shot. Useful bat, Reg Schooner. Very orthodox.

Celia (*picking up a number*) Was that a one?

Miles Yes, just a single. Ah, that's brought Rowena's little chum down to face.

Celia Terry Hogg really is an odd shape for a P.E. teacher. I think the boys call him wart or something. Wart Hogg. Quite a good name.

Miles Yes, it is. I'll remember it.

Celia How's Rowena? I carefully avoided her earlier.

Miles Oh, she's very cheerful. I think she's actually going batty but she's very cheerful.

Celia Well, she always was odd.

Miles Yes. Likeable, though.

Celia Oh yes, she's likeable. But then she's approachable, isn't she?

Miles Yes.

Celia Open.

Miles Yes.

Celia Accessible.

Miles True.

Celia Sort of comes at you.

Miles Yup. I think these are left-handed batting gloves.

Celia Toby's actually being very unpleasant.

Miles Yes. (*He calls*) Good shot. (*To Celia*) More runs.

Celia Why did I get stuck with this?

Miles Two more. That makes three.

Celia (*sorting the numbers irritably*) All right, I can count. I can count.

Miles Sorry, sorry.

Celia Then don't treat me like a child.

Miles Sorry.

Celia sorts the numbers

Well, Rowena's being super, I must say. Absolutely super.

Celia Yes, you said.

Miles She's not letting it affect her at all.

Celia Well, good for her.

Miles I mean, she could have been all heavy and jealous but she's not. She's not at all.

Celia Hooray.

Pause

Miles Is tomorrow still on?

Celia I don't know.

Miles Well, are we going or not? (*After a pause*) I booked the place.

Celia Look, there's so much to organize, Miles. You don't seem to realize.

Miles All right, I'll cancel it.

Celia It's all very well. I can't just drop things and run off to these hotels every second of the day just to suit you. I've still got two kids. I've still got a house to run. It's really not that easy. It takes a great deal of organizing. It's all right for you. You can just walk out and leave it all to Rowena.

Miles I don't do that.

Celia Oh, yes, you do.

Miles I don't leave it all to Rowena. I can't possibly leave it all to Rowena. She's never there.

Celia Well, you've got an au pair, haven't you? And a cleaning woman. And a God-knows who else. You've got a whole household of women looking after you. You're waited on hand and foot.

Miles Why are you suddenly getting at me? You've got a cleaning woman come to that.

Celia I've not got a cleaning woman, I've got Sylvie Bell. Whom I have to follow round while she does everything. Who smears polish on things and doesn't rub it off. Who makes beds without straightening the under blanket so Toby complains of lumps. Who only cleans half the bath for some extraordinary reason. And who never moves the sofa when she hoovers because she thinks it won't notice.

Miles Yes, I can see. It can be pretty hard. So—(*He looks at the field*) Ah, that's a bye.

Celia Is that a one, then?

Miles Yes.

Celia changes the numbers

Miles That came up round his nose somewhere. (*He calls*) Want a helmet, do you, Reg . . . helmet . . . doesn't matter . . . doesn't matter. (*To Grout*) That was a bye, Mr Grout, a bye. He signalled a bye. (*To Celia*) There've been about eighteen balls in this over. Do you think Toby's counting?

Celia No idea.

Miles He keeps taking things out of his pocket. I suppose that's what he's counting with.

Celia Bottle tops.

Miles My God. If he's using bottle tops he's probably littered with the things.

Celia He blamed us for his drinking.

Miles Us?

Celia Indirectly.

Miles I don't think he can blame us.

Celia He said I was screwing the lid down on him.

Miles Heavens. That's—(*shouting*)—fielded. (*He claps*) Good that little chap, isn't he? (*He watches the game for a second*) No, I think the marvellous thing about Rowena is that I don't think she really minds about us. She really doesn't. I mean, it's not an act. She's really delighted we're—together. I suppose you have to admire her.

Celia Isn't that her over there? Who's she with?

Miles Oh, that's—er—that estate agent bloke. Tobitt.

Celia Yes. Must be a sign of age when estate agents seem to get younger and younger.

Miles Hope she remembers she's got the kids with her. She does that. Went out shopping one day. Came back without them. Forgotten she had them.

Celia She seems quite organized.

Miles Oh, she can be. You see, she's really a whole load of paradoxes, is Rowena. On the one hand, she's—sorry, you don't want to talk about her, do you? I can sense it.

Celia No, I'm fascinated. Very interesting.

Miles No, no. I can sense it. (*He gets up*) Ought to get someone to throw me a ball or two. (*He looks at the field*) Oops. There's a couple more. Off the edge over the top. (*He calls*) Sneaky, Reg, sneaky ... I said, sneaky ... doesn't matter. (*To Celia*) Cloud's coming over. Hope we don't get interruptions.

Celia Would you say I was—would you say I was fun to be with?

Miles Who? You?

Celia Yes, me. We've changed the subject to me.

Miles Fun.

Celia Yes.

Miles Well.

Celia Well, don't rush, will you?

Miles No, I was considering fun as a word. You know it has strange connotations these days. Fun fur and fun runs. And fun people.

Celia I just meant fun.

Miles Jolly, you mean?

Celia No, I don't mean jolly. That's all fat and red-faced. I mean, fun.

Miles Yes, I suppose you are. Yes.

Celia You don't sound terribly convincing.

Miles Well, to be quite honest with you, Celia, I don't think that's really your forte. I mean, if you took a fun poll of people in the vicinity, voting for people with a high fun quotient, then frankly, I don't think you'd feature very near the top.

Celia Below Rowena, for instance?

Miles Well, yes. It's difficult to—yes, I think probably in terms of fun—I mean, fun—yes, you would. But then in other polls of course, you'd be streets ahead.

Celia Yes, I can imagine what they'd be.

Miles Still, as I say, it depends what you call fun. I think of fun rather when people do unexpected things to you. Jump out at you or put glue in your bedroom slippers.

Celia I don't. Fun's enjoyment, isn't it?

Miles Oh, you're enjoyable—another two. A lot of this stuff's coming up head high—Is that what you mean, enjoyable?

Celia No, I don't mean enjoyable. That makes me sound like a day trip. I simply mean, I wish I was fun to be with. (*She changes the score*) I wish we were fun. I don't think either of us are much fun at present.

Miles Me? I'm not fun. I've never claimed to be fun.

Celia Well, I think we both ought to be.

Miles You've just put a nine up there, darling.

Celia I mean, why else are we doing all this? Going to all this trouble.

Miles Trouble?

Celia All this organizing and baby-sitting and pre-arranging children's meals. I mean, the least I expect from it is a little fun.

Miles Darling, do change the score for heaven's sake. We haven't got ninety something.

Celia (*moving away*) Oh, you do it. I can't.

Miles (*getting up*) You're getting yourself in a terrible state over absolutely nothing. (*He adjusts the scoreboard*) What is it, Mr Grout? Ten? Twelve. Oh, better still. (*To Celia*) Look, darling, people are watching us. Come on. I mean, we have laughs, don't we? That's fun. We get a few laughs.

Celia I don't know that we do, really. You know, Miles, I think we must be the glummest pair I've ever met.

Miles Well, love's always—er—it's always got its painful side. It's never all that funny. But they pretend it is. It always seems to me that love's about losing your luggage somewhere and food poisoning and acute sunburn and arguing because one of you's late. Or early. I don't know. Always is, in my case. It's always about looking forward to things that don't quite turn out as they should.

Celia Oh, dear.

Miles That's just me, though. I always see a lot of other people bouncing about smiling.

Celia Would you like us to call it a day?

Miles Us?

Celia Yes.

Miles Well. . . . Look, I'm just going in to bat actually.

Celia It's just that we both seem to be putting in more than either of us are getting out.

Miles (*unhappily*) I don't know. I thought we were—shot—(*He puts up
another number*)—I thought we were . . . I'm doing my best, honestly.
Celia It's not you, Miles. It's me. I'm just not fun. I did the cliché thing. I
got married. I gave up my job. I cut myself off quite deliberately from all
the things that kept me lively, kept me alive. I lost contact. Now here I am
ten years later sterile and boring.
Miles I don't think you're boring. Promise.
Celia Oh, you're such a dear, kind man, Miles, you really are. I think I
actually love you quite a lot.
Miles (*emotionally*) Ah, well . . . God, I'm getting all choked up now. I wish
you wouldn't do this. I'm supposed to go in and bat in a minute.
Celia What's the matter?
Miles (*getting up and moving away*) Nothing.
Celia You're not crying, are you?
Miles No. Good God, no. No. Heavens, no.
Celia Miles.
Miles No, it was just then. When you said about calling it a day. It rather
took me aback. . . . Just a sec. I'd better get some batter betting gloves.
Better batting gloves. Excuse me.

Miles hurries into the pavilion

Celia Oh, dear. (*She calls to someone*) What? Is it? Well, I don't know what
the score is. What's the total, Mr Grout? How much? Oh, is it? Right, I'll
change it. (*She alters the numbers*)

Sound of a shout from the field

Is that—? Oh. He's out. Miles, someone's out. Miles.

Miles comes out of the pavilion trying to compose himself

Miles OK. OK.
Celia You all right?
Miles Yes, yes. Do I look OK?
Celia Yes, you look fine. You're sure you'll be able to bat?
Miles Oh, absolutely. Stupid. I don't normally. . . . Ridiculous. Right. (*He
sets off determinedly towards the middle*)
Celia Will you want your bat?
Miles Oh, yes. God. Yes, thank you.
Celia (*back to her scoreboard*) That's for one now, isn't it? Good luck.
Miles (*setting off again*) I'll take Reg's gloves. It's simpler.

Miles exits

Celia changes the board so that it reads fifteen for one

Celia (*to Mr Grout*) Last man what, Mr Grout? Seven? Does that go at the
bottom? Righto.

Reg Schooner comes hurrying past her to the pavilion

Well played, Reg.

Schooner (*muttering*) Lethal out there, lethal.

Schooner goes into the pavilion

Celia Really. (*She looks anxiously out to the field*) Hope he'll be all right. (*She watches the game*)

Sound of a shout from the field

My God, it's terribly dangerous. (*She shouts through the doorway behind her*) You're quite right, Reg, it looks awful. (*To herself*) It's clouding over, too. What a shame. (*She takes a cardigan from her bag and slips it round her shoulders*) Brrr. Good shot. (*To Grout*) It's quite cold when the sun goes in. (*She changes the scoreboard to sixteen*)

After a while, Lionel Hepplewick appears in the doorway of the pavilion. He is a man in his early thirties, with a look of someone with the secret of eternal knowledge and a frequent smile that suggests he knows something you don't

Lionel Afternoon, Mrs Teasdale.

Celia Oh, good afternoon, Mr Hepplewick. I'm afraid it's clouding over.

Lionel No, you won't get any rain. Not this afternoon.

Celia No?

Lionel No.

Celia Is that what the weather forecast said?

Lionel No.

Celia I've just been hearing a lot of complaints about your pitch, Mr Hepplewick.

Lionel My pitch.

Celia They're all complaining it's a bit lumpy.

Lionel Oh, yes.

Celia The ball certainly seems to be bouncing rather high.

Lionel That won't be the pitch.

Celia No?

Lionel No. No, that's the atmosphere. Atmosphere makes the ball bounce higher.

Celia Oh, really.

Lionel That pitch is like a pool table.

Celia Oh.

Lionel You'll always get that. Either your bowler's complaining because it's too easy paced or your batsman's complaining because the bounce is uneven. No way a groundsman can win.

Celia Well, they all seem to be complaining at the moment.

Lionel (*with satisfaction*) Then I reckon I've got it probably about right, haven't I?

Celia I mean, look at that. That ball went right up past his nose.

Lionel Yes, he's digging them in a bit, this lad. Nice little bowler.

Celia No, he's not. He's really quite a big bowler, isn't he? I think someone ought to do something. That looked quite dangerous.

Lionel I expect he'll be all right. Mr Coombes. I wouldn't worry about him.

Celia I'm worried about everyone.
Lionel Oh, yes?
Celia Including you.

Pause

Lionel Still, your husband's umpiring. I expect he'll see fair play, won't he?
Celia I don't quite follow you.
Lionel I expect he'll see Mr Coombes all right, won't he?
Celia I'm sure he will. There's another one. Now that very nearly hit him. This can't be right, surely?
Lionel There's nothing wrong with that. Good ball. I see Mrs Coombes over there.
Celia Oh?
Lionel By the bicycle sheds. Looking very attractive. Dressed for summer.
Celia Well, July's the time to do it if you're going to.
Lionel Right.
Celia And how's your father these days, Lionel? All right?
Lionel Oh, he gets about. He gets about. Apart from his legs of course.
Celia Yes, we do miss him at the school.
Lionel Yes.
Celia Not the same without him.
Lionel No. (*After a pause*) Good meal at *The Compass*, was it? Last Sunday? Saw you there.
Celia Oh yes, excellent. Were you eating there?
Lionel No, no. I can't afford to eat there, I'm afraid.
Celia What a shame. It's well worth saving up for.
Lionel I can't find anyone to treat me.
Celia Well, you'll have to pay for yourself, Lionel, like the rest of us.
Lionel I was just in the bar. Saw you both in there. I usually try to get out for a bit of a drink on Sundays. With one or two of the lads.
Celia Oh, you've got friends as well, have you? Are they all caretakers like yourself? Trainee groundsmen?
Lionel (*looking at the field*) Wow, there's another one. That nearly got him. (*He laughs*)
Celia I know the Headmaster's wife shouldn't say this, Lionel, not to the school caretaker but if anything happens to Mr Coombes while he's out there batting, I shall hold you personally responsible.
Lionel Me?
Celia And I shall come round to see you and I shall take my very sharp fingernails and I shall make the same mess of your face as you've apparently made of our cricket pitch.
Lionel (*amused*) Now, now, now.
Celia Now, bugger off.
Lionel Oh, right. Temper, temper. Right, I'm going. I'm going—(*He looks back at the field*) Oh, he's out. Coombsie's out.
Celia Oh, no.
Lionel LBW.
Celia He can't be out. That wasn't out.

Lionel Good bit of bowling. Kept one low, you see. Had him beaten all the way. What did he get then? What did he get, Mr Grout? Nothing? Did he get nothing? Put Coombsie down for nothing.
Celia Who's in next then? Nobody's going out there.
Lionel It'll be Dr Burgess. Oh, he got called away.
Celia Called away?
Lionel Emergency. Said I was to bat for him if he wasn't back.
Celia Well, you'd better get some things on, hadn't you? Quickly.
Lionel Oh, hell. I'll take his. I'll take them off Mr Coombes.

Lionel hurries off

Celia (*sweetly, after him*) Good luck, Lionel. I do hope you get your head knocked off. (*To herself*) What a vile man. (*She looks up*) Oh. (*To Grout*) Was that a spot of rain, Mr Grout? Yes, I thought it was. What a shame. (*She takes a hat from her bag and puts it on*)

Miles appears on the edge of the field, just removing his second batting pad as he does so. He has handed over the rest of his equipment. He tosses the pad back to Lionel

Miles (*to Lionel*) Here. Much good may it do you. I suggest you wrap it round your head. (*He storms furiously back to the pavilion, speaking to Celia*) Did you see that? Did you witness that?
Celia Yes, I did.
Miles That pitch is an absolute disgrace. He has no right to ask people to bat on it. Absolute sheer bloody suicide. Did you see it?
Celia Bouncing round your head, yes.
Miles Right up here. Not one but five in the over. Mind you, the bloody drunk umpiring was no better. Nine ball overs and he's supposed to caution them after two bouncers. (*He goes into the pavilion*)
Celia Yes, well, bad luck.

Miles reappears almost immediately

Miles I had five in a row. Five bouncers in a row. Little grinning herbert. I'll wipe the smile off his face when he comes off. Then I get one ball—did you see that last ball?
Celia Yes, it was——
Miles Three yards outside the off stump. Worst ball I've ever faced in my life. I go forward, which I grant you on that pitch is suicidal, I go forward and the thing shoots straight along the ground.
Celia Heavens.
Miles LBW. That was a deliberate, biased, petty and vindictive piece of umpiring. (*He goes back into the pavilion. From within*) He's not going to be allowed to forget this. Oh no. Not for a very long time.
Celia What are you doing? You're not getting changed, are you?
Miles No, I'm just taking my thigh pad off.
Celia Oh.
Miles Damn good job I wore this as well. (*He appears again, brandishing his thigh pad and clutching his trousers*) Well, all I can say is it's poetic justice.

Hepplewick's having to bat. I've got a few things to say to him as well.
(*He goes back in the pavilion*)
Celia (*jumping to her feet*) Oh Lord, it really is raining now. (*She moves to
the doorway*) Miles, can I come in?
Miles Hang on, darling, I've only got my trousers half on.
Celia Well, just in the doorway. I can't stand out in this. (*She moves to the
doorway*)

Sound of the rain pattering on the roof

They're all going off now. Most of them seem to be sheltering under the
bike sheds. Toby isn't. No, Toby's coming this way. Miles, Toby's
coming. Miles.

Sound of a toilet flushing

Oh. I don't think this is going to last. It's only a cloudburst

Toby comes on, jogging sedately off the field

Toby What a downpour. Wasn't expecting that. Excuse me. (*He squeezes
into the doorway beside her*)
Celia Toby, that pitch is in a terrible state, isn't it?
Toby Seemed all right to me.
Celia Toby, the ball was bouncing all over the place. It's most terribly
dangerous.
Toby Nonsense.
Celia According to Miles, it's in a——
Toby Oh well, according to Miles, yes. And he got himself out didn't he?
Celia He says he wasn't out, either.
Toby What? Absolutely plum. Never seen anything so plum. Half-baked
little forward prod. Came forward six inches, bop. No hesitation.
Celia Well, he disagrees. (*She looks into the pavilion*) Don't you? I'm saying
you disagree, don't you, Miles?
Toby Oh, there you are. What's this disputing the umpire's decision, eh?
Not very good form, Miles, is it? Letting a thirteen-year-old kid rattle
you. (*He goes into the pavilion*)

Celia stays in the doorway, looking rather anxious

Miles (*off*) You know damn well, Toby, that was a totally monstrous
decision.
Celia Now, come on, Miles.
Toby (*off*) I know nothing of the sort. It looked absolutely plum from
where I was standing.
Celia Now then, Toby.
Miles (*off*) Rubbish.
Celia It's not worth arguing about, surely.
Toby (*off*) I had an absolutely perfect view, old boy.
Celia Why don't we all break for tea?
Miles (*off*) I'm amazed you can see anything at all. You reek of bloody
alcohol.

Celia Miles, please, please.
Toby (*off*) Don't tell me I reek of bloody alcohol, matey. Don't you start
swearing at me.
Celia Please. Both of you.
Miles (*off*) I'm warning you. Don't do that.

Sound of a clatter of stumps from the pavilion.

Celia Toby.
Toby (*off*) I'll do what I like. It's my hut.

Sound of a clunk

Celia Miles.
Miles (*off*) You're not doing that. Not with my equipment.

Sound of a scuffle and a grunt

Celia If you both fight, I shall start screaming. I shall scream, I really shall.
Toby (*off*) Ah!
Celia Toby!

Miles appears in the doorway slightly breathless

Miles Right. You stay down there, do you hear? You get up. I shall hit you
again, Toby, I really will. I'm warning you.
Celia Have you hurt him?
Miles No, he's not hurt. He's OK. Just his pride

*Miles turns to move away but a cricket pad flies out of the pavilion and hits him
in the back*

Oh, well. Right now. I warned you.

Miles goes back in, determinedly

Celia (*screaming*) Toby! Miles! Somebody! Rowena! Somebody help.

*Celia goes into the pavilion momentarily but comes staggering out backwards,
clutching a cricket bag which obviously caught her when she stepped into the
line of fire*

Miles (*off*) Sorry. Sorry, darling.
Celia Oh.
Toby (*off*) Keep out of the damn way, Celia.
Celia Oh, dear God. Please, please don't fight. I'm not worth fighting over.
I'm really not.

Toby momentarily appears in the doorway

Toby We're not fighting over you, you half-witted hamster. (*He plunges
back into the fray*)
Celia Why is nobody coming to help? Nobody's coming. They're all just
standing there in the bicycle sheds, shouting and jeering

A sudden sharp shout from within the pavilion. A crash. And then silence

(*Apprehensively*) Toby? Miles? (*She looks into the pavilion very cautiously*)
Miles?

Sound of a groan

Toby.

*Toby appears in the doorway, clutching a bloodstained sports shirt to his
nose*

Toby, what's happened?
Toby (*rather muffled*) Nothing. Just a bang on the nose.
Celia What's happened to Miles?
Toby He's all right. Only his pride. I must get to a tap.
Celia Yes, I'll—(*she is torn between Toby and Miles. To Miles*) Are you all
right, darling? You sure? I'll just go with Toby, then I'll be back.

Celia rejoins Toby who is moving slowly across the field

It's not broken, is it?
Toby Take more than him to break this. (*He shouts*) What are you lot
staring at? Never seen a man with a nosebleed before? (*To Celia*) Go on,
leave me. I'll be all right.

Toby exits

Celia No, I'll come with you. I'll come with you. (*She runs back to Miles*) I'll
be back, Miles, don't go away. I'll be back, I promise. Try not to move
too much. (*She hurries after Toby*) No, it's all right, boys. You go back
under the shelter. You're getting rained on. No, the Headmaster walked
into some sports equipment. He's perfectly all right. Now, go away. Go
on.

Celia follows Toby off

*Miles stumbles into the doorway of the pavilion, looking a little the worse
for wear*

Miles (*gingerly pressing his ribs*) Aaarh. Go on, you lot. Buzz off. Well, I
walked into the other bit of sports equipment. It's your fault entirely this,
Thompson. If you'd pitched a few up in the first place, I wouldn't be in
this state. I'm reporting you to the Test Board. You wait till I'm bowling.
God. (*He sits on the steps and starts to take his boots off*) I'll be lucky. I
have a faint feeling that might have been a rather foolish thing to do. I
think that's the end of a beautiful friendship entirely. Possibly two of
them. (*He tilts his face up to the rain for a moment, his boots half off*)

*Rowena appears, wandering round the edge of the field. She is wearing a
rather large brimmed hat (male) with feathers in it*

Rowena Well done.
Miles Oh, hallo.
Rowena There was a strange optical illusion just then. From the bike sheds
there, one got the distinct impression of two men fighting in a shed.
Pavilion, beg its pardon.

Miles Was there?

Rowena Trick of the light?

Miles Absolutely.

Rowena Oh, good.

Miles What have you got on your head?

Rowena Raingear. One of the boys leant it to me. The brother of that very
nice bowler.

Miles Thompson.

Rowena That's the one. Thompson G.

Miles Thompson G. is not a very nice bowler at all.

Rowena That may be your opinion. Anyway, this belongs to his brother,
Thompson H., who is very, very much smaller, but with a pretty large
head. And a fine taste in hats. What do you think the H is for? H for hat,
obviously. What else? Thompson Hat and his brother, Thompson ...
Thompson Groin, perhaps. Upon which he is forever polishing his ball.
Or maybe ...

Miles Just a second, Rowena, just a second.

Rowena He didn't damage you, did he? Old drunk Toby. Did he topple over
on top of you?

Miles No.

Rowena Or pelt you with non-returnable empties?

Miles I don't think this is a cloud burst. I think this is setting in. Aren't you
getting wet?

Rowena No. Thompson's H. is getting wet. I'm OK.

Miles Rowena, if you could allow your mind to settle for a moment.

Rowena Plop.

Miles Would you say I was ... I mean if you were describing me to
someone, would you describe me at all as fun?

Rowena Fun?

Miles Yes.

Rowena Yes, you're enormous fun.

Miles Am I?

Rowena Oh, yes. I've had endless fun with you, Miles. Hours of fun for
your friends. Absolutely guaranteed non-toxic, harmless for children,
batteries extra. Why do you ask?

Miles I was just trying to place myself in the scheme of things. I don't think
I am, you see. I think I'm probably rather boring, actually.

Rowena Well, yes, you are.

Miles Am I?

Rowena But, you see, even boring people can be fun. In fact, practically
anyone or anything that doesn't have a sharp edge or go bang can be fun.
(*After a pause*) I think that's frightfully deep for me. Do you think that as
I get older I'll get deeper and deeper? Have you read Rowena Coombes
on this? Absolutely first rate. Picked it up from where Russell dropped it.
Frightfully good. Well, if you're all right I'll go back to the ménage
Thompson. They're looking after our three.

Miles I think we're breaking for tea, by the look of it. What's the time? Oh
yes, my watch. You've got my watch.

Rowena Oh, Miles. Now listen. I'm afraid I gave it away.

Miles What do you mean, you gave it away?

Rowena There was this old man, Miles, he was so pathetic. You should have seen him. He came up to me just along there and he said to me, "Excuse me, lady, have you got the time?"

Miles I don't believe this.

Rowena And I said, "Look, old tattered man, I have more than that for you. I have a watch."

Miles And you gave him my watch.

Rowena nods

Miles walks calmly away, turns, squares up with the pavilion runs in and kicks it

You gave him my bloody watch. The one that I've had since my twenty-first birthday. Why do you do this to me, Rowena, why do you do this . . .

Rowena holds up his watch

(*Not seeing this*) You're just stupid and thoughtless, dumb and stupid and . . .

Rowena Miles, Miles, Miles, Miles, Miles. Look, look.

Miles stops

Miles (*quietly*) You didn't give it away.

Rowena No, that was a joke, Miles. Now, remember, I told you about jokes before, darling. They're the things you go ha ha at when I nod at you.

Miles Every time you do that to me, and you do tend to do that rather a lot, let's be honest, there's a man up there somewhere with a large book. And in that book are all our names and the times of when we were born and the times we're due to die. And every time you do that, he opens that book and he knocks another couple of days off my life.

Rowena I feel we're fellow philosophers, Miles. The Masters and Johnson of modern thought. We arrived at these astounding conclusions by first hiding each other's wristwatches. Bye-bye, Miles. See you, no doubt. In the breakfast room. Or across in the other bed or something.

EITHER he says:

Miles Right.

Rowena See you then.

Miles Yep.

Rowena (*rather sadly*) Bye. Give my love to Ceel.

Miles Yep.

Rowena (*as she goes*) Oink, oink.

Rowena exits

Miles gets up, moves a little and winces. He looks at his watch

Miles Oh, that's not too bad, it's only ... It's only—(*he looks faintly puzzled, then holds the watch to his ear. He shakes it incredulously*) It's stopped. I don't believe it. She's managed to get it to stop. How can she make it stop? (*He shouts*) Rowena! The woman's a walking magnetic storm. Fifteen years this has been going. Sixteen. Nearly seventeen. God, I'm getting old. How the hell did she manage it? (*He glares at the scoreboard. He sees the nought at the bottom*) We'll have that changed for a start. I'm worth at least fifty. (*He hangs a five next to the nought*) I'm not boring. I'm very interesting. I fascinate me, anyway.

Celia comes back

Celia He's gone up to the San. Just to check. I'm sure it's not broken but anyway. You see, you both have your ministering angels. I saw Rowena come flying round.

Miles Yes. She just came round hopefully, clutching a copy of my will.

Celia Well, what a display. The Headmaster and the Chairman of the Board of Governors punching each other in the cricket pavilion. Another school first. He'd just put this place out of bounds to the kids because they'd been misusing it.

Miles Look, I'm sorry. I'm sorry.

Celia Well.

Miles Are we still packing it in then?

Celia I don't know. Are we?

Miles I think you were suggesting earlier that we should.

Celia I said, should we, that's all. I was asking you.

Miles Well, it hadn't crossed my mind.

Celia And now?

Miles I. ... Do you want to?

Celia (*softly*) No. But I think I ought to offer you a way out.

Miles Why?

Celia Because I think, knowing you as I do, you're actually a very faithful person and a very loyal person and love affairs outside your marriage are not things you're going to have a great number of. In fact, I think this is probably the one. I'm not wrong, am I?

Miles shrugs

And maybe I'm not possibly the ideal person for you to have your one and only love affair with.

Miles Oh, come on.

Celia No, I'm not saying it for that reason. I just think I might have trapped you somehow and I'm giving you the chance to run for it. I don't want you to run because I think it's my one and only love affair too. But it's very difficult for you to decide, isn't it? Between me and Rowena.

Miles Not at all.

Celia You do go on about her, Miles, you really do.

Miles I don't.

Celia You don't even know you're doing it.

Miles I'm sorry.

Celia It's all right.
Miles Well, I won't any more. You talk about Toby a bit, you know.
Celia Then I won't any more.
Miles Just us then.
Celia Sole topics.
Miles Fine.
Celia And we'll try and—have fun, shall we? Enjoy it.
Miles Oh, we'll have a lot of fun, I promise.
Celia We will. They've broken for tea. Coming?
Miles Sure.

They move away. As they walk, Celia looks at him and laughs. Miles looks a little startled. Then, getting the idea, he looks at her and laughs. They both laugh. They stop laughing and continue walking. Neither of them is totally convinced that the next few years is going to be all fun

The Lights fade to a Black-out

To: A SENTIMENTAL JOURNEY (page 69)

OR he says:

Miles Rowena.
Rowena Yes.
Miles Er——
Rowena Yes.
Miles Are you busy?
Rowena Busy?
Miles Have you made arrangements for later?
Rowena Well, if it stops raining I shall return Thompson's H., otherwise no.
Miles Can I—can I walk along with you?
Rowena You're terribly old-fashioned, Miles, but of course you may. You can stop the cabs splashing my crinoline.
Miles I wanted to say a few things to you.
Rowena Then I shall listen. You're not planning anything awful, are you? You're not going to push me into the stinging nettles.
Miles Not if you listen.
Rowena Then off we go. "Are you still wearing your box, sir?" she asked tremulously.
Miles No.
Rowena She was filled with a sense of sudden danger.
Miles Rowena.
Rowena Her heart leapt.
Miles Rowena.
Rowena Yes, Miles.
Miles If you're walking with me, you're not to talk for five minutes. All right?

Rowena Five minutes.

Miles Please.

Rowena Right, I'll try.

Miles Ssh. Not a word. (*They walk along*)

Rowena takes his arm

There. Isn't this nice?

Rowena (*breaking gently into her own version of* Singing in the Rain) Dee-dee-dee-dee-dee-dee-dee-dee-dee-dee-deeee . . .

Miles looks rather resigned that Rowena has discovered a loophole in their silence agreement. By the time they exit, Rowena is beginning to dance and even jump into puddles à la Gene Kelly

The lights fade to a Black-out

To: A 50TH CELEBRATION (page 75)

A SENTIMENTAL JOURNEY

A Churchyard. This year

The church door is closed. A gravel path leads away from it to an unseen road. A variety of gravestones border the path

We hear church bells signifying a happy occasion, followed by the sound of singing within the church. A service of Thanksgiving for Bilbury Lodge's fifty-year existence is being celebrated

In a while, Celia enters from the road and hurries up the path towards the church. She is dressed suitably for the service

Celia (*turning and calling behind her*) Come on. Oh, do come on. Miles, will you come on.

Miles appears

Miles Just a minute, just a minute. Can't leave the car unlocked, you know. You have to lock it.
Celia Come on, we'll sneak in.
Miles Has it started?
Celia Of course it's started.
Miles Oh, well, that's it, isn't it?
Celia It's halfway through. Come on.
Miles I'm not going in if it's started.
Celia We can sneak in at the back.
Miles No, it's one of my golden rules. If the show's started, I never walk in in the middle. Very bad manners.
Celia It's not a show, it's a church. Quite different.
Miles Exactly the same.
Celia Of course it's not the same.
Miles Church services are just another branch of show business. You have an audience and you have people performing. Same principle.
Celia I don't know when you last went to church.
Miles Not that long ago.
Celia It's not a hot gospel road show going on in there. It's a quiet, modest little . . .
Miles Till we go clumping in.
Celia A quiet service to celebrate fifty years of the school. There are no performers. No audiences applauding and cheering. Just a handful of people singing a couple of hymns and saying a quiet thank you. Now I'm going in.
Miles Well, I'm not.

Celia Where are you going?

Miles I think the pubs are open.

Celia You do this just to annoy me, don't you? You drive as slowly as you can all the way down here. You complain. You groan and you sulk ...

Miles Because I'm nothing whatever to do with this place now. I resigned from the Board five years ago. I've no connections. Nobody even knows who the hell I am. And I don't know anybody either.

Celia Well, that's rubbish. You know Toby to start with.

Miles Oh, yes. He'll be delighted to see us, of course.

Celia He might. After five years. You never know.

Miles Play your cards right, he might take you back.

Celia Now, why do you say that?

Miles I don't know.

Celia Why do you say things like that? We are divorced. We never see each other. We never even write. You can't possibly be jealous of Toby any more.

Miles I'm not.

Celia I'm not jealous of Rowena. I've much more reason to be.

Miles Heaven knows where she's vanished to. Or the kids. I haven't heard from them for weeks. I wonder if they——

Celia Well, I'm going in.

Miles Yes, you go in.

Celia Oh, come on, Miles, please. I don't want to walk in there on my own.

Miles Why not?

Celia Because I want you to be with me. They're all going to turn round and they're all going to stare. I want you with me. So we can say to them, "There you are, we're still together, so there." Please.

Miles That's why we've come back, is it? To show them.

Celia No.

Miles I'm not going in.

Celia Well, 1 think you're really rotten. I think that's absolutely mean of you. (*She tries the church door*) I'm locked out.

Miles I think it's the other door, isn't it?

Celia Oh, yes. What are you staring at?

Miles I was just thinking how much like your mother you're looking these days.

Celia I think this is really mean of you, Miles. Really mean.

Celia exits round the side of the church

Miles wanders gloomily about. He comes upon a tombstone

Miles (*reading*) "In memory of Joseph John Hepplewick, aged seventy-five." Good Lord, I didn't realize he'd gone. Quite young. (*He reads*)

> This will not be the last of him you've seen.
> His poetry will linger evergreen.

Well, I suppose it might at a pinch. (*He sits on a gravestone. He looks up at the church clock. He looks at his own watch. He bangs it irritably*) This has never worked since, blast her. Oh, well. (*He rises and starts to move down the path*)

Rowena appears round the side of the church

Rowena Miles?
Miles Hallo.
Rowena Hallo. I saw Celia creeping in, I——
Miles Rowena, I wondered where you were.
Rowena Where I was?
Miles Yes, you seemed to—you didn't answer anything. Phones, letters. I sent some things for the kids. Money and things.
Rowena Oh yes, we got all that. Thank you.
Miles I'm glad you did. Are you well?
Rowena Yes, oh yes.
Miles You never say very much. I don't want to pry. You're all right, then?
Rowena Yes.
Miles Do you—is someone with you? Are you—living with anyone? At the moment?
Rowena No, I'm on my own.
Miles Ah.
Rowena You know I was with Terry.
Miles Yes, yes I did.
Rowena But he—well, he was with us for about a year but he—he got rather nasty to us all. I don't think actually he's a very nice person. You were absolutely right about him, Miles. I wish I'd listened to you. You always know about people.
Miles Well, sometimes.
Rowena He started hitting me and things. And I can't stand that, as you know. So we told him to go. I took a vote with the kids. We do everything very democratically now. We decided, after you left, that we were going to run things as a republic. You know, when the king abdicates. So we vote. And the majority rules. We do jolly well, I think. So we're not having anybody else living with us at all. We don't need them. So there. (*After a pause*) I only came out of the service because they got to a bit I didn't believe in. I have to pop out now when they get to those bits. Then I go back in again. After they've finished. I think you must protest if you don't agree with something, don't you? I think that's only honest. I used to jump up and argue but then they asked me not to come, so I promised I wouldn't argue any more. I just walk out instead. It still makes the point. God notices. He's been very helpful lately. He really has. He sees when you're a bit lost or something and then He comes and helps you, you know.
Miles Good, good.
Rowena You look well.
Miles Yes, I'm well.
Rowena (*listening*) Ah, they've got back to a good bit.
Miles Ah.
Rowena I'll see you then. Bye-bye.

Miles Bye-bye. Rowena, take care, won't you?
Rowena Oh, yes.
Miles Give my love to the kids.
Rowena My love to Ceel. I don't think I'll talk to her.
Miles Right. Bye.

Rowena goes back inside the church

(*Pacing about*) Meeuurrr-nah-meeuurrr ... I think we both agree, Celia, that the course we've trodden—chosen. The choice we've made ... well, we've run our natural, in fact I think we're beyond it to a certain extent. It's just occurred to me, Celia, it's just this second occurred to me ... no, it's—my God, Celia, this sudden thought has just struck me. What the hell are we both doing? Just this second. What are we thinking of? What are we?

Celia comes round the side of the church

Celia What are you doing?
Miles Is it over?
Celia Yes. I noticed Rowena rushed straight out here. Did you see her?
Miles Yes, we exchanged a quick hallo.
Celia How is she?
Miles Oh, fine. Absolutely terrific. Did you see Toby?
Celia Briefly. He's very well. Stopped drinking completely. Put on a little weight, which hasn't done him any harm. In fact, he looks better than I've ever seen him.
Miles Good. Tempted to rush back to him, are you?
Celia Look, is that what you want, Miles?
Miles No.
Celia You keep suggesting it. You seem to be more and more anxious to get rid of me.
Miles No.
Celia Well, it seems that way. Just say the word, I'll go.
Miles No, don't do that. It's not that. I don't know what it is. Let's get back in the car. It's getting cold.
Celia I think the problem is really that we've both—we both feel somewhere that we've perpetrated acts of betrayal, if that's the right expression. I don't know that necessarily we have but we feel we have. Which amounts to the same thing. It's our conventional upbringing, Miles, I'm afraid, telling us to do the decent thing. So we're finding it very hard to live with ourselves. Let alone each other. It's not fair really. We shouldn't need to feel like this. But we do. Too bad.
Miles Yes, I suppose that might possibly be true. I certainly do worry about Rowena.
Celia But there's something else, isn't there, besides that?
Miles Is there?
Celia Remember you used to say to me, "A very small degree of hope is sufficient to cause the birth of love." Stendhal, do you remember?
Miles Yes, yes, of course.

Celia Well, I think the thing is we've rather lost hope, Miles. That's the truth of it. Come on.

Celia goes off towards the car

Miles (*nodding to himself*) Possibly. Possibly . . .

He follows her off

The Lights fade to a Black-out

A 50TH CELEBRATION

A Churchyard. This year

The church door is closed. A gravel path leads away from it to an unseen road.

A variety of gravestones border the path

We hear church bells signifying a happy occasion, followed by the sound of singing within the church. A Service of Thanksgiving for Bilbury Lodge's fifty-year existence is being celebrated

The church door opens and Toby stumbles out, looking very dizzy and in need of some fresh air

In a second, Celia comes out after him anxiously, closing the door behind her

Celia Now, breathe in. Breathe deeply.

Toby Just a minute, just a minute. I'm all right.

Celia You're not all right. You nearly fainted in there.

Toby What do you expect? It's absolutely boiling. That church is like a greenhouse. You could grow tomatoes in the pews.

Celia Toby, it is freezing cold in there. People are singing hymns with their gloves on.

Toby Well, I couldn't stand it.

Celia Because you're not well. You must take things quietly.

Toby Quietly? I've retired from my work. I don't teach. I never see anybody. If I get any quieter I might as well lie down over there and wait for them to cover me over. I don't know what we're doing here anyway.

Celia You're the one who wanted to come. Don't blame me. A two hour drive on my one day off. I could have done without, thank you.

Toby Well, I suppose it's the school's fiftieth anniversary. Quite good going, fifty years. Several years of my life thrown in there, too. I thought at least we'd come to the service. I can do without the rest of the bally-hoo. A staff production of *Charley's Aunt* will be well worth avoiding. But it's always a mistake to come back. Nobody knows you. The people who do remember you pretend they don't. Old headmasters, they're like old suits. Wrong style, no longer fit anywhere and rather worn around the seat and elbows.

Celia If you'd see a doctor . . .

Toby I promise you this. When I'm ill, I'll see a doctor. If I'm fainting at the moment, it's probably through sheer boredom. You're out all day.

Celia Somebody has to work. Look, you don't have the kids. They're being looked after. You could read. You could write. I don't know what else I'm meant to do. I mean, I really think that whatever it is I've done or I'm meant to have done, I've paid for it, haven't I, Toby? I must have paid by now.

Toby What are you on about?

Celia My—passionate few weeks with Miles.

Toby Oh, God.

Celia I think after five years that is buried now, isn't it?

Toby As far as I'm concerned.

Celia Well.

Toby No. I've always been deeply appreciative of the sacrifice you made in coming back to me. Must have been a huge wrench for you.

Celia The thing is, I made the decision. I decided in favour of you. Why can't you accept that?

Toby I'd accept it if it were true, Celia. But it isn't. You're as inscrutable as a gibbon on heat. Totally transparent. Miles went back to Rowena and left you at a loose end.

Celia That's not true.

Toby I don't mind. I just can't stand you wandering about looking as if you've done the decent thing by me. You did the only thing. You jumped overboard because you thought the ship was going down, you climbed on somebody else's life raft and when he shoved you off, you had to crawl back on board here again. Now, that's perfectly all right. You made an error of judgement and you are totally forgiven but don't expect me to say thank you very much for rescuing you.

Celia I'm going back in. Are you coming?

Toby No, I'm going to the pub. I'll make one more nostalgic trip.

Celia If you drink again, you'll drop down dead, you know that.

Toby Splendid, splendid. Tell them, I'd like that little area over there if they can spare it. Perhaps you'd ask them for me. I'll see you by the car.

Toby goes off towards the road

Celia (*standing, staring after him*) I don't know what I'm supposed to do. What more am I supposed to do? (*She wanders a little. She comes upon a tombstone and reads*) "In memory of Joseph John Hepplewick, aged seventy-five." I didn't know he'd died. He wasn't very old, either. (*She reads*)

> This will not be the last of him you've seen.
> His poetry will linger evergreen.

Yes. I suppose his awful son's still around. Oh, dear. (*She sits on a gravestone. Rather guiltily, she lights a cigarette*)

Miles comes out of the church, rather anxiously. He sees her

Miles Ah. Is he all right? Toby. Is he all right?

Celia Yes, he's all right.

Miles Ah. (*He closes the church door*) Hallo, then.

Celia Hallo.

Miles Long time.

Celia Yes, it is.

Miles I saw you both sneaking in late at the back. Glad you could come. I was going to catch you both for a word afterwards. Then I saw you helping Toby out. . . . I had to wait for an opportune moment in the service. . . . It's a very pleasant service.

Celia Yes, it is.

Miles Do you know we've got four ex-headmasters in there? Well, three now. It's terrific, the people who've turned up for the celebrations. From all over the place. Kenya, Bridgnorth, all over.

Celia The school still doing well?

Miles Oh yes. Oddly enough in these times, yes. No shortage of pupils. Splendid.

Celia Good.

Miles How are you both?

Celia I'm working again, of course. Which is nice.

Miles Back on the conferences, are you?

Celia No. That would take me away too much. No, I'm a receptionist at the—at a local hotel. It's very interesting work. Fascinating.

Miles Meeting people.

Celia Yes, you do. You meet a lot of people.

Miles Yes, I imagine it's a job where you would meet people, yes.

Celia I enjoy it. Poor Toby's not—not really able to do much since his illness. He's a lot better than he was but of course he refuses to see another doctor ever again. So there's a limit to his progress. . . . But the children are happy and that's the main thing. How are yours?

Miles The brood? Oh, fine, fine.

Celia Rowena?

Miles Oh, mad as ever. (*He laughs*)

Celia smiles

It really is very good to see you. I—er—still think about our—our fling, you know. Do you think about it?

Celia No.

Miles Ah. Probably wise of you not to. I—er—I mean, I sometimes wonder—whether we did . . . the right thing . . . or perhaps we should have . . . you never know, do you? Never mind.

Celia No.

Miles I think, on the whole, weighing it up, it probably was the right decision we both made, don't you? I don't think either of us was equipped for that sort of existence. We're sort of honest people, I think. Curse it. I think if you're going to plunge into that sort of life, you can't care too much about who you hurt. Either that or you need to be a little mad like Rowena. She can cope with it. (*After a pause*) Oh. Here's another quote for you. Another Stendhal nugget I came across. Been saving it up in case I saw you. "The more one pleases everybody, the less one pleases profoundly." I think that's my problem really. You staying for the show this evening?

Celia No.

Miles Rumour has it, it's pretty good. Hogg's playing Fancourt-Babberley.

Apparently surprisingly well. Of course you can't see his legs under the skirt which probably helps. (*After a pause*) Well, take care.

Celia And you.

Miles Give my regards to Toby if I don't see him.

Celia (*moving away*) Yes. Mine to Rowena.

Miles I'm glad I—I'm glad we——

Celia Goodbye, Miles.

Miles (*desperately, after her*) What I'm saying is, I don't think we possibly appreciated it at the time but we did have fun, you know. We really did.

Celia Goodbye.

Celia goes off towards the car

Miles (*calling after her*) Just—thanks for all the fun we had. That's all I'm saying. (*To himself*) Great fun. It really was. Great fun.

Miles goes into the church

The Lights fade to a Black-out

INTIMATE EXCHANGES is a related series of plays totalling eight scripts

This is the Sixth

A GAME OF GOLF

preceded by *How It Began* (page 3);
A Visit from a Friend (page 5) and
Dinner on the Patio (page 17)

CHARACTERS
APPEARING IN THIS SERIES OF SCENES

Celia
Miles
Sylvie
Josephine
Toby
Irene
Rowena

A GAME OF GOLF

*The tenth green of a golf course. Five weeks later. It is the morning of
Saturday, July 24th*

*Leading off from one side of the green is the tenth fairway and on the far side
of the hole there is a deep bunker, overhung with trees. It is not a good hole to
overshoot. At present, all is deserted*

*There is the sound of birds singing. Suddenly a golf ball drops on to the green.
The birds stop singing and there is silence. After a second, they cautiously
restart*

*In a moment, Miles appears with his rather worn and ancient golf bag slung
over his shoulder. He stops at the edge of the green as he sees where his ball is
positioned*

Miles (*not displeased*) Ah. Not so bad. Not so bad. (*He looks back along the
fairway and calls*) I've—er——(*he breaks off realizing no one is about*)
Where the hell's he gone to? (*He shrugs*) Well. (*He unslings his golf bag,
nearly dropping it because of the broken handle*) Oh, this damn thing. (*He
selects his putter and laying his clubs down on the grass just off the green,
starts to circle his ball. He walks round it a couple of times, examines the lie
from all angles and then, with great concentration, squares up for his shot.
The tension is unbearable*)

*As Miles hits the ball there is a shout from off. It is the vast voice of Irene
Pridworthy*

Irene (*off*) Oy! Coombes!

Miles's ball skids away to a far corner of the green

Miles Oh, bloody hell. Look, do you mind, I was just ...

*Irene Pridworthy appears. She is a large woman in her early sixties, and is
swinging a driver rather menacingly. She seems very irate*

Irene Coombes ...
Miles Look, Irene, that was appallingly bad etiquette. I was just about to
sink a birdie three and you caused me to miss-hit ...
Irene Never mind that.
Miles ... so I'll be lucky to get down ...
Irene I said, never mind that.
Miles ... I'll be lucky to get down in ...
Irene I said, Coombes, never mind about that. One, you've absolutely no
right to be here and two——

Miles What are you talking about? I'm a member. I'm a fully paid-up member of this club.

Irene Then, as such, you ought to consult your Clubhouse notice-board and read your circulars that we, the Committee, spend pounds every year sending out to you. The course is closed today to everyone, for the Ladies' International Friendly.

Miles Oh, Lord.

Irene So if you don't want a dozen angry Dutch women setting about you, I'd clear right away.

Miles Yes, I will. I'm terribly sorry. I'll just finish this . . .

Irene Two. Secondly, what are you going to do about him?

Miles Who?

Irene Who? I'm talking about that oaf back there. Teasdale. I'm talking about Toby Teasdale. He's your responsibility isn't he?

Miles Well . . .

Irene Isn't he?

Miles Yes.

Irene Well, put him on a lead or something, will you? Absolute bloody menace.

Miles Where is he?

Irene He's at present ambling to and fro across the fourth fairway holding up fourteen other people. I mean, which hole is he meant to be playing, for God's sake?

Miles Er—this one, I thought.

Irene This is the tenth. What's he doing on the fourth?

Miles I don't really know. Did you ask him?

Irene I did. He was most offensive.

Miles Look, he's still learning the game, Irene. There's no point in getting impatient.

Irene Yes, but he's been learning it for weeks, hasn't he? He's here every damn weekend. Endangering members' lives, ploughing up four foot divots. I mean, members are expected to exercise their discretion over their choice of guests. That is clearly stated in Rule 14. Not invite every homicidal trainee farmer who wants to take pot luck.

Miles Yes, yes.

Irene I have Mrs Van der Hoogh back there waiting.

Miles Yes, of course.

Irene What is he, drunk or something?

Miles No, he's not drunk.

Irene Get on, he's always drunk.

Miles He's had very little. He's been extremely moderate for over a month now.

Irene (*scornfully*) Hah.

Miles It's true.

Irene He's fooling you, Coombes. They're a crafty little wagon-load, alcoholics. I should know. My mother drank. Used to keep a bottle strapped to her leg, under her skirt.

Miles Really?

Irene When she got really blotto, she'd forget to cork it. Terrible mess when she lay down for her afternoon nap.

Miles Must have been.

Irene We were under the impression for years she drank so much she'd started piddling raw whisky.

Miles Ah.

Irene Nobody dared look, you see. She was a tough customer.

Miles Yes, I can imagine.

Irene So. Be a good chap, exercise a bit of discretion. I mean, this isn't the first time it's happened, is it, Coombes? We had all that trouble before when you brought your wife round.

Miles Yes, that was some years ago.

Irene Possibly. All I know is many of the greens still haven't recovered.

Miles Now, I apologized to the Committee, I offered to pay for the damage . . .

Irene Now it's happening again with this Teasdale man. Why can't he play the holes in the same order as everyone else? Doesn't he teach maths?

Miles I think he's just off course. He does hook rather badly.

Irene He must have hit it straight over his head to reach the fourth from the tenth. I mean, if he wants to play clock golf, why doesn't he go to the seaside?

Miles Yes.

Irene I'm sorry, Coombes, he's your chum but you know what I think of the man, don't you?

Miles Yes, Mrs Pridworthy. You make that abundantly clear at the School Governors' meetings.

Irene He's the three D's, Coombes, the three D's. You know what the three D's are? Disruptive, devious and dangerous. I don't think children's minds should be exposed to that kind of filth.

Miles Filth?

Irene Teasdale's a knocker. He knocks what's good and he knocks what's decent. Easiest thing in the world, you know, to knock. Takes no ability. No dedication. Do you know what I'd do with all knockers?

Miles No.

Irene I'd lock them up. Lock up the knockers. Good slogan, eh?

Miles Splendid.

Irene Get him off the course, there's a good chap.

Miles I'll do my best, Irene.

Irene Incidentally, have you lost any balls this morning?

Miles No.

Irene We've lost three. I've a nasty feeling there's a bit of pilfering going on as well.

Miles Really.

Irene Kids, probably. Hiding till you're out of view. If I catch them, I'll wop them with this. I suppose that wouldn't be Teasdale, would it?

Miles What?

Irene Pilfering. Nicking golf balls.

Miles No. He may be a knocker, he's not a nicker. (*He laughs*)

Irene Pardon?
Miles Now then. (*He lines up his shot*)
Irene That you?
Miles Yes.
Irene Not so hot, is it?
Miles It isn't now.
Irene How many are you? Two?
Miles No, four.
Irene Four? My God, this is a birdie three.
Miles I know it's a birdie three.
Irene You'll be lucky to make par from there.
Miles I'm probably giving it up anyway.
Irene What's your handicap?
Miles At the moment, about six hundred. It's usually about twenty-two.
Irene I'm not surprised if you take four on the tenth. I'm down to seven.
Miles Seven?
Irene Handicap. Not bad, eh?
Miles No.
Irene Sixty-two this year.
Miles Oh. Game's gone off recently, has it?
Irene No, I am. Sixty-two years old. (*She mutters under her breath*) Stupid ass.
Miles Ah.
Irene I must get back to Connie. I'd ditch that chap if I were you. That's my advice. Ditch him. Before he brings you down with him. Put the flag back when you've finished, won't you, there's a good chap.
Miles Yes, thank you, Irene. I do know about these things.
Irene Just your friend who doesn't, is it?

Irene exits back along the fairway

Miles (*glowering after her and muttering*) Stupid old boot. (*He returns to his game*) I was down in three. Definitely. Would have been down in three. (*He lines up for his shot again with more elaborate preparations, brushing the ground, examining the lie from a worm's eye level and practising one or two shots alongside the ball*)

Celia enters and stands silently watching him

Miles, deep in concentration, fails to notice her. Finally ready, he prepares to make his shot

Celia Miles.

Miles's shot shoots off in another direction

Miles (*hysterically*) Oh, dear God.
Celia Hallo.
Miles (*savagely*) Hallo.
Celia (*startled*) What's the matter?
Miles (*recovering*) Nothing, nothing at all.

Celia Were you involved?
Miles No, no. I was just trying to—um—to get the ball in that hole, that's all.
Celia Oh. (*She indicates the ball*) It's over there.
Miles (*irritably*) I know it's over there. I hit it over there.
Celia (*puzzled*) But the hole's over there.
Miles I'd—er—rather not talk about it if you don't mind, Celia. What did you want?
Celia Well. Where's Toby?
Miles He's on the fourth. He was. He's probably at the sixteenth by now.
Celia I thought you were playing together.
Miles No, I think he's making his own way. Did you want to see him?
Celia No.
Miles Ah.

Pause

Celia I thought I saw Rowena back there.
Miles (*alarmed*) Rowena?
Celia With the kids.
Miles Are you sure?
Celia It looked like her.
Miles On the course?
Celia Yes, I couldn't be sure. It looked like her.
Miles I hope to God it wasn't.
Celia Does she play?
Miles She most certainly doesn't.
Celia No, I shouldn't think she's a lot of energy left for golf.

Pause

Miles Is it something important, Celia?
Celia Don't say it like that.
Miles Like what?
Celia Well—is it something important, Celia. It sounds so—so unfriendly.
Miles I'm sorry.
Celia I thought we were friends, Miles.
Miles We are.
Celia At least.
Miles Yes.
Celia That's what you led me to believe.
Miles Yes.
Celia A month ago.
Miles Well, we are friends.
Celia Yes. And?
Miles Friends.
Celia Nothing more?
Miles Oh, God, Celia.
Celia What?
Miles Well . . .

Celia What?

Miles We're in the middle of a golf course, for God's sake.

Celia Is it me? Have I done something?

Miles No.

Celia Well, what's happened? What's happened to everything we said that night? What happened to all that?

Miles It—well—it . . .

Celia Didn't you mean it?

Miles (*guardedly*) Yes.

Celia I'm in love with you? And Stendhal and all that?

Miles Yes.

Celia I mean, you can't just say all that and walk away. As if you hadn't said it. It's not fair.

Miles Well, you weren't really very forthcoming at the time, Celia, let's face it.

Celia Well, I was . . .

Miles You didn't exactly shout whoopee, did you?

Celia No, maybe I didn't but . . .

Miles Hard cheese, that's what you said. I remember that. It stuck in my mind.

Celia Well, I was . . . I was in a terrible dilemma then. I'm not now. I wanted you to be sure. I didn't want you to rush into things without thinking.

Miles Oh, that was all for me, was it?

Celia Yes, mostly.

Miles And locking me up all night in your revolting garden shed, that was also for me?

Celia What else was I to do? Toby arrived.

Miles I was in there till four o'clock in the morning, Celia.

Celia I had to wait till he went to sleep. He never goes to sleep.

Miles Oh, come on, Celia. You gave me the elbow. Fair enough. I said I loved you. You said hard cheese and locked me in your shed. End of romance. I sort of took the hint.

Celia No. That wasn't it. That was just me saying . . .

Miles That was just you saying, no, thank you very much.

Celia No, it wasn't. That was me saying—possibly.

Miles Well, frankly, Celia, if that was you saying possibly, I'm bloody glad you didn't say no thanks, that's all.

Celia Oh, Miles.

Miles I dread to think what that would have been like.

Celia I think you're being very, very unfair to me. (*With a tremulous voice*) You can't just dump me like this. As if I was a bag of golf clubs or something. I don't think you know what I've been through. I don't think you do.

Miles I think I do, Celia, I really do.

Celia I mean, things between Toby and me, they've just reached. . . . You've no idea, Miles. I thought once he'd cut down on his drinking he'd appreciate me more. I always thought it was the drink that stopped him from appreciating me. Now he's stopped, I don't think he can stand the sight of me at all. At least when he drank he used to sit at home and shout at us. Now, he's not even there to do that.

Miles Oh, dear.

Celia I never see him.

Miles No.

Celia All this ridiculous golf and things. He never used to do all this. What's come over him?

Miles I think he's actually trying to make an effort, Celia. I mean, you were always saying to him he ought to get a grip.

Celia Yes, but not like this. What's the point of him making an effort if I don't get the benefit?

Miles He's looking a lot better.

Celia Maybe he is, I wouldn't know. I haven't seen him. I blame you, Miles, I really do.

Miles Me?

Celia You've lured him away from us.

Miles Oh, come on.

Celia You're always phoning him up. What about going to this? What about doing that?

Miles Sometimes he rings me.

Celia What about me?

Miles You want me to ring you?

Celia No, I mean I'm just left out. It's as if I don't exist.

Miles I'm sorry.

Celia I work hard all day to make a home for him. He's never in it. What's the point? I'm just redundant. Unwanted. I need to feel wanted, Miles.

Miles Well, we all do.

Celia Now, he doesn't want me. You don't want me. What's the point of me?

Miles The kids want you.

Celia Oh well, they've no choice, poor things. (*She weeps*) It isn't fair. I don't deserve it.

Miles Oh, don't cry, Celia, please.

Celia Well ...

Miles Why don't you take up golf?

Celia Oh, don't be so stupid.

Miles Why not?

Celia I'm far too busy to chase after balls all day.

Miles A lot of women play ...

Celia Maybe they do.

Miles Irene Pridworthy plays.

Celia That's a great recommendation.

Miles And Connie van der thing.

Celia What?

Miles Nothing.

Celia So. This is goodbye, is it?

Miles What?

Celia I'm saying, you're saying goodbye to me, are you?

Miles Oh, come on, Celia, I'm not saying goodbye to you. I'll probably see you this evening. What are you talking about?

Celia You know what I mean.

Miles I can't say goodbye to you. Not in that way either. I mean, how can I? I haven't even said hallo.

Celia Whose fault's that?

Miles Yours entirely.

Celia Mine?

Miles God, what more could I have done, Celia? I rolled on my back, kicked my legs in the air and spouted romantic poetry. I debased myself in front of you, Celia. But finally, getting close to you was like trying to scale the north-west face of Annapurna in bedroom slippers. To put it crudely, you're a bit daunting, Celia. Unyielding.

Celia Am I?

Miles You do not give up your secrets easily, as they say in climbing circles.

Celia Why are we suddenly talking about mountains?

Miles I've no idea.

Celia Do I remind you of a mountain?

Miles Well, let's say a pretty steep hill.

Celia weeps afresh

Celia, come on. (*He laughs weakly*) Come on, Celia. Right, Celia, I'm going to play this shot now. Celia, you're standing in the middle of the green. Oh, God. Celia, if you don't move, I'm going to have to take another shot as well. Just to get round you. OK, that's going to make it at least six. (*He lines up for a putt*)

Celia sobs. She is in a direct line between Miles' ball and the hole

Look, it's terribly hard putting under normal circumstances. Even Nicklaus would find this tricky. (*He putts around her*) Five. All I'm saying, Celia, is there's nothing I can say. Or do. I'd offer you my handkerchief, only I've been cleaning the ball on it. What can I say? Except, well, frankly, hard cheese. (*He putts again*) Six. (*This time he sinks it. Or if he doesn't, until he does*) Now look, Celia, we've got to get off the course. There's a vanload of Anglo-Dutch Valkyries coming this way waving their sand wedges. They will not take kindly to your standing there. They will no doubt blame me for it and I will have my membership cancelled. Now, are you coming?

Celia stands, unmoving

Oh, Lord. OK. Well, I'd better hang on for Toby. Tell him if you see him. I'm going to whack a few off the eleventh, OK? Right. I'll be back. Cheerio, then.

Miles replaces his putter, takes out a driver and three balls and exits

Celia (*tearful; muttering*) What does he want me to do? Throw myself at him? I'm not throwing myself at him. I've never thrown myself at anyone. I'm certainly not going to start now. Not at my age. He'd never have respected me if I'd done that. He wouldn't have wanted me then, would he? Of course he wouldn't. He doesn't want me now either. I don't know. You can't win. I don't know what they do want, any of them. What does a woman have to do? Behave like Rowena Coombes? Running after people in the street with her skirt over her head. Well, I'm not behaving like that. I'm sorry. Oh, no.

Toby (*off*) Look out!

Celia Oh, God.

Celia ducks as a ball apparently screams over her head. It zips through the foliage and into the bunker

Toby enters a second later, swinging an iron with a bag of clubs over his shoulder

Toby What the hell are you playing at?

Celia Toby, that nearly hit me.

Toby Well, what are you doing standing there, woman? You can get killed. They're very dangerous these balls. You need to stand clear. Once you've hit them, you know, they can go anywhere. No control over the damn things at all. You see where it went?

Celia I've no idea. It shot over my head. Over there.

Toby Oh, my God. You any idea what number hole this is?

Celia How should I know?

Toby Hang on. (*He pulls a crumpled map of the course from his pocket*) I started there. And then that put me over there. Then my second didn't take me very far and then my third got me to the ninth. Then my fourth and fifth took me across to the third and then six, I was on the fourth. Seventh I came back across the fourth. Then I met up with old Pridworthy. Then eight, across the fourth yet again and then nine, on to the road. Ten, back through the sheep. Eleventh to the eighth. Then twelve and thirteen to here. Which ought to be the tenth. Which is the one I wanted. Success.

Celia It's certainly the one Miles was playing just now.

Toby Miles?

Celia Yes. He said he's gone on to whack a few off the something.

Toby Ah, right. Probably to the eleventh.

Celia Presumably. Since this is the tenth.

Toby Don't you believe it. There's absolutely no logic to this game at all.

Celia Then why are you playing it?

Toby Well, you get a bit hooked, you know. I never thought I would. I used to drink with all these appalling men who talked about nothing but bogies and birdies. Bored me rigid. But I can see the attraction now.

Celia So, I'm to be another golf widow, am I?

Toby Look, Celia, I tell you. My aim is quite simple. I've borrowed these clubs from Terry Hogg. I even borrowed the balls. Well, the first dozen I did, anyway. All I'm aiming to do is to get round this bloody course once during the hours of daylight. I've nearly cracked it. I started at eight o'clock this morning. It's now noon and I'm over halfway. I could be

through by teatime. Then that's it. No more golf. I've cracked that. I'll try
something else. Ice hockey or something.

Celia Then you still won't be home, will you?

Toby Probably not.

Celia You'll either be working or off with Miles.

Toby I expect so.

Celia I mean, you spend more time with Miles these days. . . . Well, frankly,
I think it's a bit unhealthy.

Toby Unhealthy?

Celia I mean, friendship is one thing but you're practically never out of
each other's sight. It can't be healthy.

Toby What's all this health business? I've never felt healthier.

Celia I mean, surely it's normal to spend a little time with the woman you
married and your children. Men normally spend time with women.
Normal men.

Toby I can't think why.

Celia Because they want to. Need to.

Toby I don't think they do, you know.

Celia Of course they do.

Toby Well, early on. Not when they get to our age. I mean, people just all
merge together these days. I mean, recently, I'm not even aware whether
I'm talking to a man or a woman most of the time. Member of staff comes
up to me, starts wingeing away, I've no idea what sex it is. As for the kids,
well, they're completely indistinguishable. They're like Persian kittens,
they are. You have to turn them upside down and hold them up to the
light.

Celia I wish I knew what you were talking about. I don't know what you're
talking about half the time.

Toby I'm saying, I don't these days particularly yearn for a woman's
company. Not just because she's a woman. Thank God. I used to. I used
to have an urgent need over and above her company for certain—
ancillary services which she could offer me. I can now do without those
services thank you very much so the field's wide open. Men, women—
talking dolphins, it doesn't matter. If I prefer men on balance, it's only
because they don't keep making you cups of tea and insisting you use the
ashtrays. The point is if I see a woman these days I don't say to myself,
good heavens, there's a woman over there. I must go and sit next to her
immediately.

Celia I should hope not. Anyway, I wasn't talking about women. I was
talking about me.

Toby Oh, you.

Celia Yes.

Toby Well, there'd be no point in sitting next to you either, would there,
Celia? Because we'd sit there in absolute silence. Speechless. We've
absolutely nothing in common and haven't had for years.

Celia Of course we have.

Toby I can't think of anything.

Celia The children.

Toby Yes. Ish.

Celia Ish?

Toby I don't think I've got a lot in common with them either. They like ghastly music. I don't. They like botany and studying things through microscopes. I don't. They're clean and tidy with an absolute obsession with washing their hands and cleaning their shoes. I find them appallingly conventional. And now Lucy's got religion, it's even worse. I keep falling over her kneeling everywhere praying for me. I mean, it's a bit depressing. You do your best to bring them up to mistrust everything, rebel, question, never take yes for an answer and you finish up with a daughter who wants to be a right-wing nun.

Celia She's nine years old. It's a phase. A girl growing up, it's a disturbing experience.

Toby It can be fairly alarming for boys as well.

Celia James is all right.

Toby Probably. I don't know. He never talks to me.

Celia So you don't care about your children.

Toby Well. It's all right for you, you had them. The bit I was involved in, well, by the time they arrived it was so much water under the bridge, if you'll pardon the expression. I couldn't even remember it. I'd forgotten. As I was intended to presumably. I mean, it was probably a wonderful occasion and I'm sure it gave both of us a great deal of fleeting pleasure at the time. But since you didn't start flashing on and off with the letters NOW CONCEIVING, your eyes didn't spin round to three plums and a bell indicating a possible jackpot feature, there was no indication whatsoever that in nine months' time you were about to pay out.

Celia You don't care about the children. You don't care about me. That's what you're saying.

Toby I don't know, Celia. It's not a question you should ask. It's not important.

Celia My God, what's more important than that?

Toby Plenty of things, plenty of things.

Celia What?

Toby Practically everything. Look around you. Read the papers. Look, I've lost this damn ball. Even that's more important. (*He wanders away*)

Celia I wish people could hear this conversation. I really do. They wouldn't believe it. What are you doing?

Toby I'm looking for the ball.

Celia Toby, we're talking about our lives here.

Toby I can't do anything about our lives, Celia. Not yours and mine. I'm sorry. Nothing at all. Whereas this ball—yes, I can. I can look for it. I can find it. Or it can stay lost. And if I find it, I can carry on playing with it. Absolutely straightforward. With us, I regret to say, there is no solution. Because you, in your heart of hearts, don't want me and I don't want you. You're not very fond of me and I don't like you. Full stop. That's it. I've had a go. Tried my best. I'm sure you have too. But it's no use pretending any longer. Now you can either be extremely dramatic and do what you've been threatening to do for months and leave me, taking the kids.

Or we can rub along as we have been doing. But there aren't going to be any miracles, Celia. So don't wait for them. I'm not going to leap out of this bunker and turn into a handsome prince. You're not suddenly going to look beautiful because you're wearing glasses. As we get older, we're going to look ghastlier and ghastlier to each other and that's it. (*After a pause*) Well, somebody had to say it.

Celia (*recovering*) It's a bit ironic being left for Miles Coombes.

Toby Oh, don't be so stupid. He's a good friend, that's all.

Celia You said you preferred his company to mine.

Toby I do. But I'm not going to marry him. I'm not making that mistake twice.

Celia Well, I hope he's as good a friend as you think he is. I hope he doesn't disappoint you.

Toby I don't see why he should.

Celia He wasn't above making a dead set for me when your back was turned.

Toby Miles did?

Celia Yes.

Toby When?

Celia Oh. A few weeks ago. At that dinner you didn't turn up for.

Toby Did he?

Celia Yes. He—got quite passionate.

Toby Really?

Celia I—nothing happened. I wouldn't let him.

Toby Good for you.

Celia Some of us have a little loyalty and decency left in us.

Toby Splendid.

Celia Well, I'll go home. The kids'll want their lunch. Some of us have to carry on, Toby. We don't get your choice.

Toby Oh, don't look so persecuted, Celia, there's a love. Be a bit pleased. I'm down to practically zero alcohol consumption. I'm eating food. I'm drinking tea and coffee like a maniac. I'm playing hearty sports. There are roses in my cheeks and I feel five years younger. I probably look ten years older but that's beside the point. So rejoice, as someone biblical once said.

Celia I'm delighted. Congratulations to Miles. He managed something I never could. Goodbye.

Toby Bye-bye.

Celia exits

Toby wanders around still looking for the ball. He climbs to the edge of the bunker and looks inside

Toby Oh dear, oh dear. There you are. Got an attraction for sand, haven't you? Now, how are we going to get you out of there? Wait there. (*He wanders back to his bag*) Well, take your pick. (*He selects a club at random*) This looks fairly vicious. Might frighten it out of there with any luck. Right, I'm coming to get you. (*He climbs up and into the bunker with his club*) One, two, three, hup. (*There is a flurry of sand*) No, that's not counted. I had my eyes closed. Hup. (*More sand*) Right, we'll count that one. Fourteen. Hup, out you go. (*More sand*) Fifteen. Hup. (*More sand*) Sixteen. Oh, dear God. Get out of it, you little bastard.

Rowena wanders on. She is holding up her skirt in front of her carrying something in its folds. She stops to listen to the sounds emanating from the bunker

(*With a final triumphant hoik*) Heeupah . . .

Rowena follows the path of the ball over her head and back offstage along the fairway

Toby emerges from the bunker

Gotcha. Hah. Seventeen. Oh, hallo, Rowena.

Rowena Toby. Thank God. I thought it was some awful troll burrowing his way to the surface.

Toby Where did it go?

Rowena The ball?

Toby Yes.

Rowena Over there somewhere.

Toby Damn it. That's where I've just come from.

Rowena You having trouble?

Toby Just a bit.

Rowena (*showing the contents of her skirt*) Well, have one of these.

Toby My God, where do those come from?

Rowena We've been collecting them. Well, the kids have. We came up for the mushrooms actually, but there aren't any. So we've been collecting balls instead. I'm giving them a penny for every ball they find. Sandy's made fifteen p already. I'm going to sell them in the Oxfam shop for a vast profit. Isn't that brilliant?

Toby You're sure they don't belong to anybody?

Rowena Findies keepies.

Toby Not if they're still playing with them.

Rowena Nobody was about. Do you want one?

Toby No, no. I want to find mine.

Rowena They're all the same. Except some have got spots on and some haven't. Has yours got spots?

Toby No, mine's got a split in it.

Rowena Oh, those are the smiley ones. Timmy says those ones are smiling back at us.

Toby Really? In that case mine's laughing its head off.

Toby exits

(*Off*) Aha, there you are. I'm going to knock it back that way. Keep an eye on it, will you?

Rowena (*perching on the edge of the green*) OK.

Toby (*off*) Right. Mind your head. Heyupah! Eighteen.

Rowena follows the ball over her head and back into the bunker. It thuds

through the foliage again. She releases her skirt. A large number of golf balls
spill out on to the green

   Toby returns triumphantly

Toby Right now. Did you see where . . . (*he stops and surveys the green*) Ah.
   Which one is it?
   What?
Rowena Go on, have a guess. If you touch the right one, I'll tell you. Five
   guesses. If you don't guess correctly, then I get it for my collection.
Toby Oh, for the love of mike.
Rowena Five guesses.
Toby Look, I'm in the middle of a game here. Rowena.
Rowena So am I.
Toby There's dozens of them. (*He touches one at random*) This one.
Rowena No. That's one guess. Is Miles with you?
Toby He's somewhere around. I don't know. That's his bag. This is going to
   take hours.
Rowena Are you very fond of him?
Toby Miles? Yes, he's a very old, dear friend. Yes, I am.
Rowena I see.
Toby (*indicating another ball*) This one.
Rowena No. Two. Only we—the kids and I—we're very fond of him too.
   And we'd like him back sometime, please.
Toby What?
Rowena We'd like him back. We never see him.
Toby There may be a reason for that.
Rowena There is. He's with you.
Toby Maybe he's not very happy at home.
Rowena How do you know?
Toby He told me.
Rowena What did he tell you?
Toby That—er—he's not very happy. With you. Well, for God's sake, you
   know why he's not very happy. You can't carry on like you have and
   expect your husband to stay happy.
Rowena Did he tell you we weren't sleeping together?
Toby (*embarrassed*) Er—possibly. (*He indicates another ball*) This one.
Rowena No. Three. Two more. We haven't been for months. Quite a
   problem. It is for me anyway. Not so much for Miles. He sublimates it
   with games of golf and things. I'm forced to go outside.
Toby Look, I'd rather not . . .
Rowena It's no secret. Everybody knows. I mean, I don't talk but the men
   do.
Toby Men?
Rowena Man.
Toby You said men.
Rowena Well. Men, yes.
Toby And you wonder why he doesn't come home.
Rowena But if he came home there wouldn't be any men. Simple as that. I

think I'm what they used to call in the bad old days a nymphomaniac. Now known as a perfectly healthy normal woman. You know, I always wanted to be one of those when I was at school. What do you want to be when you grow up, Rowena? Please, Miss, a nymphomaniac. I did everything I could to top up my appetites so I'd be really insatiable. So I'd leave men strewn exhausted all over my boudoir. My God, is there no one can satisfy this woman, they cried. One awful girl told me that coal was an aphrodisiac. I ate about a hundredweight. Nearly ruined my chances altogether. This dreadful creature with a black tongue and anthracite teeth.

Toby (*indicating another ball*) This one.

Rowena Nope. One more to go.

Toby Anyway, I don't know what it's to do with me. It's up to Miles whether he comes home, isn't it?

Rowena Yes. But if you were to go home to Celia, maybe he would come home to me.

Toby Ah. Well, that's between me and Celia surely?

Rowena Not if it affects me.

Toby Things between Celia and me are drawing to a close.

Rowena Thank God, at last.

Toby Don't worry. All is due to end shortly.

Rowena I wonder. I don't think she'll ever let you go, you know. You're all she's got. I think she'll hang on.

Toby Unlike you who are spoilt for choice.

Rowena Not at all. Miles is all I've got. I'm just more enterprising about bridging the gap. Want another guess?

Toby Would you—er—I mean, are you very choosy about who you sleep with? Or is it with anyone who comes along?

Rowena Well. . . . They have to want it too.

Toby And that's the only criterion?

Rowena Really, yes.

Toby My God. Would you with me?

Rowena Yes.

Toby Just like that?

Rowena Are you asking me?

Toby Wouldn't it worry you?

Rowena Why?

Toby Well, Miles for one thing.

Rowena I think that's your problem. He's your best friend. He's only my husband.

Toby All right, I'm asking you.

Rowena OK. Now?

Toby No. God, no.

Rowena It'll cost you.

Toby Cost me?

Rowena I don't do it for nothing.

Toby Oh, you're joking.

Rowena No. I always charge people something. That way, no one goes

away with the idea that it has anything to do with love. It's pleasure and
expedience. The only person who gets it for nothing is Miles.

Toby How much do you charge?

Rowena Oh, not money. Things. You, I'll charge three golf balls, all right?

Toby New?

Rowena Nearly new, I'm not greedy. Terry Hogg pays me in polo mints.

Toby Dear God, I feel old-fashioned.

Rowena You don't want to go through with it?

Toby No.

Rowena Two golf balls.

Toby No, no.

Rowena Two very very old golf balls.

Toby No, Rowena, do stop it.

Rowena Ping pong balls. One squashed ping pong ball. I'm not proud.

Toby Listen, I only. ... I only asked you because Miles had apparently
approached Celia.

Rowena Oh. Did he?

Toby It was—er—nothing. She sent him off—apparently.

Rowena Good old Ceel. Not a girl to lie down for ping pong balls.

Toby Certainly not.

Rowena New living-room curtains, possibly.

Toby So now it's all square.

Rowena He asked her. You asked me.

Toby Exactly.

Rowena I think you got the easy end, squire.

Toby Would you really have gone through with it?

Rowena Well, that you will never know now, will you, Toby? The price has
just gone up alarmingly. It's now two million new golf balls and the deeds
to Gleneagles. Come on, last guess.

Toby It must be this one.

Rowena Wrong. Dong.

Toby Oh, God.

Rowena Hard luck. (*She starts to gather up the balls*)

Toby Look, I've taken eighteen shots to get here.

Rowena Too bad. Is this Miles's bag, did you say?

Toby Yes.

Rowena I'll load him up then. (*She begins to drop the balls into the bag*)

Toby Well, I'm calling that nineteen. (*He produces his card*) That's ninety,
ninety-five, a hundred and four so far. Getting better. I think if you want
Miles, you're going to have to get him back yourself. (*He starts to go*)

Rowena I sure will. (*She calls after him*) Hey, Toby.

Toby (*turning*) Mm?

Rowena Catch. (*She throws him a ball*)

Toby Is this mine?

Rowena No. That's your deposit back.

Toby Thank you.

Toby exits

Rowena Where have those kids gone? (*She calls up the fairway*) Sandy! Col!
Sandy . . .! Is Timmy all right? Yes, let him play in the sand. Don't let him
get in the way of the golf balls, will you? No, that's a good girl. What?
Fifteen. Well done. (*She gathers up the rest of the balls and puts them into
Miles' bag. She examines the clubs*) I suppose if I'd been an awfully good
wife, I'd have knitted little hats for these. Ceel would have done. And
mittens. Right. Let's have a swing. (*She puts the last ball down in the centre
of the green, selects an unsuitable iron and lines up for a mighty swing*) Here
she goes. The amazing Rowena Coombes. Putting for a bogie birdie
twenty-six. One, two, three——

Miles appears

Miles (*alarmed*) Rowena!
Rowena Oh. (*She stops in mid-shot*)
Miles What are you doing?
Rowena Hi.
Miles You're on the green, for God's sake.
Rowena Yes.
Miles You can't do that. Not on the green.
Rowena Sorry.
Miles You'll carve a hole in it the size of the Cheddar Gorge. Now give me
that.
Rowena (*handing over the club obediently*) Yes, Miles.
Miles And the ball.
Rowena Yes, Miles. (*She does so*)
Miles What are you doing here anyway?
Rowena Coming to see you, Miles.
Miles Have you got the kids with you?
Rowena Yes.
Miles Where?
Rowena They're playing in the sandpit over there.
Miles You know perfectly well that is not a sandpit. That is a sand trap.
Which is completely different.
Rowena You try explaining that to Timmy, darling. He sees a hole full of
sand exactly like the one at nursery school, he assumes it must be for him.
How's he to know it's reserved for grown-ups to romp around in. He's
only four.
Miles I know he's only four.
Rowena I thought you might have forgotten.
Miles Well, I wish you'd take them home. It's terribly dangerous.
Rowena Yes, I will. We were just all hoping to catch a glimpse of you, that's
all, as you passed. Jolly nice to see you, darling.
Miles Everything's OK. Nothing wrong, is there?
Rowena No, fine. What news can I bring you up to date with? What's
happened since you were last home? Sandy's got married and she now has
three children—Peter, Paul and Mary. Colin's a test pilot, of course. Well,
you knew that. And Timmy's running a brothel in Rio. They all send their
love and hope to see you around Christmas as usual.

Miles I'll be home later.

Rowena Miles.

Miles Toby's waiting.

Rowena Just one teeny moment.

Miles What?

Rowena Now you know I'm the last one ever to suggest we should talk, darling.

Miles Rowena, I'm in the middle of a golf game.

Rowena But I think something should be said—(*She speaks louder*)—and if you walk away while I'm saying it, Miles, then I shall just have to shout. And as you know I have a very loud voice when I want to and that would mean that everyone within half a mile would hear what we're talking about. And you might not want everyone to hear what I have to say—(*she speaks more quietly*)—though I don't mind in the least, suit yourself.

Miles All right. All right. (*After a pause*) Well?

Rowena I've forgotten what I was going to say now.

Miles Oh, for heaven's sake.

Rowena No, I haven't. I've just forgotten how I was going to say it. Er . . . (*she frowns*)

Miles The suspense is indescribable.

Rowena Er—I love you. I think that's what I wanted to say. Yes, that's it. Right. Cheerio. On with your game. (*She starts to go*)

Miles Just a minute.

Rowena Yes?

Miles Er . . . (*he hesitates*) Thank you. I—er——

Rowena Yes.

Miles This is a hell of a place to talk.

Rowena I like it.

Miles Irene Pridworthy's going to heave into sight in a minute.

Rowena Gosh. Will you be able to control yourself?

Miles I'll try.

Rowena Shall I put on forty-eight stone for you, darling? Is that what you crave? An affair with an amorous rhino.

Miles No, I . . .

Rowena Talking of kindness to animals, did you really have a go at Celia?

Miles Who told you?

Rowena Oh, it gets about. Came up at the last WI meeting, I think.

Miles I behaved rather stupidly.

Rowena Well, you were always a bit stuck on her.

Miles Yes—I—no, not really. I began to sort of fantasize about her, that's all. Possibly because I could never imagine her doing it. I've always been fascinated by those sort of women.

Rowena How on earth did we get together?

Miles No idea.

Rowena Did you do your poetry at her?

Miles Oh, God.

Rowena Did you?

Miles No.

Rowena You did, didn't you?

Miles No, I didn't

Rowena Oh, Miles.

Miles Well, yes, a bit.

Rowena Oh, Miles.

Miles This is awful. It makes me sound——

Rowena It's sweet. I used to love your poems. I wish you hadn't stopped.

Miles Makes it sound like some cheap thing I do whenever I ...

Rowena Not cheap. Not you.

Miles (*thoroughly embarrassed*) Oh, God. You started me on all that, anyway.

Rowena I did not.

Miles I never did all this poetry before I met you.

Rowena You never did anything before you met me. You met a woman, you were like a rabbit in the headlights. You just stayed there crouching with fear.

Miles Rubbish.

Rowena You did. I remember. I had to spend hours with you, Miles, just making little lettuce noises.

Miles I don't know why you bothered.

Rowena I was at my wits' end. Will he ever speak? Are we both going to be sitting here night after night for ever, year after year and then, one evening, came this very strange grinding, rusty noise and a voice said— (*sepulchrally*)—

Shall I compare thee to a summer's day.

And I said, "My God, it's him." And I was yours in an instant.

Thou art more lovely and more ...

Miles This is all rubbish.

Rowena Would you do a poem again for me sometime? Please? Will you?

Miles Well ...

Rowena Please.

Miles Possibly. Not at the moment.

Rowena Aren't you inspired?

Miles No. Not here. Not now.

Rowena Oh.

Miles Anyway, you'd laugh.

Rowena No, I wouldn't.

Miles You always do. That's the trouble. I sometimes think that's all I am to you really. One endless source of mirth.

Rowena What an extraordinary idea.

Miles It's true. I come home from work in the evening exhausted. I say something perfectly straightforward and sensible. You and the kids are rolling about. Hallo, everybody. Ha, ha, ha, ha, ha. It's like a bloody variety show. Now the au pair's started. Hildy. She thinks I'm hilarious as well. And she doesn't even speak English.

Rowena It's because we love you.

Miles Yes, well, sometimes it's rather debilitating. I mean, you've really got to be on top form to take that sort of barrage of mirth non-stop. And it is non-stop. I think that's—I think that's principally the problem in—in bed, if you must know.

Rowena Is it?

Miles Possibly.

Rowena You mean if I stop laughing, it'll be all right again?

Miles Well, there's a chance. I don't know. One's not in control of these things really.

Rowena My God, it can't be as simple as that.

Miles I don't know if it is. It could be that.

Rowena Come on. If only you'd said this before.

Miles What are you doing?

Rowena Darling, let's set about this at once. Seriously. No laughs at all, I promise.

Rowena rushes up the slope and jumps into the bunker

Miles Rowena, don't be ridiculous.

Rowena Ridiculous?

Miles Quite apart from anything else, it's a contradiction in terms. We can't possibly have a so-called serious sexual experience lying in a bunker on a golf course in the middle of a Ladies' International Friendly. (*After a pause*) Rowena, come out. Come on, please.

Rowena (*in broken English*) Hallo, hallo.

Miles Come on.

Rowena You speak English, please? The war, it is over? Do you hear that, Hans? The war is over.

Miles Oh, God. This is what I mean, you see. Rowena, come out.

Rowena I'll come out if you give me a pome. I want a pome first.

EITHER he says:

Miles I can't.

Rowena Celia had a pome. I want a pome. Come and sit here and give me a poem.

Miles (*reluctantly going to her*) Irene Pridworthy will be here in a minute. If she finds us. . . . (*He sits on the edge of the bunker*) Just one.

Rowena Yes.

Miles Er—I can't even think of one. This is ridiculous. You have to be in the mood, you know.

> Down in the valley
> Green grows the grass.
> I saw a billy goat
> Sliding on his overcoat . . .

No?

Rowena No.

Miles I don't know. This is terribly difficult.

> I loved thee though I told thee not,
> Right earlily and long.
> Thou wert my joy in every spot
> My theme in every song
> And all the charms of face or voice
> Which I in others see
> Are but the recollected choice
> Of what I felt for thee.

(*After a pause*) That's it. Is that any—aaah!

With a violent tug, he is pulled backwards into the sand trap and vanishes

Rowena . . . aah . . . please, we. . . . Hang on, I've got a mouthful of sand. Now, come on.

A ball drops on to the green driven from the fairway

All right, you said no laughing. No laughing. Sssh.

Irene (*off*) I think that's me on the green, Connie. I think you're away to the left.

Connie (*off*) I'm very much afraid, Irene, I am in the bushes there.

Irene (*off, laughing*) I think you may be. Want a hand?

Connie (*off*) No, no. It's OK. OK.

Irene appears with her golf bag

Irene Oh, yes. Super. Look at that. Yes. (*She calls*) What? May I go ahead? Right, thank you. (*She puts down her bag, pulling out her putter, removes the flag from the hole and starts to prepare for her shot*)

Miles (*from the bunker*) Ow, God. Damn ball. Ow.

A golf ball sails out of the bunker and lands on the green. Irene straightens up, startled

Irene Hallo? Hallo, someone there?

Miles (*from the bunker*) Oh, God. Someone's there. Someone's there.

Irene Hallo. Who's there? Who's there?

Miles appears over the edge of the bunker

Miles Hallo. Oh, hallo, Irene. Hallo.

Irene Coombes, you're still not playing this hole surely?

Miles (*struggling with his clothing*) Yes. Afraid so.

Irene You've been here nearly an hour.

Miles Yes. Waiting for Teasdale.

Irene Well, I'm sorry, you're going to have to shift.

Miles Yes, I'm sorry, Irene, I'm sorry.

Irene Nice little chip shot of yours. Very neat.

Miles (*moving over to Irene*) Thank you.

Irene What were you using?

Miles Pardon?

Irene What club were you using?
Miles Er—none, actually.
Irene None?
Miles My foot. Used my foot.
Irene Your foot?
Miles Found it's better. Much more effective.
Irene You can't use your foot. It's illegal.
Miles Ah well, new rules, Irene. For those who can't afford clubs. Hup,
   hup, hup, hey. (*He dribbles his golf ball round the green and finally kicks it
   down the hole*) There you are, look at that. Down in eight. Carry on.
Irene You're potty, Coombes. You've gone completely potty.
Miles Probably.
Irene I shall certainly report this to the Committee.
Miles Splendid.

Rowena's dress comes flying over the side of the bunker

Irene What the blazes is that?
Miles Oh, just my caddy. Hot work. Excuse me. (*He jumps back into the
   bunker*)
Irene I don't like the smell of this at all.

She is about to investigate further when someone calls from the fairway

   What's that? No luck? Right, hang on, Connie. I'll come and help you in a
   second.
Miles (*from within the bunker*)

> Oh, cease we then our woes, our griefs, our cries,
> Oh, vanish words, words do but passions move

*Irene, hearing this, moves suspiciously back to the bunker and peers down the
side*

Irene Oh, dear God. They're no better than rabbits. (*She stamps back
   towards the fairway*) They're no better than filthy little rabbits. Connie.

   Irene exits

Miles (*from within the bunker*)
> Oh, dearest life, joys sweet, oh, sweetest love

The Lights fade to a Black-out

To: EASTER GREETINGS (page 105)

OR he says:

Miles There was a young sailor from Crewe. . . .

   No, honestly, Rowena, this isn't going to work. There's a hell of a difference between spouting verse at two a.m. in the morning after three vodkas, a bottle of wine and a large Italian meal and standing here, stone cold sober at noon in the middle of a golf course. I'm sorry.

Pause. Rowena emerges slowly from the bunker

Rowena Oh well, all right then. We are coming out with our hands up. Don't shoot. We were only joking.

Miles But I also don't think trying to wind the clock back is going to work either. If you try and pick up something you dropped back there, the best that can happen is you finish back where you were again.

Rowena You tried with Celia.

Miles Precisely. Absolute disaster. All it did was nearly ruin our whole relationship.

Rowena Our relationship?

Miles Mine and Toby's.

Rowena Oh, yes. Sorry. Well, I think I'd better sneak away then. Leave you two bosom chaps together.

Miles Yes.

Rowena Toby's probably halfway across Buckinghamshire by now. Putting his way down the M4 to Bristol. Just one word of advice, darling, from my ragbag of useful philosophical tips. Much as you search for fresh pastures, and much as you search for people who'll treat you better or at least differently—very little of that is liable to happen until you first change yourself. I know that much because I've found it out the hard way. We get what we deserve. I suppose if I took myself more seriously, other people might. But I'm buggered if I'm going to. Bye.

Rowena exits

Miles (*staring after her*) Row . . . (*He gives up*) I don't know. I don't know. What would be the point? Hell.

> I loved thee though I told thee not,
> Right earlily and long.
> Thou wert my joy in every spot
> My theme in every song.

A golf ball drops on to the green. He fails to notice it

> And all the charms of face or voice
> Which I in others see
> Are but the recollected choice
> Of what I felt for thee.

I suppose that would have done. Oh well, too late now. (*He notices the ball*) Ah.

Irene (*off*) I think that's me on the green, Connie. I think you're away to the left.

Connie (*off*) I'm very much afraid, Irene, I am in the bushes there.

Irene (*off, laughing*) I think you may be. Want a hand?

Connie (*off*) No, no. It's OK. OK.

Irene appears with her golf bag

Irene Coombes, you can't still be here.

Miles Afraid so.

Irene Not still playing.

Miles No, I've finished playing. (*To Connie off*) Afternoon.

Irene What the hell have you been doing? I mean, you were six foot away from the hole about an hour ago. (*She lays down her bag and selects her putter*)

Miles No, well, I've been reassessing my game.

Irene (*sizing up her shot*) I wish to blazes you'd do it in the Clubhouse and not in the middle of the green. (*She straightens*) Yes, that's quite sweet. Swallow that for three, with any luck. (*She calls*) Connie. (*To Miles*) She's having trouble with the wind. Hits them too high for this course. Need a flat trajectory. Once you're over tree level, it can carry you into the town centre. You all right?

Miles Yes.

Irene You look dreadful. Didn't hit you with that, did I?

Miles No.

Irene Going to say, if I did, thanks very much for the bounce. (*She laughs, turns and calls*) Any luck . . .? I hope it's not another one gone. We've lost six already. Damned fishy. What? May I? Play first, can I? Thank you. Be with you in a sec. Thanks.

During this last, Miles picks up his golf bag. He is in a sad and rather trance-like state and so fails to notice as Rowena's collection of golf balls pour out of the bottom of it and on to the green. He wanders off towards the eleventh

(*Turning back*) OK then. I'll just sink this and then . . .(*she sees the balls*) Oh, good God. Coombes! Right, this is going before the Committee, this is. I've got you red-handed. Do you hear that, Coombes? Red-handed.

The Lights fade to a Black-out

To: A TRIUMPH OF FRIENDSHIP (page 109)

EASTER GREETINGS

A Churchyard. This year

The church door is closed. A gravel path leads away from it to an unseen road. A variety of gravestones border the path

We hear church bells signifying a happy occasion. It is Easter

In a moment, Miles comes strolling from another part of the churchyard with his head down, deep in thought

Celia, carrying a bunch of daffodils, hurries up the path from the road

Miles (*as they nearly collide*) Oh, I do beg your pardon, I——
Celia (*staring at him frostily*) Oh.
Miles Ah.
Celia Well . . .
Miles Hallo. (*After a pause*) I was—er—How are things?
Celia Thank you.
Miles Good, good.

Pause

Celia That must have been Rowena in the car.
Miles Yes.
Celia Crouching under the seat.
Miles Yes. (*After a pause*) She's got a bit of a cold. So she didn't get out. Keeping the kids amused.
Celia Haven't been back for a long time, have you?
Miles No. Er—three and a half—no, four years.
Celia Are you still living in——
Miles Yes, still there. Just back briefly. Spot of leave. Came back to see the in-laws.
Celia Yes. How is it in——?
Miles Brisbane? Oh, glorious. Well, hell of a jolt to start with, of course. Didn't think I'd like it at all. Rather overwhelming the Australians, initially. Then you sort of get the hang of it and shout back at them. Stop trying to shake hands with them and just punch the ones you like. We're all very happy now. Kids love it.
Celia And Rowena?
Miles Oh, heavens, yes. Right up her street.
Celia Yes, I imagine she'd be very popular there.
Miles Oh, yes.
Celia I can picture her in the outback.

Miles Yes. Well, we're not——

Celia She'd make a lot of friends. But then people there aren't quite so fussy, are they?

Pause

Miles I was—er—I actually just came to—er—. Look, I'm most terribly sorry about Toby. Tragic.

Celia Oh, yes. Three years ago now. I think we're all more or less over it.

Miles Yes. I only heard it much later. Which is why I didn't write. Terry Hogg's brother told me. He's over there, you know. Runs our local liquor store. Grog Hogg, he's known as. It's a small world. (*After a pause*) Was it very sudden? Toby.

Celia No, not really. I mean, officially it was a series of heart attacks but, of course, it was quite obvious what it really was.

Miles Booze?

Celia Of course.

Miles God. I thought we'd cured him of that. I really thought we'd cracked it.

Celia Oh, Miles. That's dreadfully naïve of you, surely.

Miles Well, when I last saw him, he was coping.

Celia Yes, and as soon as you left, he started again.

Miles Did he?

Celia Of course he did. Surely you knew he would? Worse than ever.

Miles Oh.

Celia I did what I could but, of course, he never listened to me.

Miles Oh, that's awful. You mean, the minute I left . . .

Celia Oh, yes.

Miles I'd no idea.

Celia Well, don't blame yourself, will you? Heavens, you had your own life to live.

Miles Well, it was a pretty good offer. I mean, we're far better off financially.

Celia Well, that's the main thing, isn't it? The money.

Miles Are you—back at work, are you?

Celia Yes. I've been forced to get a little job. The school's been very kind. Mr Ashburn, that's the new Headmaster—he's not married—I'm helping him a little with some of the secretarial stuff. It's only part-time but it all helps. That was Irene Pridworthy who arranged that, would you believe?

Miles Really?

Celia She's been amazing. Very supportive. Quite a revelation.

Miles Yes. I think she was one of the reasons I left, actually. I mean, once I'd got drummed out of the golf club there wasn't much left to live for round here. (*He laughs*) I mean, in a manner of speaking.

Celia Yes, she told me about that incident. I must say, it did all sound a little unsavoury.

Miles Oh. Well. Sandy not unsavoury. It was quite fun, actually. (*He laughs*)

Celia Yes, you've got quite Australian, haven't you? Well, excuse me, I must ... (*she moves away*)

Miles Those for Toby, are they? The flowers?

Celia Lord, no. These are for the church. Easter. Toby never cared for flowers.

Miles Ah, yes.

Celia Give my regards to Rowena, won't you? Tell her not to overdo it out there.

Miles No. Quite.

Celia goes into the church

Miles My God, what's happened to her? (*He stops to read a nearby grave*) "In memory of Joseph John Hepplewick, aged seventy-five." He's gone as well. (*He reads*)

> This will not be the last of him you've seen.
> His poetry will linger evergreen.

Is that a promise or a threat? (*He moves to the gate, then turns back to the church as if to follow Celia inside. He shrugs and shakes his head*) No, why should I? What the hell.

The clock chimes

Miles checks his watch absentmindedly and sits on the bench

> The chief defect of Henry King
> Was chewing little bits of string ...

Rowena enters, rather muffled up

Rowena Coming?

Miles Right.

Rowena Did you see Celia? It was Celia, wasn't it?

Miles Yep.

Rowena We all dived under the seat. Timmy saw her. He said, "Look out, Mummy, here comes the witchwoman." You know how he always used to call her that. He remembered her. So we all threw ourselves flat.

Miles She still saw you.

Rowena Ah, well. She looked awful. More like a witch than ever.

Miles Yes.

Rowena How was she? Did you talk?

Miles A bit.

Rowena You all right?

Miles Yes, I—yes.

Rowena What's happened? You were perfectly cheerful a minute ago.

Miles Nothing.

Rowena God, this bloody cold. (*She snuffles*) The minute we get back to England, I get a cold.

Miles You'd better get in the car.

Rowena This place really has shrunk, hasn't it? I mean, the whole village is tiny. To think it used to be our whole world, didn't it? Well, mine certainly. At least you went to work. Now, it's—it's like going back to your old nursery school. All those tiny little chairs and weeny little loos. And coathooks two foot off the ground. You feel like Gulliver. That's what I feel like here. Better watch where I tread or I'll squash the verger. Did you find Toby's grave?

Miles (*indicating*) It's over there. (*After a slight pause*) It's ironic. I was just thinking, if we hadn't taken this job, if we'd stayed on here instead, Toby might still be alive.

Rowena Really? How come?

Miles Well, at least I might have been able to stop him drinking himself to death.

Rowena Possibly. Then again, if you'd stayed here, you might have been able to prevent a large section of the East Coast of England from falling into the North Sea. You never know.

Miles No, really?

Rowena Yes, really. It's just as likely. And if we hadn't gone, then Timmy's chest would never have cleared up and I would have finally died of cold from another winter here. As my friend, Ted, at the gas station is very fond of putting it—"Well, Row, you win a few, you lose a few. That's the way the roo's shit crumbles".

Miles Yes, he says that rather a lot, doesn't he? Whenever he's round to see us. Him and Stan whatsisname and big Bru. And Stu. Not forgetting Grog and Titcho.

Rowena Well, they're your friends as well.

Miles No, they're not, Rowena, they're really not. I support the wrong cricket team and I'm not very fond of canned beer. They're far more your friends than mine.

Rowena Oh.

Miles That was my friend over there. OK, we'd better get going. Come on.

Miles exits

Rowena (*scowling in the direction of Toby's grave*) I bet you're laughing, Toby Teasdale, wherever you are.

Rowena goes off after Miles

The Lights fade to a Black-out

A TRIUMPH OF FRIENDSHIP

A Churchyard. This year

The church door is closed. A gravel path leads away from it to an unseen road. A variety of gravestones border the path

We hear church bells signifying a happy occasion and from within the church, the sound of a service just finishing

After a second's pause, Celia creeps furtively out of the church, closing the door behind her

Simultaneously, Miles, in an equally secretive manner, comes round the side of the building. They see each other and stop guiltily

Celia Oh.
Miles Ah. (*After a pause*) Sorry, I was—er—I came round this way so—you—we wouldn't run into—each other.
Celia No.
Miles Both seem to have had the same idea.
Celia Yes. (*After a pause*) Silly.
Miles Sorry, I—sorry.
Celia No, well. (*After a pause*) We can both be grown-up, can't we?
Miles I just came for the service.
Celia Yes. (*After a pause*) Moving, wasn't it?
Miles Yes. Fifty years of the school. Quite a landmark.
Celia Toby—didn't come.
Miles No, no. He had a bit of a cold.
Celia Oh, dear.

Pause

Miles The new Headmaster looks pretty on the ball.
Celia David Ashburn. Yes, he's very bright.
Miles Fine sermon.
Celia Oh, yes. Very, very. Avarice.
Miles Yes.
Celia Extremely topical.
Miles Rather. Well . . .(*he begins to move away*) I must . . .
Celia First time you've been back here, isn't it?
Miles Yes, for—well, since I resigned from the Board, yes. Four years. Must be. Four and a half.
Celia Have things changed, do you think?
Miles Not a lot, no. You haven't. You're working, I hear?

Celia Yes, I'm right back in the swing, would you believe? My old job.

Miles Conferences.

Celia Yes. All very hectic. Employing nannies and all that.

Miles Yes, you're looking good.

Celia Thank you. You're——

Miles I'm fine.

Celia Yes. (*After a slight pause*) How's Toby?

Miles Oh, terribly well.

Celia Apart from his cold.

Miles Yes, apart from his cold.

Celia And you're still working with . . .?

Miles Still down among the micro-chips, yes. Toby worked there for a bit. In the—er—in the dispatch section. Only he didn't fancy it very much. Posting off invisible things to people. Not his scene.

Celia So what's he doing now?

Miles Well, he's—er—he's doing a little bit of private tuition and—er—no, he's not doing an awful lot at the moment. You know Toby, he's—can't quite sort out what he wants to do really.

Celia Sitting at home and being mother, is he?

Miles No, no. No such luck. No, he's being a bloody nuisance actually. (*He laughs*) You know Toby. Dear old Toby.

Celia (*laughing*) Yes. (*After a pause*) He can be awfully . . . if he doesn't get his own way.

Miles Oh, yes. Yes. (*After a pause*) You—er—you haven't seen anything of Rowena at all, have you? I don't often hear from her. I just wondered if she . . . at all?

Celia No, not for a long time. I think she's—she's travelling.

Miles Travelling?

Celia Yes.

Miles What about the kids?

Celia I think they're travelling as well.

Miles Oh, God.

Celia Well, you know her. You know what she's like. She—she got very sort of gloomy—terribly unlike her really. And she suddenly said to me one day, "I can't stick this place a minute longer". And then it must have been a week later, I got a phone call from the station—reversed charges— and it was her saying, "I'm off, see you sometime". And that was that. I thought you must know. The house is all shut up.

Miles Where on earth have they gone?

Celia Well. She muttered something about India.

Miles India?

Celia Or Indonesia. One of those.

Miles Oh. She said nothing to me.

Celia No? Well, that's her really, isn't it, Miles? She only phoned me because she forgot to cancel the milk. She really is a. . . . Not that I'll have a word said against her. I mean, after Toby—resigned and just walked out on us, she was tremendously supportive. Wonderful. I really misjudged her. I don't think I could have coped otherwise. I think I think I might have done something really silly if it hadn't been for her. I grew to like her quite a bit.

Miles Yes, she was ... she was ...

Celia I certainly don't think it was very bright of you to swop her for Toby. I really don't.

Miles Well.

The clock chimes

I must make a start back.

Celia Long drive, is it?

Miles Oh, about an hour and a half. Quite pleasant. Of course we miss the countryside a bit but ... (*After a pause*) You see, if only he'd stop drinking, Celia. That's the whole problem in a nutshell. I mean, he's killing himself slowly but surely.

Celia Yes, yes.

Miles I keep telling him but he won't listen. He won't eat. I stick food in front of him. He refuses to touch it. He just gets abusive.

Celia Calls you everything under the sun.

Miles And some besides.

Celia Oh, yes.

Miles He told me I had a brain like a dead lightbulb this morning. That's not a very nice thing to say.

Celia No. Very hurtful that sort of thing. When he tells you you have a smile like congealed porridge or something, it sticks. You remember it for days. You daren't smile at all.

Miles Well, he doesn't think.

Celia No, he doesn't. Have you trained him to put clean clothes on? That was always my pet hate. I mean, his socks. He'd go for days.

Miles God, yes.

Celia You'd have to wrestle them off him.

Miles He never seems to notice, no.

Celia You'd think he would. It's all right this time of year. But in summer.

Miles Quite.

Celia And I bet he still stubs his cigarettes out in the saucers.

Miles Yes. The times I've asked him ...

Celia Oh, that used to drive me mad. I'd put ashtrays here, there.

Miles Everywhere, yes.

Celia Everywhere. Would he ever?

Miles No. Never.

Celia No. Oh, he's an infuriating man. I think it's so courageous of you, Miles, I really do. Taking him on. I mean, I—well, I was going to say if you ever need any help but I don't honestly think I want to get involved in all that again. But I do feel for you.

Miles (*shrugging*) Well.

Celia It is good to see you. I'm glad you came back. I know you're not attached to the school now, but——

Miles It's good to see you, too, Celia.

They smile at each other

Celia Still quoting Stendhal, are you?

Miles Er—no—not as much as I used to.

Celia Shouldn't think he'd go down so well with Toby.

Miles No. He calls him the soggy frog.

Celia Yes.

Miles I'm glad things seem to have worked out for you, anyway. I wondered how you'd be.

Celia It's funny. One always lands on one's feet.

Miles Yes.

Celia Jolly brave of you to come back.

Miles Oh.

Celia I mean, there was a lot of talk obviously.

Miles Oh, yes.

Celia I don't know if you saw Irene Pridworthy's face when you slipped in at the back of the church there.

Miles Yes, I did, actually.

Celia Oh, good. I'm glad you did.

Miles She was one of the reasons I came back. Get my revenge on her for having me chucked out of the golf club. Well . . .

Celia (*smiling at him and then impetuously clasping his hand*) Dear Miles. Dear, dear Miles. If there's anything—you know—anything I can do, seriously. Advice or something . . . I did live with him for years and years so I'm quite experienced.

Miles Thanks. I might ring you.

Celia Do. Please, do.

Miles Goodbye, Celia.

Celia Goodbye.

Miles goes off towards the road

What a dear man. What a dear, sweet man.

She smiles affectionately to herself as she goes off around the side of the church

The Lights fade to a Black-out

INTIMATE EXCHANGES is a related series of plays totalling eight scripts

This is the Seventh

A ONE MAN PROTEST
Preceded by *How it began* (page 3)
and *A Visit from a Friend* (page 5)

CHARACTERS
APPEARING IN THIS SERIES OF SCENES

Celia
Miles
Sylvie
Rowena
Toby
Lionel

CONFESSIONS IN A GARDEN SHED

The same. Five days later. It is the afternoon of Saturday, June 19th and is another sunny day

We now see the garden from a slightly different angle. The shed is far more centrally placed and we are able to look into its interior. It is extremely cluttered. The dustbins behind it are also in view, as is the back fence and a gate which leads across a wide cinder track to the playing field. Consequently, we see considerably less, if anything, of the patio and the house itself

Miles is hovering at the gate, looking anxiously towards the house

Miles (*calling urgently*) Come on, Rowena, come on. Rowena.

Rowena (*off*) All right, all right.

Miles There's nobody in. Obviously. (*He hops about, uncomfortable at them trespassing in other people's gardens*)

Rowena enters, much less concerned at whether or not she is trespassing. She is about the same age as Miles, a lively woman, attractive and who, with three children, manages most days to look several years younger

Rowena I think they must be out.

Miles They said they were.

Rowena Yes, I knew Toby would be out. He'll be up at the school. I thought Celia might be there.

Miles (*irritably*) Well, she isn't, is she? Anyway, I don't want to see her. I don't want to see either of them.

Rowena What's the matter? You used to like her, didn't you? What's wrong?

Miles Nothing.

Rowena You used to go all—soft over her.

Miles No, I didn't.

Rowena Whenever she was mentioned. I think she quite likes you too, actually. In so far as Celia can like anybody. Have you had a tiff?

Miles Oh, don't start all that, Rowena. It's so stupid and childish.

Rowena Well, I am stupid, aren't I, Miles? (*She looks around*) It's an awful tip, isn't it, this garden?

Miles Look, do come on, it's going to rain in a minute.

Rowena No, I am the one Celia doesn't like. I think she loathes me. Can't think why. You see, they could plant things along here. Herbs and things. It would be lovely.

Miles Are you coming?

Rowena There's no hurry.

Miles This happens to be someone else's garden.

Rowena They're not going to mind.

Miles Yes, they are. I would. People tramping across my garden. Peering in through all the downstairs windows.

Rowena I wanted to look. Honestly. Sometimes you're so old, Miles, you really are. You call me childish but sometimes I feel I'm going out with a grandfather.

Miles Oh, thank you.

Rowena Anyway, after what you did for Toby, I should think we have absolute right of way. You saved his job, didn't you?

Miles I suppose I did.

Rowena Of course you did. But for you, he'd have been sacked for the old drunk he is. They ought to red carpet the lawn for you.

Miles We're supposed to be going for our walk. It's our annual walk.

Rowena We are going for a walk.

Miles I'm not going for a walk. I'm standing still.

Rowena Well, I'm walking.

Miles You're not walking. You're going round and round in circles snooping through other people's property. Now come away.

Rowena One of the reasons for the walk was to visit them, wasn't it?

Miles One of the reasons. Only they're not here so come on.

Rowena One of the reasons?

Miles Yes.

Rowena What was the other one?

Miles I wanted to talk to you.

Rowena Oh, God. (*She looks into the shed*) Oh, what's in here?

Miles Rowena, will you come away. That is a private shed.

Rowena Private shed. How can you have a private shed? Private shed. Major shed. Brigadier shed. Second lieutenant shed reporting for duty, sir. It's full of tooools. Straaaaange tooools. What do you think Toby does with all these straaaange tooools? They can't all be bottle openers, can they?

Miles glances at his watch, resigned

Why can't we talk at home? Why do we always have to walk when we talk? Walkie talkie.

Miles Rowena, will you try, please and be a little adult.

Rowena Yes, of course I will, Miles. I'll be a very small adult indeed. (*She crouches down in the shed*) Is this short enough for you?

Miles It's going to rain, you know.

Rowena "Rubbish," cried the dwarf. What do you want to talk about then? As if I couldn't guess. (*She comes out of the shed*)

Miles Can we get out of their garden first?

Rowena (*looking off towards the field*) Look, they're all going for a run. Dozens and dozens and dozens of small boys. Well, you can't call it a run. It's more of a scamper really. Who's that with them?

Miles Terry Hogg.

Rowena Oh yes, so it is.

Miles You know damn well it's Terry Hogg.

Rowena (*delighted*) Look at him, he can hardly keep up. He's supposed to be the P.E. instructor. He can hardly keep up with them.

Miles I wouldn't imagine you'd have much trouble recognizing Terry Hogg. With or without his running shorts.

Rowena (*looking at him coolly*) Really? Well, once you're undressed, darling, you all look rather alike. I can only tell men apart when they've got their shirts on.

Miles You know, you're actually a female sexist. I didn't know there were such things. I just think it's a little bit corny with a P.E. teacher, isn't it?

Rowena Well, I'm corny as well, Miles, you know that. I'm corny and stupid and childish and ill-educated. What do you expect?

Miles I expected a little more from you, that's all.

Rowena Ssh.

Miles (*getting angrier*) I'm sorry but I do.

Rowena Let's not start shouting, Miles. Let's enjoy the walk. You want to talk, we'll talk at home. That's what homes are for. For shouting at each other. That's why we build them. So that people next door can't hear us shouting. Only they do of course.

Miles We can't talk at home. It's perpetually swarming with people. Hildy, the kids, Mrs Boatman—a continual stream of workmen taking out what they failed to install properly the previous week. . . .

Rowena (*more interested in the race*) There's a poor little fat boy at the back desperately trying to keep up. Oh, do look, Miles. It's terribly sad. I've an awful feeling Timothy's going to be like that in three or four years.

Miles It's a girl, actually. It's a little fat girl.

Rowena Oh dear, that's worse.

Miles I'm sure you need glasses.

Rowena Poor thing, look at her.

Miles Do her good.

Rowena I bet she's so self-conscious and embarrassed.

Miles Best thing for little fat girls. Chase them all round and round fields, that's what I say.

Rowena I'm sure she wouldn't mind being chased. It's having to run after everyone, that's what's so awful for her. The only boys she'll ever meet will be the weeds or ones with a stitch.

Miles Serve her right.

Rowena Oh, you're so mean sometimes, Miles. Mean, mean-faced. Look at it, all mean.

Miles Not at all.

Rowena It's your lemon-sucking look.

Miles Oh, do shut up.

Rowena You used to be enormous fun, Miles, you really did. You used to care about things and talk about them. Make jokes about them. There were so many things you used to like and enjoy. Now you don't like anything very much, do you?

Miles I'm merely forty instead of thirty, that's all.

Rowena But you're not forty.
Miles Damn nearly. So are you.
Rowena I am not damn nearly forty, thank you. I am thirty-six and a bit.
And that is nearly thirty-five if it's anything. All right, come on if you're
coming.
Miles You're going to refuse to talk about anything, aren't you?
Rowena What's the point in our talking, Miles? It never did any good.
Miles Yes, I realize it's not a frightfully efficient means of communication,
especially when employed by two people like us but it's the best person to
person system so far devised, Rowena. You make noises. Then I make
other noises, slightly deeper noises . . .
Rowena Occasionally.
Miles Yes, I meant deep in register rather than philosophical content.
Rowena So did I. You can get very shrill. You practically squeak.
Miles (*choosing to ignore this*) And in that way, our respective noises tell us,
each other, what we're both thinking. So that we know. I can find out
whether I can look forward to thirty more years of marriage or whether
I'm to come home one evening to find you've buggered off with the local
kung-fu expert. Does that seem unreasonable?
Rowena My God, you were right. It's raining.
Miles Oh, no. (*He hurries towards the gate*) Come on, come on.
Rowena We can't. We'll be soaked.
Miles We will just standing here. Come on.
Rowena In here, quick.

Rowena goes into the shed

Miles Oh, Rowena.
Rowena Quick, quick, quick. It's dry.
Miles (*deeply frustrated by everything*) Oh. (*He goes into the shed after her*)
Rowena I know, I know, it's a private shed. It's only a shower. It won't be
long.
Miles (*looking out gloomily*) It's pelting down.
Rowena Poor little fat girl's going to get wet.
Miles So's Terry Hogg with any luck.
Rowena I'm not saying anything, Miles. You're not going to get me to say
anything. I'm saying nothing. So there.

Pause

The rain patters on the roof

Whatever I say, you'll twist round, make me look a fool. (*After a pause*) I
don't think I'm that stupid. I do think though you do an awfully good
job, sometimes, convincing me that I really am more stupid than I really
am.
Miles I've never said you were stupid.
Rowena Oh yes, you do. You wouldn't understand this, old girl. I'm afraid
this is far beyond your ken, old tiny brain.
Miles This is absolutely slanderous. What a load of rubbish.

Rowena Yes, you do. (*After a slight pause*) You do.

Miles I have *occasionally*, very very occasionally remarked that you deliberately choose not to understand things when you deliberately go into your professional idiot act.

Rowena What does that mean?

Miles All this, "I don't understand cars at all, that's all beyond me. Oh, is that the petrol tank, good gracious. Oh dear, I'm an absolutely silly when it comes to figures."

Rowena (*with dignity*) There are some things I have the grace to admit I am not very good at. I do not understand cars at all.

Miles You understand a damn sight more about a lot of things than you make out.

Rowena Oh, really?

Miles Nobody could be that stupid. (*After a slight pause*) I didn't mean that.

Rowena I'll ignore it then. The point is, all I'm saying's if you treat someone as if they were stupid, don't be totally amazed if they become stupid.

Miles And all I'm saying is, that if you pretend to be stupid for long enough don't be totally amazed if people treat you as stupid.

Pause

Rowena I told you we shouldn't talk. I'm not clever enough to argue with you. You're absolutely brilliant, Miles. What a brain. Like a laser beam. Golly, wow, gosh. (*After a pause*) Trouble was, I was educated before they started to take girls seriously. Allowed us to take our rightful place in the world. Puffing round fields in the rain with the rest of the chaps. I was never taught anything. If I am a professional idiot as you refer to me, it's the way I've managed to survive. It gave me a sort of attractive plumage. What was it attracted you to me in the first place, Miles? Was it my idiocy or my sheer professionalism?

Miles I don't think it had much to do with either of those.

Rowena (*smiling*) No, it didn't, did it?

Miles No.

Rowena But who'd have thought it'd have led to all this though? Look at us today. Married, in someone else's garden shed. Isn't life just full of adventure? Why don't you have an affair, Miles? I'm sure it would do you an awful lot of good. I think it would do us an awful lot of good. I think you need a bit of danger, Miles, I really do.

Miles I don't need danger, thank you. Life is quite dangerous enough. I travel to work every morning. That's dangerous. Every day of my life. I have to fight men larger and fitter than me just for a seat on the train. I have to walk through central London. God, that's dangerous. I have a temporary secretary with green hair who reads magazines advocating compulsory castration for all men over twenty-one. My whole world is fraught with danger, thank you very much.

Rowena You'd have enjoyed all that in the old days. You'd have argued with old green hair or sent her up until she saw the funny side. Remember all the things we were going to do? Do you remember we were going to walk all round England once, right round the coast. England, Scotland, Wales. Remember?

Miles Good Lord, yes. Now we should have done that. Why didn't we?

Rowena I think I got pregnant.

Miles Oh, yes.

Rowena Would have unbalanced the rucksack. We were going to take a year off.

Miles That's right.

Rowena It wasn't all my fault. There were Test Matches as well, I seem to remember.

Miles Yes, well, that would have done it.

Rowena They've always managed to do it. I think but for Test Matches, we would have had a very full and active marriage, really. No, honestly, Miles, you should have an affair. Seriously. Do you good.

Miles You talk about it as if it were a health farm.

Rowena Well, it would be in a way. More fun than colonic irrigation.

Miles I think you're just trying to offset your own guilt.

Rowena Guilt? I'm not guilty.

Miles You're not denying it now, are you?

Rowena No.

Miles Well then.

Rowena Miles, try and understand. Imagine you've married a pianist. Now it so happens that my own piano has gone slightly out of tune so I'm having to practise elsewhere.

Miles My God.

Rowena I'm not giving concerts, I'm practising. There is a difference.

Miles I think this is one of the most distasteful metaphors I have ever heard.

Rowena It's rather apt.

Miles Well, if you're off with Terry Hogg then you're practising on the bloody banjo, that's all I can say.

Rowena Bitchy, bitchy. Why don't you try Celia? She's available. She's just about to walk out on Toby as she's been telling everybody for weeks. She'd probably welcome any man provided he was sober.

Miles Rowena, I do wish you'd think before you say all this. You're just saying these things without thinking. That's your trouble, you're——

Rowena I'm stupid.

Miles Well, yes. No. Yes, sometimes you are, you know. You really are on occasions almost unbelievably bovine.

Pause

Rowena (*nodding*) And you wonder why I have affairs. When I'm forced to stand in a shed and listen to somebody calling me bovine.

Miles I'm sorry.

Rowena I won't say I'm getting old, Miles, because I'm not. But I am getting older and I need loving. I thought as you got older you needed less loving but, in fact, you need more.

Miles Well, you're not going to get love, are you? Not from——

Rowena (*angrily*) I know I'm not going to get it from Terry bloody Hogg.

Do you think I don't know that? Or from Frank Arrowsmith. Or Geoff Hampton. Or Malcolm Smith. Or Ronnie Chalmers. Or any of the rest of them.

Silence

Miles (*stunned*) Have you—have you—am I to understand you've been with all of those?

Rowena (*meekly*) Yes.

Miles That's—that's practically my entire Squash Club, do you realize that?

Miles sits down on a box

Rowena Yes. I'm sorry, Miles. (*After a pause*) I was only trying to . . . (*after a pause*) I was trying to keep interesting. I know that sounds . . .

Miles Well, you're certainly never boring, I'll give you that. Geoff Hampton?

Rowena nods

Yep. Just confirming.

Rowena Are you very hurt?

Miles I don't know what I am. I'm just trying to acclimatize myself to this new global view of things. I mean, the reason I came out for a walk with you was to discuss some mild sexual skirmish. Now I see you've actually embarked on world conquest. Has it stopped raining?

Rowena (*looking out*) Nearly. Do you want to go?

Miles No.

Rowena What do you want to do? Do you want to shout at me?

Miles No.

Rowena Would you like to hit me?

Miles No.

Rowena Thank God. Kill yourself?

Miles No.

Rowena Kill me?

Miles Oh, Rowena, please, do you mind?

Rowena (*exploring the shed*) Plenty of stuff here. Rope, you see? (*She strangles herself*) Yaark. Oh—aha!—half a shovel. (*She pretends to strike herself on the head*) Dong! Or even better—(*She picks up a packet*)—weedkiller. (*She clutches her throat*) Aargh. The squash club murders. Fifteen nil Service. Service to—aaarrgh. (*She rolls about in the shed gasping*) Don't—eat—the—squash—ball. It's . . . pois . . .

Miles (*shouting*) Rowena, if you don't go away in a minute, I shall break your neck!

Rowena (*twisting her head*) Snap! Right. (*She moves to the door*)

Miles (*pleading*) Please leave me alone, Rowena, please. If there's one thing worse than having a multiple unfaithful wife, it's having a funny multiple unfaithful wife.

Rowena Well, at least I make people laugh occasionally.

Miles Yes, but mostly at me, though.

Rowena (*going through the door*) Bye-bye, then.

Miles Goodbye.

Rowena I'll leave you in peace. (*She pushes the door to, making a vocal creaking sound*) Uuurrrkkk! My God, cried the butler, there's something in the shed ... (*She closes the door on Miles and as an afterthought, turns the key on him. She moves away and looks up*) Oh, it's stopped.

She peers in through the shed window as she passes. Miles is still seated motionless

Good grief. They have a gnome in their shed exactly like my husband.

Rowena exits through the gate

Miles sinks his head in his hands and groans. After a moment, he stands up. He sees the weedkiller. He looks at it

Miles I honestly don't know, Inspector. I really don't. I can only suppose the weedkiller must have somehow toppled off the shelf and bounced into her tea. (*He shakes his head. He picks up the rope*) She always was an impetuous woman, Inspector. I think what must have happened was, she obviously snatched up this piece of rope thinking it was her scarf and rushed out to meet me without realizing the rope was attached to the door handle. . . . (*After a pause he picks up the shovel*) She was just swinging the shovel round her head in sheer high spirits. She was that sort of woman. (*After a pause he picks up an old fertilizer bag filled with straw or woodshavings. He cradles the sack in his arms*) I don't know how she suffocated, Inspector, I really don't. I can only assume the entire Squash Club must have sat on her at once. (*He sits on the sack savagely. He shakes his head. He moves to the shed door and tries to open it. He rattles the handle*) Oh, no. (*He is almost in tears*) She hasn't locked me in! (*He rattles the handle*) That's it. She's now locked me in the shed. (*He calls*) Rowena! (*He yells*) Rowena! God damn it, Rowena! I shall kick down this ... (*He screams in total uncontrollable fury*) Damn it, damn it, damn it! I just picked her up, Inspector, I don't know what came over me. I just picked up the stupid, bloody, brainless bitch and threw her out of the window. It was a pure accident. Rowena! (*He hurls the fertilizer sack on the floor and jumps on it with two feet. He stands panting, slowly calming down. He looks out of the window and speaks more calmly*) She's running round that field with that fat girl. That's what she's doing. Both of them. Chasing Terry Hogg for all they're worth. (*He shakes his head*) Oh, dear God. (*He sits and mutters to himself*)

As he does so, Sylvie comes from the house. She is dressed for housework and is carrying some rubbish to the dustbin. She passes the shed. Miles does not notice her. Nor she Miles. She empties her rubbish (some old bottles)

Miles reacts to the noise but is unable to locate the sound

Sylvie finds a book amongst the rubbish and studies it

(*Muttering*) I mean, what a childish thing to do. To lock someone in a shed. I ask you, what is the point of locking someone in a shed? Absolute kindergarten behaviour.

During this Sylvie looks around puzzled. She puts the book back in the dustbin and replaces the bin lid. She starts to move towards the house

I mean, I suppose I'm going to be stuck in here all night, aren't I? Not that she'd bother. Couldn't give a damn. A thirty-six year old woman with three children, you'd think she'd actually learn to behave with a little more dignity.

Sylvie, on her way back to the house, hears the sound again. She frowns, pauses, then somewhat cautiously looks in through the shed window. She sees Miles

Sylvie Oh.
Miles (*stopping as he sees her*) Hallo.
Sylvie Hallo.
Miles I wonder if you'd mind opening the door.
Sylvie Oh, yes. Just a minute. (*She unlocks the door*)
Miles (*coming out of the shed*) Hallo, there.
Sylvie Afternoon, Mr Coombes.
Miles Good afternoon, Sylvie. Thank you very much.
Sylvie You're welcome.

Pause

Sylvie stares at him

Miles (*self-consciously taking deep breaths of fresh air*) It's good to be out.
Sylvie Yes.
Miles I got locked in.
Sylvie Oh yes?
Miles My wife. It was a joke.
Sylvie Yes.
Miles It was raining, you see, earlier.
Sylvie Yes. (*She looks up*) Stopped now.
Miles Yes, yes. (*After a pause*) Are you working here today for Mrs Teasdale?
Sylvie Yes.
Miles On a Saturday, eh? That's very keen of you.
Sylvie I missed Wednesday.
Miles Oh, I see. You usually do Wednesday?
Sylvie Yes.
Miles Ah.
Sylvie Except when Mum has her treatment. Then I stay home to look after the youngsters.
Miles Oh dear, your mother, is she——?
Sylvie Yes.
Miles Oh, dear.
Sylvie Yes.
Miles Worrying for your father.
Sylvie No.
Miles No?

Sylvie No, he's dead.

Miles Oh. (*After a pause*) You're the eldest, are you?

Sylvie Yes.

Miles And how many of you are there, then?

Sylvie How many of me?

Miles No.

Sylvie (*smiling*) Just the one of me.

Miles (*laughing rather excessively at this very small joke*) No, no, I mean how many in your family.

Sylvie There's me, Gerald, Marcie, Janet, Tubsy, Jeannine and Leroy. Leroy's the baby.

Miles Oh, that's unusual.

Sylvie (*after a pause*) That's my sister running round there.

Miles Which one?

Sylvie The fattie. The fattie one at the back. That's Tubsy. Her name's Rachel, only we call her Tubsy.

Miles Oh.

Sylvie Look at her. Do her good, that.

Miles She's gone a very bright colour, hasn't she?

Sylvie Do her good. (*She yells suddenly*) Run up, Tubsy. Go on, girl. Get some of it off your arse.

Miles (*laughing nervously*) Quite an expense for your family, wasn't it? Sending your sister to this school.

Sylvie (*looking at him slyly*) You mean, she doesn't belong there.

Miles No, that's not what I meant.

Sylvie She's a scholarship.

Miles Oh, is she? (*Remembering*) Rachel Bell, of course. I didn't make the connection.

Sylvie She's the brains, that one. Science. Wants to be a scientist. She's only nine.

Miles Good, good.

Sylvie She blew a hole in our kitchen.

Miles Good heavens. What was she doing?

Sylvie She was trying to make a mortar bomb.

Miles Ah. Well.

Sylvie She did, too. (*After a pause*) Look at her. She's going to collapse in a minute. He's a right mean sod, that one. Him. Terry Hogg. Likes seeing them all cry. He's a real mean bugger, that one.

Miles Yes, I can imagine he would be.

Sylvie He loves it. (*She looks at Miles*) Quite good-looking though, wouldn't you think?

Miles —er—no, not really, no.

Sylive smiles at him

What's that?

Sylvie Nothing.

Miles Have you got a boyfriend then, Sylvie?

Sylvie Yes, sort of.

Miles Oh.

Sylvie Lionel Hepplewick.

Miles Oh yes, he's the school caretaker, isn't he?

Sylvie S'right.

Miles Took over from his father when the old man retired. He looks a nice boy.

Sylvie He isn't a boy. He's quite old.

Miles Is he?

Sylvie He's knocking thirty-four.

Miles Yes.

Sylvie Anyway, he thinks he's with me but I'm not so sure I'm with him.

Miles Why's that?

Sylvie Think I can do better, that's all. All he's looking for is someone to look after him and his father. That's all he wants. More to life than that.

Miles Right.

Sylvie You got to be careful, if you're a woman, or you get stuck with them. I'd be running round after his dad till I'm ninety-one, wouldn't I?

Miles Be a waste, that would.

Sylvie It would.

Miles So what do you want to do?

Sylvie I don't know. Something exciting. I don't want to do what my mum did, anyway. You know, she's never been more than thirty miles away from here in her life. Except a couple of times. For her brother's funeral in Birmingham and that. Now she's dying. And what's she seen? Nothing. Except our backyard. All that washing. And the kitchen. Dark little kitchen. Smells of dog. 'Cos she won't have him put down. And the oil stove. With all the knickers hanging round it. That's about the limit of her experience really. You say to her, "What about them Russians, then, mum?" She says, "Bugger them, you eat your tea." "What about the Americans, then?" She says, "To hell with the Americans, what about this rain and my washing?" Got real world vision, my mum. Well, I'm not staying here to wash Lionel Hepplewick's socks, I can tell you.

Miles (*nodding*) Well, I think you've got very much the right idea, Sylvie.

Sylvie You don't believe women belong in the home then?

Miles Not at all. I believe a woman should be as free as the next man. However free that is.

Sylvie You're not one of them chauvinists?

Miles I hope not. I try not to be.

Sylvie Let her do as she pleases, eh?

Miles (*a little uneasily*) Er—how do you mean?

Sylvie Do what she wants.

Miles Well . . .

Sylvie A lot of men don't. Women gets out of hand, they clout her.

Miles Well, I don't think that's the way.

Sylvie Sometimes necessary.

Miles No, I don't think violence is ever necessary. I think people sometimes get the feeling that it is because they've allowed themselves to be

manœuvred into a position where there seems to be no alternative. But
there's always an alternative somewhere. Always.

Sylvie Maybe there is where you come from.

Miles (*warming*) No, no, not just where I come from. No.

Sylvie Only language some people understand.

Miles Well, if that's true, it's a very very sorry world.

Sylvie It is a very very sorry world, isn't it?

Pause. Miles considers this

Why did she lock you in there, then?

Miles I told you, she—she——

Sylvie Why really though? It wasn't a joke, was it?

Miles Yes, it really was a joke. It does seem strange, but—if you knew
Rowena, it's fairly typical. And like most of her jokes, I don't quite know
what the point of it was. Rowena's got a—well, she's got a sense of
humour, let's face it. Always has had. When we first married, she used to
be the most appalling practical joker. You know, those cushions that
made noises and plastic spiders. Beetles in the bed. She adored all that
sort of thing.

Sylvie Plastic dog shit on the carpet.

Miles Yes, I think we even had that. Yes, we did. And, well, thank God all
that stopped—she's gone through that phase. She still has these mad
moments. Of course the kids adore it. Now they've started, of course.
Second generation of plastic spiders. But she's a sort of contradictory
personality really because she's really—well, you'd imagine from all that,
that she'd be rather hearty and vulgar, wouldn't you, and yet there's this
other side of her that's very gentle and vulnerable and quite touching,
really. Two different people.

Sylvie Probably a Gemini.

Miles A what? Oh, possibly. I don't know.

Sylvie When was she born? What date?

Miles Er—second of June, I think. Yes, second of June.

Sylvie She's a Gemini.

Miles You believe in that, do you?

Sylvie No. When it suits me. Today was supposed to be a good day.

Miles Oh, really?

Sylvie So it said in the paper. Said I'd meet someone interesting.

Pause

Miles smiles

If you're that fond of her, why do you let her do things like that? With
him. That Terry Hogg.

Miles Oh, now look, I don't really want to——

Sylvie She behaves like that, she belittles you, that's all.

Miles I don't know. Possibly.

Sylvie She can't think much of you, can she?

Miles Well, maybe I deserved it. I don't know. I don't really——

Sylvie She'd no business doing that. No right. Not that publicly.
Miles It is fairly public, I take it, is it?
Sylvie Oh, yes.
Miles I thought as much.
Sylvie You can't have a secret affair round here, that's for sure. (*After a pause*) You want to get your own back sometime. That's what I'd do. If I were you. Teach her a lesson.
Miles Yes, well funnily enough she did actually . . .
Sylvie What?
Miles Nothing.
Sylvie Well, I must do my work.
Miles Yes.
Sylvie Get rid of all their rubbish. They collect some clutter they do.
Miles Do they?
Sylvie Empties mainly.
Miles Oh.
Sylvie His.
Miles I don't think I want to go discussing——
Sylvie No use for a Headmaster, is it? Surprised he can teach. Hardly stand up some days.
Miles Now, Sylvie, Mr Teasdale is a very old friend of mine——
Sylvie —I should have a word with him then——
Miles —and I don't think we should be talking about him, if you don't mind.
Sylvie Somebody should for her sake. She's all right. Mostly. Mrs Teasdale. Quite nice. (*She smiles at him*) You're a bit sweet on her, aren't you? Seen you round here.
Miles I'm sorry. I can't have any more of this. I'm sorry. Go on. Off you go. (*He laughs*) Cheeky thing. Go on.
Sylvie (*grinning*) All right. (*She starts to move towards the house*)
Miles (*good-naturedly*) Get on with your work.
Sylvie (*smiling*) Be quite strong when you want to be, can't you?

Sylvie goes into the house

Miles laughs to himself. He moves as if to go off to the playing fields, then hesitates, stops and looks back towards the house. He seems reluctant to go

In a moment, Sylvie comes out with some more rubbish

Sylvie Still here?
Miles Yes.
Sylvie Right. (*She dumps her rubbish in the dustbins and starts back, moving around Miles*) Excuse me. (*She heads on towards the house*)
Miles Er——
Sylvie Yes.
Miles (*laughing*) I was just curious to know . . . why do you think I should have an affair?
Sylvie Did I say that? I didn't say that, did I?
Miles You said I should get my own back, didn't you?

Sylvie Well, it's another way to teach her, isn't it? If you don't want to clout her.

Miles Yes, true.

Sylvie Just a thought.

Miles Who with? Mrs Teasdale?

Sylvie I shouldn't think with Mrs Teasdale. Not if Mr Teasdale's an old friend.

Miles No.

Sylvie That wouldn't be right, would it?

Miles No.

Sylvie You'll find someone, I expect. There's always somebody around looking for a bit.

Miles Yes, probably there is. I don't really think I'd want to—well, go to all that time and trouble just for "a bit". I'd like it to be more than just that.

Sylvie A bit more.

Miles Yes.

Sylvie Well, it's like most things, isn't it? The more you're prepared to put in, the more you'll get out most likely.

Miles You mean money?

Sylvie No, I don't mean money.

Miles Sorry.

Sylvie Money would help. Let you do things that otherwise you wouldn't be able to do.

Miles Get away from here for instance.

Sylvie Oh, you'd need to do that. Still, I shouldn't think that's a problem, is it, for you?

Miles Not—desperately. No.

Sylvie Now, all you've got to do is find someone you want badly enough to ask and then you have to ask her. That's how I'd go about it.

Miles Would you think it frightfully rude of me to ask how old you are?

Sylvie I'm answering to twenty this year.

Miles Yes.

Sylvie I'm over age.

Miles Oh, yes.

Sylvie I can go into pubs.

Miles Good.

Sylvie Smoke cigarettes.

Miles Good. Well, you seem quite mature for your years.

Sylvie My dad used to say we're born knowing everything, we spend the rest of our lives unlearning it.

Miles Yes, I think that's been said before.

Sylvie Probably. My dad was nothing if not unoriginal. How old are you then?

Miles Well, I'm answering to thirty-seven this year.

Sylvie That's a bit old, isn't it?

Miles Is it?

Sylvie A little bit. You'll have unlearned quite a bit by now.

Miles Nothing that's important. Has your mother got blue eyes?

Sylvie She's got bloodshot eyes from staring at the telly. You've got brown eyes, you have.

Miles Yes.

Sylvie Like a cow. My dad said, people with brown eyes——

Miles Yes, your dad was obviously the local Kierkegaard.

Sylvie I don't get that.

Miles She gave me eyes, she gave me ears;
And humble cares and delicate fears;
A heart the fountain of sweet tears;
And love and thought and joy

Sylvie (*after a slight pause*) I get that all right. You make that up?

Miles I'm afraid not.

Sylvie Somebody else's?

Miles Yes.

Sylvie You're as bad as my dad.

Miles I've—er—I've always wanted to walk right round England, you know.

Sylvie Walk?

Miles Yes.

Sylvie There's probably a bus if you wait.

Miles No, no, seriously. All round the coastline. Right up through Scotland, down the East coast, down to the foot, up again through Wales. Take a year off. Just do it. I meant to when I was your age. I never did. And now the older I get, the more I realize every day there go another million things I'm never going to see. Ever. I mean, I've given up on India and China. And America. I'm reduced to Britain. If I wait much longer, it'll be the Isle of Wight. But wouldn't it be fascinating? Round some of that glorious coastline? Fascinating.

Sylvie I suppose it would.

Miles Quite an adventure.

Sylvie It would be.

Miles You think it would?

Sylvie Better than here, anyway.

Miles I mean, we'd—I'd stay in hotels and things. Hostels, farmhouses or whatever. Wouldn't be totally roughing it.

Sylvie No.

Miles Couldn't be doing with that. Not now.

Sylvie Youth hostels, you mean?

Miles Well, middle-aged men's hostels really.

Sylvie You've got a thing about your age, haven't you? My dad used to say, what was it—er—a woman gradually forgets her age while a man gradually becomes aware of his.

Miles Did he? Well, I think old man Bell's hit the target again, hasn't he?

Sylvie He had his moments. (*She moves towards the house*)

Miles Sylvie . . .

Sylvie I'd better get on. She'll be back in a minute. She's only gone shopping.

Miles (*rather desperately*) I mean, does that sort of thing interest you? Walking round the place? With someone.
Sylvie You inviting me?
Miles Yes.
Sylvie Well ... it's a bit sudden.
Miles Yes.
Sylvie I'd need to think first.
Miles Oh yes, fair enough. Yes.
Sylvie It's a big thing to do.
Miles Quite.
Sylvie A long way to walk.
Miles Yes.
Sylvie I'll let you know.
Miles Soon?
Sylvie Very soon.
Miles It's a—it's a big thing for me too, you know.
Sylvie I'm sure of that. (*She turns to go in*)
Miles (*calling after her*) How will you let me know?
Sylvie (*as she moves*) I'll find a way.

Sylvie goes into the house

Miles is both elated and rather dazed

Miles My God, what am I doing? What the hell am I doing? What on earth's come over me? You see, Inspector, this girl just let me out of a shed, you see and—er—well, it sounds ridiculous. It was love at first sight. Twenty seconds later we were planning to run away. Right round the British coastline. I can't believe this. Now, should we start at an obvious place like Land's End? No. We start in the North-west in spring and then with any luck by the time we get to autumn, we'll be coming down the East side. Winter in the South, tea in Penzance. That makes sense. I don't believe this is happening. (*He shouts*) Did you get an eyeful of that, Hogg? You jogging, wife-stealing sadist. You got the fat one, I got the pretty one. That'll teach you. "In the highlands, in the country places". We'll need some boots. Some good walking boots. "Where the old plain men have rosy faces". I wonder what size she takes. Quite small feet. "And the young fair maidens, quiet eyes." No, damn it, why the hell should I worry about Rowena? As far as she's concerned, I'm still locked in the shed. That is not going to concern me.

Celia enters. She has on her mac and has obviously just returned from shopping

Celia Oh, you're out of there. Good. Did Sylvie let you out?
Miles Yes.
Celia Good. Fine. Want a cup of tea?
Miles How did you know I was in there?
Celia Rowena just phoned. As I came in. She said you were in our shed. Apparently she'd locked you in.
Miles Yes.

Celia Rather a batty thing to do, wasn't it? No, I'm sorry but she is very batty occasionally, isn't she, Miles? You must admit it. Almost stupid.

Miles Oh, yes. Thick as a brick.

Celia It was lucky she caught me. I only just came in the door.

Miles If you hadn't come back, I could have been in there all night.

Celia Well, no. Sylvie was here.

Miles Rowena didn't know that, did she?

Celia Well, she's stupid, Miles. I keep telling you. She doesn't think half the time. You're wonderful the way you put up with her.

Miles Thank you.

Celia Did you say yes to tea?

Miles No, I think I'd better get back now, thanks very much, Celia.

Celia Kettle's on. Look, Miles . . .

Miles Yes?

Celia Look, I'm afraid I was rather rude to you when you were last here.

Miles Oh no, that's all right. Forget it.

Celia It's just that—Toby and I had just had one of our do's.

Miles Yes.

Celia But he is—we're both awfully grateful for what you did, Miles. You must have put up a hell of an argument to convince the Governors.

Miles Colonel Malton was a bit tough.

Celia Anyway, Toby's trying to cut back on the booze, he really is. I think things just got him down. He—well, I get on his nerves a bit as well, I think.

Miles (*vaguely*) No.

Celia The point is I'm—if you ever, with or without Rowena this is, want to pop round, have a biscuit, have a chat about things . . . I'm putting this frightfully badly but—you know—I realize you've got problems as well with Rowena . . . a trouble shared and all that. I think that's what I'm saying really. That's all.

Miles Yes. Certainly will.

Celia I mean, even tomorrow even. Sunday tea. I think Toby's out but I'm in. He's taking the kids to some model aeroplane rally or something. Well, I'll be here stuck on my own, anyway.

Miles I don't know that tomorrow's a frightfully good time for me, Celia. I've got one or two things to catch up on. Paperwork.

Celia Oh, yes. Fine. Righto. OK. Just a thought. Right. I'll go and organize Sylvie. Sorry about our shed. It's a frightful mess, isn't it? Cheerio.

Miles Bye.

Celia (*turning back*) Oh. Nearly forgot. Sylvie said—now, what did she tell me to tell you? Something extraordinary. Oh, yes.

EITHER she says:

Celia You were apparently asking her about her hobbies or something, weren't you?

Miles (*uncertainly*) Er—yes, yes.

Celia Well, she said she was interested in—now, let me get it right—cooking, films, travel and meeting new people. But going for long walks is apparently very bottom of her list. Is that any help?

Miles Ah.

Celia Apparently it isn't.

Miles Yes, it is. Thank you, Celia.

Celia What did you want to know that for?

Miles Oh, it's—research for my firm. Spare-time job.

Celia Oh.

Miles savagely crashes the dustbin lid down on the dustbin

(*Startled*) Miles? Are you all right?

Miles Yes.

Celia You look awfully low suddenly.

Miles No.

Celia Sure you won't have tea?

Miles No, Celia, no. Home to Rowena. I'll go and lock her in a coal bunker or something.

Celia Oh, that's the other message.

Miles What?

Celia I've got dozens of messages—I'm forgetting them all. Rowena, when she phoned. She had to go out, she said. A Squash Club meeting or something. Does that make sense?

Miles Yes, that makes sense as well.

Celia I didn't know Rowena played squash.

Miles Oh, yes. Continuously. Right. (*He wanders rather jadedly back into the shed*)

Celia What are you doing?

Miles Would you mind most awfully if I sat in here for a while?

Celia Not if you want to.

Miles It's become rather like home, you see.

Celia Miles, are you sickening for something?

Miles Probably. It's a choice of weedkiller or rope, isn't it?

Celia What?

Miles Would you shut the door?

Celia Of course. You're welcome to sit in the lounge.

Miles does not reply. Celia shrugs and closes the door

I think I will make you some tea.

Celia moves away but stops as she hears Miles' voice and stays to listen

Miles We found him in the shed, Inspector. It was a ghastly sight. He must have chewed through a whole packet of weedkiller while simultaneously strangling himself with a rope and hitting himself over the head with a shovel. It was horrible, horrible.

Celia moves away, shaking her head and goes into the house

In the country places

Where the old plain men have rosy faces
And the young fair maidens, quiet eyes.

Miles gets up, opens the door gently, removes the key from the other side, closes the door and locks it. He stands staring out of the window The fat girl jogged to a sudden halt. For there, staring from the window of the shed, were the eyes of a madman. A man sworn to a terrible cause: the destruction of all women, male or female. I'm never coming out, do you hear me? Never again.

I'm never coming out, do you hear me? Never again.

The Lights fade to a Black-out

To: A ONE MAN PROTEST (page 135)

OR she says:

Celia You were apparently asking her about her hobbies or something, weren't you?

Miles (*uncertainly*) Er—yes, yes.

Celia Well, she said she was interested in—now, let me get it right—cooking, films, travel and meeting new people. But going for long walks is apparently very top of her list. Is that any help?

Miles (*with a smile*) Oh, yes. Thank you very much, Celia, it is. It's a great help. It's wonderful.

Celia I didn't know she liked walking. She always catches the bus up here. Why did you want to know?

Miles Oh, it's—research for my firm. Spare-time job. Thank you for your shed. Thank you very much indeed.

Celia Quite all right.

Miles It's one of the very nicest sheds I've ever been in. (*He laughs*)

Celia Miles, are you all right?

Miles I feel marvellous, Celia. Absolutely marvellous. (*He pulls off his jacket*)

Celia What are you doing?

Miles (*moving away towards the end of the garden*) I'm just going to make someone else's day.

Celia How do you mean?

Miles I'm going to chase that fat girl round the field.

He gives a whoop and clearing the fence is gone, rushing off in pursuit of fat girls

Celia (*staring after him in bewilderment*) Mad. Completely mad.

She shakes her head and goes inside as the Lights fade to a black-out

To: LOVE IN THE MIST (page 177)

A ONE MAN PROTEST

The garden. Five weeks later. It is Saturday, July 24th, late in the morning. There are now two chairs by the patio table. On one of them sits Toby Teasdale, a rather crumpled red-faced man in his early forties. He sits with his paper and an undrunk cup of tea. He is smoking and coughing while he reads

In a moment, Celia comes out of the house. She seems very bright and perky. She walks down the garden

Celia (*as she moves*) He should be ready for his pudding by now.

Celia disappears round the back of the shed. Her voice is heard brightly, if indistinctly

Toby glares briefly after her, then continues reading

In a moment, Celia returns with an empty, dirty plate on a tray

Well, he ate all that. Every scrap. His appetite's really come back.

Celia goes into the house

Toby glowers, first after her and then at the shed. He mutters something to himself and then continues reading

In a moment, Celia comes out of the house carrying another tray upon which is a covered pudding dish and a spoon

I hope he likes this. He liked the apple crumble the other day. He had seconds.

Celia disappears round the back of the shed

Toby (*muttering*) Hope it bloody chokes him.

In a moment, Celia returns empty-handed murmuring happily

Celia (*to Toby*) You've not forgotten we're out to lunch?
Toby No.
Celia At the Fognorths.
Toby No.
Celia (*pausing for a breather*) It's so much easier now we've got that hatchway round the back. It means I can pass his trays straight through to him. Much better than leaving it outside the door. Like we used to have to. I mean, everything got stone cold. He's really quite practical, Miles, isn't he? Surprising. I wouldn't have thought he would have been. He's

done a beautiful job on the hatch considering he had to cut it from inside. Very neat. I wish he'd have a look at our kitchen window. (*After a pause*) He's looking better. Of course, he gets the sun through that little back window first thing in the morning. I think he's even got a little suntan. I think so. Of course it's very difficult to see him that clearly. (*After a pause*) I wonder if he needs his bucket emptying yet. (*After a pause*) I expect he'll leave it out if he does. When there's no one around. Oh well . . . (*She turns to go in*)

Toby Celia . . .

Celia Mmm?

Toby This can't—go on, you know . . .

Celia I'm sorry?

Toby This—him in there. It really can't.

Celia What do you mean?

Toby I mean, I think that's it. He's got to come out.

Celia There's no point in saying that.

Toby One way or the other, he's got to come out. Either he comes out or I'm going in to get him. Best friend or not, I won't have him in there any more. That is my shed. I want it back.

Celia You never use it. You never even go in there.

Toby True. Any more than I'm given to standing in the gaps between our cavity walls but I'd still resent other people living there. It's got to stop.

Celia He needs time.

Toby He's had time. He's had five weeks. That's his lot.

Celia You've just no idea at all, have you?

Toby Eh?

Celia If you could just forget your own selfish point of view for a moment, Toby, and look at it from his angle. What do you think it must be like for him cooped up in a shed, never coming out, day after day, week after week. . . .

Toby He doesn't have to stop in there. It's his fault.

Celia What harm is he doing?

Toby He's ruining my life. I want to be able to sit in my garden without having hoards of women keening away outside my shed door, whispering through the knot-holes at him, cantering backwards and forwards with plates of apple crumble. It's altogether too much, Celia. I've had enough.

Pause

Celia We're out to lunch in a minute.

Toby So you keep saying.

Celia Well, oughtn't you to change?

Toby I am changed.

Celia You're going like that?

Toby Yes.

Celia I see.

Toby What do you expect, a morning suit?

Celia I thought a suit.

Toby Not for batty old Fognorth. I'm not putting a suit on for him. The rate his twitchy wife flings food down your front, the only sensible garb to wear in their house is a polythene overall.

Celia Nonsense.

Toby She shot her bloody cheese dip all down me last time.

Celia You shouted at her.

Toby I did not shout at her.

Celia You said something.

Toby I merely told her she had no soul. And I said it very quietly.

Celia No wonder. What a terrible thing to say to a vicar's wife. Anyway we'd better be off in a minute or two. (*She begins to move inside*)

Toby The point is, Celia, Ben Gunn there, our friend in the shed, is coming out today. All right? I don't want you to get upset but he's coming out today.

Celia We'll see. We'll see. (*After a pause*) I don't know why you're complaining. He's no trouble. No noise. He doesn't speak. He hasn't spoken to anyone.

Toby He clumps about though.

Celia He needs some exercise.

Toby Well, why doesn't he go for a walk like everybody else?

Celia You know why.

Toby I'll tell you something. If you'd stopped feeding him every ten minutes he'd have come out a long time ago. If you'd stop treating that shed like a glorified Wendy House ...

Celia I couldn't let him starve.

Toby He wouldn't have starved. Not Miles Coombes. He's a man hell bent on survival. If you hadn't fed him, he'd have rushed out and savaged a sheep or something. Eaten next door's poodle. As it is, he's got it made, hasn't he? All mod cons.

Celia It's very uncomfortable in there. I'd like to see you do it. You couldn't have done it.

Toby You're damn right. And I'm not loopy enough to try it, either.

Celia Dr Burgess said there was no harm in him being there. It might actually be beneficial. Give Miles a chance to sort himself out quietly. He's been through the most appalling traumas. You can't rush these things.

Toby What traumas?

Celia Emotional ones.

Toby Yes, that's generally the sort. What? I mean, has his car failed its MOT? Has he just had his heating bill for the last quarter? What is this trauma?

Celia Nothing.

Toby Exactly.

Pause

Celia I suppose you ought to know. I was never going to tell you but I suppose you ought to know. The fact is he—well ... Miles ... he——

Toby Celia, you're standing there squeaking like a constipated chihuahua. What is it?

Celia Miles was—is—was—I don't know, a little bit in love with me. To put it perfectly bluntly.

Toby Miles was?

Celia Yes.

Toby With you?

Celia Yes.

Toby Nonsense.

Celia I'm afraid it's the truth.

Toby How do you know?

Celia One knows.

Toby Did he tell you?

Celia No.

Toby Then rubbish.

Celia A woman doesn't necessarily have to be told. You get these—little signals. Sometimes you know instinctively that somebody loves you.

Toby What little signals?

Celia Oh, Toby. Intimate signals.

Toby Whistling? Flapping his ears? Hopping up and down on one leg?

Celia Oh, Toby.

Toby What a load of old wellingtons, Celia.

Celia It's not.

Toby I've never given secret signals.

Celia You haven't. You're abnormal. You've never even been romantic. Not even on our honeymoon.

Toby Quite right. Nobody could possibly get romantic in Llandudno. It's full of Welshmen for one thing.

Celia Anyway that's the reason he's in there, I suspect.

Toby Bloody silly way to carry on a love affair, isn't it? One of you incarcerated in a garden shed. Or do you creep Thisbe-like down to him in the middle of the night?

Celia Of course I don't. Don't be disgusting.

Toby You have done.

Celia Only in that cold spell. With a hot water bottle. Oh, and then there was the night-light.

Toby (*disgustedly*) A night-light.

Celia He was crying, Toby. I heard him. All alone in the dark with just shovels and things. What did you mean, Thisbe-like? That's one of those things you throw, isn't it?

Toby I think that's a Frisbee.

Celia Oh.

Toby I still don't see why he's in there. I mean, normally, a normal chap if he fancies another man's wife, he whips her away for a quick bang in the Holiday Inn. He doesn't sit crying in sheds.

Celia Toby, he is in the shed because he is in love with me and he realizes how hopeless it is.

Toby Being in love with you?

Celia Yes.

Toby Well, he's got a point.

Celia So.

Toby He's pining.

Celia If you want to put it that way.

Toby So what are you planning to do about it? Apart from cramming him with carbohydrates. Or is the theory that he'll eventually get so huge he'll burst out of the shed like a day-old chick?

Celia I wish that just once in your life, Toby, you'd fall in love with somebody. Not necessarily me, it's a bit late for that, but somebody. Then you might understand. You might have a little sympathy. If you knew what the rest of us have to go through sometimes.

Toby Us?

Celia Yes.

Toby Are you referring to the human race *en masse* or someone more specific?

Celia What do you mean?

Toby I mean, is this love mutual? Are you in love with him?

Celia No. Of course not.

Toby Right.

Celia No—I'm—I'm very fond of him. I think he's a man who needs—affection. And care. And he hasn't had much of that. Certainly not from Rowena. She's destroyed him. She's eaten away at his confidence and made him feel inadequate. I'll never forgive her for that. What she's done—she's just—he's worth ten of her. Ten of her.

Toby God forbid there were ever ten of Rowena Coombes. Well, maybe you're right. Maybe I'm no longer part of the mainstream of the human race. Probably not. Hope not. I've been swimming desperately long enough trying to get out of it. Nevertheless, it does appear even to one as distant, remote and ill-informed as myself that you are, Celia, undeniably nuts about the man.

Celia I—I care, that's all.

Toby Splendid. Well, don't get too involved, will you? With your Wendy House.

Celia Jealous?

Toby Not a lot. Don't want you to get hurt, that's all. I'm sure he's good fun to play with but, sooner or later, Rowena's going to want her dolly back. . . .

Celia Oh no. I'm afraid she's shot her bolt there. There's no way he'd go back to her.

Toby How do you know? He hasn't spoken for five weeks. How do you know?

Celia He hasn't spoken to her either. Despite all her—cavortings and gigglings, he's ignored her. He's seen through her once and for all. And you needn't worry about her coming back either. I've told her, so far as she is concerned, this garden is out of bounds. From now on, I'm taking full responsibility for him. By very gentle degrees, I'm going to coax him back so that he can face the world.

Toby He is due to face the world today, Celia.

Celia You'd better not try anything. You'll have me to reckon with.

Toby We'll see.

Celia Anyway, you can't use force. Remember what the Board of Governors said. No violence, no publicity. Nothing that would reflect on the school. Think what the press would say——

Toby I'm actually thinking of selling the story. School Governors' Chairman and Headmaster's Wife in Potting Shed Love Tryst. Smiling happily together, over a large plate of summer pudding, pasty thirty-seven year old Miles Coombes and ageing academic sex-kitten Celia Teasdale . . .

Celia Oh, do be quiet. I'm warning you, you leave Miles alone. God, look at the time. We should be off and I haven't made his coffee. He'll wonder where on earth his coffee is.

Celia hurries indoors

Toby Terrific. The only shed in the country with an Egon Ronay recommendation. An unpretentious little bistro gaily decorated with old lawnmowers and gardening tools, it springs many a gastronomic surprise for the unsuspecting horticultural gourmet. Accommodation is limited so it is advisable to book early. Among the specialités du shed to be recommended by the maître de hut are sieved gumboot on a bed of crisp shredded fertilizer bag topped with a delicious sauce of turps substitute and weedkiller. . . . (*He calls*) Coombes? Miles? I'm putting your rent up, do you hear? Miles? Oh, God. Miles? (*He rattles the door handle of the shed*) I honestly don't know why you refuse to talk to me, Miles. I'm not in love with you, I promise. Listen, you're an oaf. Do you realize that? There's absolutely no woman in the world worth locking yourself in a shed for. Well, not for five weeks. Twenty minutes possibly. Providing you've got a bottle of Scotch and a good book with you. But not for five weeks, old boy. You've missed a wonderful Third Test as well. Want to know who won? Bet you're dying to know, aren't you? Well, I'm not telling you. You'll have to come out and find out. Miles, I have to warn you. I'm sending in the bailiffs today. So. Be a good chap. Move out now. Save a lot of trouble.

Sylvie comes out of the house with a cup of coffee

Sylvie Morning, Mr Teasdale.

Toby What are you doing here?

Sylvie I've come to help Mrs Teasdale.

Toby On Saturday?

Sylvie Yes.

Toby Why?

Sylvie I just have. I came on inclination.

Toby Did you. What's that?

Sylvie What?

Toby That which you are holding.

Sylvie Oh, this. This is for Mr Coombes.

Toby I see.

Sylvie He doesn't take sugar.

Toby No. You staying here long, are you?

Sylvie Long?
Toby All through lunchtime.
Sylvie Maybe. Why?
Toby As soon as you've given that to Mr Coombes, you go home. All right?
Sylvie Mrs Teasdale said you were both going out.
Toby We are.
Sylvie He'll be on his own then, Mr Coombes.
Toby I daresay he'll manage.
Sylvie What if he needs something?
Toby Just go home, do you hear me?
Sylvie (*unhappily*) Yes, Mr Teasdale.
Toby Saturday. You should be out with your boyfriend having fun. Not hanging around garden sheds.
Sylvie I'm happy here.
Toby Go away.
Sylvie Yes, Mr Teasdale.

Sylvie goes round behind the shed

Toby (*muttering*) I think she's been getting secret signals as well.
Sylvie Hallo, Mr Coombes, I've brought your coffee.
Toby Don't know what everyone sees in him. If I went and sat in a shed, no one would take a blind bit of notice.

Sylvie reappears

Sylvie I think he smiled nearly just then.
Toby I should think he's laughing his head off.
Sylvie You off then?
Toby Yes.
Sylvie Enjoy your lunch.
Toby I doubt it. I'll probably be spending the next hour or so scraping it off my shirt. You go home.
Sylvie Yes, Mr Teasdale.

Toby goes indoors

Mr Coombes? It's Sylvie again, Mr Coombes. You enjoying your coffee? I made it. I hope it's not too strong. . . . Anything else you want, Mr Coombes? No? It's a lovely day. Really warm. What did I do this morning first thing? I went shopping for my mum. . . . She's a lot better, thank you. I got some new kitchen gloves because the others had worn out. Soap powder. Teething syrup for Leroy. Two new pairs of pants for Marcie. Toothpaste. Beefburgers and a cauliflower. Oh, and Mr Coombes, I went in the bookshop to see if they had any maps. You know. Of the coast line. Only they hadn't. They said there was no call for them seeing as we were inland. It's rubbish, isn't it? As I was saying the other day, Mr Coombes, I think that walking idea, you know, it's the sort of idea that grows on you. All that walking. I'm really getting quite interested now. Mr Coombes, I know why you've locked yourself in there and that and—and I don't blame you. I've been thinking. I think we've all let you down, that's what it is. My mum's Busy Lizzie's recovered. We thought it was dead. Rachel, you know, my sister Tubsy, she brewed up some stuff to revive it. Nearly killed it. The pot started smoking. But it's OK now . . . I wish you'd talk to me, Mr Coombes. There's only me here now. You can say what you like. What was that poem you said? I'm still trying to remember. She gave me eyes, she gave me something. And something and something and fountains. It was good that. Oh, there was one in the paper last night I thought you'd like. I learned it for you.

> All gold and silver in the world
> Has value we can measure
> But one small smile of human love
> Surpasses worldly treasure.

Good, isn't it? I think Mr Hepplewick wrote it. You know, Lionel's dad. So if you're ever in a mood for a walk, Mr Coombes, all I'm saying is, I'm coming round to it. Bit by bit. So.

Lionel enters from round the back of the shed carrying two lengths of flexible trunking as from a standard vacuum cleaner, a drum of extension cable and some wide heavy duty adhesive tape

Oh, hallo.
Lionel 'llo.
Sylvie What are you doing here?
Lionel I might ask you the same question.
Sylvie I work here.
Lionel So do I today.
Sylvie No, you don't. This is the Headmaster's garden. It's private. Buzz off, you. Lionel bloody Hepplewick.
Lionel Buzz off yourself.
Sylvie What's all that smoke, then?
Lionel Where?
Sylvie (*indicating beyond the shed*) Out there.
Lionel Just a bonfire.
Sylvie Who lit that then?
Lionel I did.
Sylvie You'll burn their fence down.
Lionel Who were you talking to, just then?
Sylvie Never mind.
Lionel Mr Coombes was it?
Sylvie Mr Coombes?
Lionel Oh, come on. I know he's in there.
Sylvie You're not supposed to know. It's supposed to be secret.
Lionel Everybody knows. He's been in there for weeks. He's sulking because his wife's been sleeping about.
Sylvie Oh, is he?
Lionel Yes. Coombesie's sulking.
Sylvie It's more than that.
Lionel No. He couldn't hold her. Too much woman for him.

Sylvie Ssh. He can hear you.

Lionel Good. (*He peers in the window*) Hallo, Coombesie. You in there, are you?

Sylvie Stop it.

Lionel Look at him. Sitting on the table like a monkey. (*He pulls a face*) Hallo, Coombesie. Monkey's on the table.

Sylvie (*furiously*) Lionel, you stop it. You just stop it at once. Leave him alone. Do you hear me?

Lionel (*surprised at her vehemence*) All right, all right.

Sylvie You leave him alone.

Lionel I'd have sorted her out. His wife. If she'd been mine.

Sylvie Oh yes?

Lionel She wouldn't have gone off with anyone else if she'd been with me.

Sylvie How do you know?

Lionel She wouldn't have had the energy.

Sylvie Oh, terrific.

Lionel I'd have put my foot down. Brought her to heel. I fancy her. About my mark she is.

Sylvie If she started on you, in ten minutes time there'd only be your ears left.

Lionel Hah. (*He looks in again*) He's a funny colour, isn't he?

Sylvie So would you. He hasn't been out for five weeks.

Lionel He's crawling under the table, look at him.

Sylvie Yes, he often does that.

Lionel Bet it niffs in there.

Sylvie No, it doesn't. Mrs Teasdale brings him his bucket to wash in morning and evening. And then we empty the other one regular.

Lionel What a carry on.

Sylvie We don't mind.

Lionel Not much for him to look at. Lot of old junk.

Sylvie He's not interested in looking at things.

Lionel No.

Sylvie No. He's busy with his thoughts.

Lionel About Rowena Coombes.

Sylvie No. He's not in there because of her.

Lionel No?

Sylvie No.

Lionel Why then?

Sylvie Not saying.

Lionel Why?

Sylvie Nothing to do with you.

Lionel Somebody else then, is it?

Sylvie Maybe.

Lionel Who? Mrs Teasdale?

Sylvie Mrs Teasdale?

Lionel Who else is there?

Sylvie Never mind.

Lionel Nobody else, is there?

Sylvie Plenty of people.

Lionel Not who he'd go for.

Sylvie You'd better go. I've got to get on (*She moves towards the house*)

Lionel Hey. You don't mean you, do you? It's not you you're talking about? He been after you?

Sylvie I'm not saying.

Lionel (*greatly amused*) Never.

Sylvie Why?

Lionel He wouldn't go for you.

Sylvie How do you know?

Lionel You're not his type.

Sylvie How do you know?

Lionel Did he go for you, then?

Sylvie Ssh.

Lionel Get on.

Sylvie Well, he did. So there.

Lionel Honest?

Sylvie Yes.

Lionel Bloody hell. What, you mean you both been ...

Sylvie No, we haven't.

Lionel What have you done then?

Sylvie Nothing. He—he just told me a poem and then he asked me to walk with him.

Lionel Well. Great romance.

Sylvie Shut up.

Lionel What happened then?

Sylvie I said I wouldn't.

Lionel Sleep with him.

Sylvie No, walk with him. And so he shut himself in the shed. Because I refused him. I wasn't prepared to make myself available just like that. Only I don't think he wanted that anyway. He just wanted to talk.

Lionel He's a rum bugger, isn't he? So you've been having it in the shed then.

Sylvie No, we haven't. You've got a terrible mind, you have. Terrible. Like a cess pit full of centipedes.

Lionel Ta.

Sylvie There's a lot more to love than just having it.

Lionel What?

Sylvie Plenty.

Lionel I can't think of nothing.

Sylvie Go on. Go away.

Lionel No.

Sylvie I'll tell Mr Teasdale.

Lionel Mr Teasdale asked me in the first place. So there.

Sylvie Asked you?

Lionel I'm here on a special mission. At his express request.

Sylvie Cleaning the drains, are you?

Lionel Nope.

Sylvie What?
Lionel Special mission. Top secret. For my eyes only.
Sylvie Oh, hell.
Lionel I'm getting him out of there. Mr Teasdale's orders.
Sylvie How?
Lionel He said he was leaving it to my discretion. Anything short of brute force, he said. Only I have to do it before Mrs Teasdale gets back from her lunch otherwise she'll have a tizzy.
Sylvie You'll never get him out of there.
Lionel Want a bet?
Sylvie How?
Lionel Wait and see.
Sylvie You're not going to do anything dangerous.
Lionel Your lover'll be all right, don't worry.
Sylvie What are you going to do, Lionel?
Lionel I'm going to smoke him out.
Sylvie How?
Lionel With smoke. Like they do with wasps' nests.
Sylvie You're not going to burn the shed?
Lionel No. Scientific, this is. No danger. You see, I've got the big school vacuum out the back there. The heavy industrial one. Brought it down in the cart. I've lit the small bonfire round the back there and what I'm going to do is stick one end of the nozzle into the smoke, the other end through a hole in the shed, switch it on to blow and Bob's your uncle. Pump the smoke in this end, out it comes that end.
Sylvie That's dangerous.
Lionel No, it's not.
Sylvie He might suffocate.
Lionel That's up to him. He's only got to open the door, hasn't he?
Sylvie You'll knacker the vacuum cleaner as well.
Lionel Good cause.
Sylvie I still think it's dangerous.
Lionel Foolproof plan. (*He joins the two lengths of hose using the adhesive tape*)
Sylvie Anyway, he'll just come out and then as soon as the smoke's cleared, he'll go back in again.
Lionel No, he won't. I'll be hiding round here, you see. As soon as he runs out, choking and gasping and mopping his eyes and throwing up, I'll whip the key out of the door and lock it from the outside so he can't get back in.
Sylvie I don't know why you can't leave him alone. He's doing no harm.
Lionel Headmaster wants him out. He's trespassing.
Sylvie I'm having nothing to do with it.
Lionel Doesn't bother me. I don't need you anyway. Bye-bye.
Sylvie Goodbye.
Lionel Might take you out in a day or two if you behave yourself.
Sylvie Oh, ta. As it happens, I'm busy anyway.
Lionel Busy?
Sylvie Walking.

Lionel Walking?
Sylvie I'm getting into practice. Bye.

Sylvie goes in to the house

Lionel (*calling after her, holding up the extension lead*) I'll need to plug this in at the kitchen there.
Sylvie (*off*) Don't ask me.
Lionel (*to himself*) Need a thirteen amp. I've got my extension. It's all planned. Soon have him out. (*He moves to the shed*) Coombesie, you in there? Oh, there you are. I don't know if you heard any of that, but I'm under instructions to get you out of there, Mr Coombes. By reasonable means. Mr Teasdale's instructions. You understand that? Nothing to do with me. God, he's sitting there looking like a dead budgie. Mr Coombes? I've been asked by Mr Teasdale to read you a statement by him to give you one final chance. To come out peacefully. (*He fumbles in his pocket*) Hang on, you listen to this. (*He unfolds a piece of paper and reads*) "Miles, you dozy buffoon. This is your last chance to get out of my shed under your own steam, you oaf. Otherwise I'm setting this maniac Hepplewick on you"—that's me—"and God help you. Just remember what he did to the cricket pitches"—that wasn't my fault. I just measured them out in metric, that's all. Have to keep up with the times, don't you—"so I would run for it while you still have all your limbs. Sorry but I can't stand any more of it. You are driving me potty. Yours, Toby." That's Mr Teasdale. He's signed it. (*He holds the paper up to the window*) See? All right? Right, I'm getting going. Hold on to your hat, then.

Rowena appears round the side of the shed

Rowena Hallo.
Lionel (*picking up the flexible trunking*) Oh, afternoon, Mrs Coombes.
Rowena Heavens, what's that?
Lionel It's just a—just a bit of tube.
Rowena Thrilling. What are you going to do with it?
Lionel Er—blow things down it mostly.
Rowena What fun. Anything in particular?
Lionel No. Smoke chiefly.
Rowena Smoke? God, what are you on? It must be two hundred per cent.
Lionel No, it's bonfire smoke.
Rowena Really? Does that do things for you?
Lionel Pardon?
Rowena You're something else altogether, Mr Hepplewick. First of the bonfire freaks. Guy Fawkes night will never be the same. We'll all be sitting there with Roman Candles up our noses.
Lionel I'm afraid I don't quite follow this.
Rowena Is Mrs Teasdale around?
Lionel No, I'm afraid she's just gone out.
Rowena Good.
Lionel So has Mr Teasdale.

Rowena Then I can pay my wifely visit. I take it he's still in there, my husband?

Lionel Oh, yes.

Rowena (*looking in the shed*) Yes, there he is. Hallo, darling, it's me. How are they treating you in there? Look. Good news. I think we've found a new lawyer. He says we've a good chance if we appeal. Don't worry, darling. We could have you out of there in a matter of days. The dead man's brother's sister's mother's wife's uncle has just come forward unexpectedly. He was under the bed and saw it all. Isn't that wonderful news, darling . . .? No, he doesn't look too overjoyed. He hasn't been the same since he ate that file I brought him last week and tried to saw through the bars with the cake.

Lionel Who's this brother's sister's uncle?

Rowena Aha, surprise.

Lionel I don't get it.

Rowena Family joke, Mr Hepplewick.

Lionel Ah.

Rowena I hope he comes out soon. The kids refuse to see him any more. I mean, at first it was a bit of a novelty. Having a secret daddy at the bottom of the garden that no one was supposed to know about. Nobody else's father at school lived in a shed. Now he's become a bit like one of those Third World homemade toys you buy at Christmas from charities. It doesn't do very much, just sort of sits there staring at you, making you feel guilty for having the money to spare to buy it in the first place. Hallo, darling. (*She gives up*) Oh, well. (*To Lionel*) Don't let me interrupt you. Smoke away if you want to.

Lionel Yes. (*After a pause, slyly*) Had any good squash matches lately, have you?

Rowena Sorry?

Lionel Squash matches?

Rowena I'm afraid I don't play.

Lionel I heard you did.

Rowena No. Do you?

Lionel No. (*After a pause*) You think I should?

Rowena It's very good for you, I understand.

Lionel So I've heard. (*After a pause*) Do you reckon me as a player?

Rowena A squash player?

Lionel Yes. What do you reckon then?

Rowena Well. . . . It's not something one can tell just by looking. I'd have to be able to see you in action to be able to tell.

Lionel Ah, well.

Rowena You look as if you'd move quite well.

Lionel I do, I do.

Rowena All you need is equipment.

Lionel I've got equipment.

Rowena Oh well, then. Away you go.

Lionel I'm in with a chance then, am I?

Rowena I'd have thought so. You look pretty good to me.

Lionel Thank you.
Rowena As I said, I'd have to see you in action.
Lionel Right.
Rowena You look well-built.
Lionel I'm well-built.
Rowena You've strong legs, I take it?
Lionel Oh, yes.
Rowena You need strong legs.
Lionel Oh, these are strong. I've got good calf muscles.
Rowena Have you? Really?
Lionel Want a look, then?
Rowena (*gratefully*) May I?
Lionel Right. (*He pulls up a trouser leg*) There.
Rowena (*impressed*) Heavens. Is the other one the same?
Lionel (*rolling up his other leg*) You bet. Look at that.
Rowena Gracious.
Lionel Good, eh?
Rowena Like whipcord.
Lionel Yes.
Rowena If those are your calves, what on earth must your thigh muscles be
  like.
Lionel Oh, well. They're all right too. Like these, only bigger.
Rowena No.
Lionel Yes.
Rowena No.
Lionel Yes. You want to——?
Rowena Would you?
Lionel Just a quick look.
Rowena Thank you.
Lionel My pleasure. Just a tick. (*He unfastens his trousers*) Clean on today.
Rowena Good.
Lionel (*exposing a thigh*) There you are.
Rowena Well. What can I say? I think I've seen it all now, Mr Hepplewick.
Lionel Lionel.
Rowena Lionel. Wow!

Lionel starts to pull his trousers up

  Just a minute. Don't—you wouldn't——
Lionel I'm not taking any more off.
Rowena No.
Lionel Not in the garden here.
Rowena No, I was just wondering how you would look in shorts.
Lionel Shorts?
Rowena When you were playing squash.
Lionel Ah. Have to use your imagination a bit . . .
Rowena Go on. You're still decent. No one's looking.
Lionel Well. (*He hesitates*) All right. (*He steps out of his trousers*) There.
Rowena My God.

Lionel All right, eh?

Rowena Just look at them. I bet you can run.

Lionel Oh, I can run. You want to see me run.

Rowena Please.

Lionel Watch this then. (*He darts a few yards, possibly disappearing offstage and reappearing*)

Rowena (*delightedly*) Do it again.

Lionel Right. (*He hands her his trousers*) Hold these, would you?

Rowena Of course.

Lionel Watch this. I'll run on the spot for you.

Rowena Super.

Lionel I can't run about too much. Not like this.

Rowena You'd start a riot.

Lionel Eh?

Rowena Off you go.

Lionel Right. Now you time me. I'll run for a minute, all right, flat out. I won't even be out of breath.

Rowena I don't believe you.

Lionel Want a bet? You time me. Say when.

Rowena (*glancing at her watch vaguely*) Er—when.

Lionel Right—(*He pounds away on the spot flat out*)

Rowena Lord, carefully.

Lionel Easy. I do this every morning.

Rowena Incredible.

Rowena wanders off behind the shed for a moment and returns without the trousers

Lionel (*tiring slightly*) Say when it's time.

Rowena Right.

Lionel (*running some more*) Been a minute yet?

Rowena Not quite.

Lionel (*still running*) Must be getting near.

Rowena Keep going.

Lionel (*still running*) I must have had a minute.

Rowena No.

Lionel slows down slightly

Don't stop, you're nearly there.

Lionel (*desperately short of breath*) I can't believe this.

Rowena Keep going, keep going, keep going—oh, Lord, I think it's stopped. I'm so sorry.

Lionel What?

Rowena I'm sorry, it's stopped. My watch has stopped.

Lionel (*collapsing on the ground*) Jesus. (*He lies there panting*)

Rowena I'm terribly sorry, Mr Hepplewick. Are you all right?

Lionel is unable to reply

Lionel? Golly, I hope he's all right. (*She smacks her watch*) Silly thing. Oh,

look, it's working again now, I do that to watches, for some reason ...
Lionel I nearly blacked out there, you know.
Rowena Oh, dear.
Lionel You shouldn't do that for that long.
Rowena No. Perhaps you need a bit more training.
Lionel How do you mean?
Rowena Before you play squash. I think you probably need a bit more training, Mr Hepplewick, that's my opinion.
Lionel Is it?
Rowena I don't think you're quite up to it yet.
Lionel Oh, I'm—I'm up to it.
Rowena I don't think you are really.
Lionel (*crawling to his knees*) I can't do that too often though. Where are they then?
Rowena Sorry?
Lionel My trousers. What have you done with them?
Rowena Oh, Mr Hepplewick, what do you need with trousers? It's a crime to cover up legs like that.
Lionel Where are my bloody trousers?
Rowena On you they are little more than an obscenity. It's like putting a bra on the Venus de Milo.
Lionel Where are my flaming trousers, you stupid bitch?
Rowena I have burnt them, Mr Hepplewick. Consider yourself liberated.
Lionel You've what?
Rowena They're on the bonfire where they belong.
Lionel On the bonfire? You put my trousers on the bonfire?

Lionel rushes out behind the shed

Rowena laughs

There is a yell of fury

Lionel returns with the smoking remains of his trousers

Look at these then. Look at them. You stupid loopy cow.
Rowena Oh, dear.
Lionel You should be locked up in the shed with him. How am I going to get home?
Rowena You could run.
Lionel Very funny. You done this deliberately. (*He throws the trousers down angrily*)
Rowena If you're really shy, Mr Hepplewick, I could lend you my skirt.
Lionel I don't want your skirt. Look at these. Ruined these are, ruined. I'll ask Sylvie to lend me a pair of Mr Teasdale's. (*He picks up his drum of extension cable*) You'll be hearing more about this.
Rowena See you at the Squash Club, then?
Lionel Not bloody likely.

Lionel goes off into the house

Rowena I hope you heard all that, Miles. You see it isn't quite true to say

I've embarked on world conquest, darling. Just now, that was me saying no thank you, gracefully. Just to show you I can. Miles ...? Darling, I think it's time you came out. ... You went in there to punish me and you've done it. You punished us all. The kids are miserable. Jasper has worms and Hildy's pregnant. We all need you, darling, desperately. And we're saying grovel, grovel for being so awful to you. And failing to appreciate the sort of man you are. Come out, Miles. Your terms. Your conditions. Promise. I'll give up—everything—I promise. Miles, please, please. ... Miles, you'll have me crying in a minute. I never cry. Please, I really swear. I swear it on my—I was going to say on my honour but that may be the wrong place. On my everything else, Miles, I swear. Pleeeeease.

Sound of the shed door being slowly unlocked. Rowena watches, holding her breath. The shed door slowly opens

Miles emerges very shakily. Due to the care and attention he's received, he doesn't look too bad. He blinks in the daylight

Darling, thank God. (*After a pause*) Miles. (*After a pause*) Are you all right?

Pause

Miles (*croakily*) Hallo.
Rowena What?
Miles Lovely day.
Rowena I don't think I should talk too much, darling. Not at first. Not if you haven't spoken for five weeks.
Miles No.
Rowena It's wonderful to see you, it really is. What on earth have you been doing in there?
Miles Working things out.
Rowena Working things out?
Miles Yes.
Rowena And?
Miles I've worked them out now.
Rowena You've worked them out now?
Miles Yes.
Rowena And?
Miles I feel much better.
Rowena You feel much better. Good. So it's all OK again, is it, darling? Can we go home, please? Are you coming home? I promise not to ... are you coming home? We all want you home.

EITHER he says:

Miles No.
Rowena No?

Miles I'm sorry, Rowena. It's taken me five weeks to make up my mind but
... I have to go away somewhere. Away from all of this. I must start
again.

Rowena Miles, that's silly, darling.

Miles No, it's not silly.

Rowena You can't start again. None of us can start again.

Miles We can try. We have the choice. We must try. When you see that all
the choices you've made so far are getting you nowhere, straight into a
wall, you have to break out and start again.

Rowena Oh, God. Make all the same mistakes again?

Miles Not necessarily.

Rowena Nothing changes. We are what we are. You can give up smoking
or—wear different clothes or—get your nose altered but victims stay
victims and bullies stay bullies—and people like me will go on being
thoroughly selfish and frivolous and people like you, vulnerable people,
you're never going to grow a thick skin. You might possibly learn to duck
occasionally. That's the best you can hope for. But all in all, *fait accompli*.

Miles I don't believe that. It's the only way out. I'm going to have to take it.

Rowena I see.

Miles begins to move off

Where are you going?

Miles Home to have a bath. God, I need a bath.

Rowena Anything I can do?

Miles Not really.

Rowena Right. (*She watches him*) I do love you, Miles.

Miles Yes, yes . . .

Miles exits stiffly down the garden

Silence

Rowena (*pounding the ground with her fists*) Bugger-bugger-bugger-bugger-
bugger-bugger . . . If you cry, Rowena Coombes, I will slap your stupid
face. (*She pulls herself together, although she is clearly under more
emotional stress than is normally apparent*) OK then, kids. Here we go.
World conquest it is. Think I'll start with the Junior Chamber of
Commerce and build up to the Rotarians in easy stages via the Rugby
Club. (*She picks up the trousers*) Alas, poor Hepplewick. (*She looks inside
the shed*) God, how on earth did he survive in here? Ugggh. I hope I'm
never in a war. I couldn't bear not having a bath every morning. Anything
else. If they wanted me to confess, all they'd have to do is switch off my
immersion heater. (*She tosses the trousers into the shed. She sees something
just inside the doorway and picks it up. It is the cardboard wrapper in which
the weedkiller was once wrapped. It has been opened flat and something
written on the inside. She closes the shed door*) What's this? (*She reads*)

> She gave me eyes, she gave me ears;
> And humble cares and delicate fears;
> A heart the fountain of sweet tears;
> And love and thought and joy.

(*She drops the wrapper, then after a pause*) Oh, dear. (*She slaps herself around the face*) I warned you. Well. Anyone who writes that isn't going to walk out, is he? That's one consolation. (*She begins to move off*)

A heart the fountain of sweet tears.

Oh, do dry up, Rowena Coombes, you sentimental lump.

Rowena exits down the garden

A moment later, Lionel comes back from the house. He still has no trousers on. He is paying out his extension cable which is apparently plugged in in the house

Lionel (*shouting*) I still don't see why I can't borrow a pair. Only borrowing them. No harm in that, is there? Sylvie? He wouldn't mind, would he? (*He listens for a reply*) Oh, to hell with it. Now then. Get a bit of power to the cleaner, we're away. Smoke him out. That'll teach him. Had my way, I'd use dynamite. Bang! Put her in there as well with him. Red-headed tart. Burning my trousers. She hasn't heard the end of that, by a long chalk. I'll find out her phone number. Write it on the wall in the Gents by the bus station. That'll teach her.

Lionel exits behind the shed

In a second, we hear the whine of the vacuum as it is switched on and then off

(*Off*) That's working.

Lionel returns and looks in the shed window

Coombesie? Where are you? You're hiding under that table again, aren't you? Where is he? I know you're in there, Coombesie. This is your last chance to come out. You coming? (*After a pause*) No? Right. Good.

Sylvie comes out of the house. She carries a bucket of water in one hand and a very old dirty mac in the other

Sylvie Here.
Lionel What's that?
Sylvie Something to put on.
Lionel What is it?
Sylvie Cover you up. Hide the hairy matchsticks.
Lionel Watch it.
Sylvie Here.
Lionel I'm not wearing that.
Sylvie Go on.
Lionel I'll look like a flasher in that. Get me arrested.
Sylvie You'd get arrested anyway if you don't put something on. It's all right. Go on. It's his old one. He won't mind this.
Lionel (*taking the coat reluctantly*) All right. I'll be the only person wearing a mac. It's not even raining. (*He puts on the coat*) How do I look?
Sylvie Peculiar.
Lionel Said I would.
Sylvie (*laughing*) How come she burnt your trousers, then?

Lionel Never mind.
Sylvie Hot stuff, is she?
Lionel Belt up.
Sylvie Old hot pants.
Lionel I'll come and do you over in a minute.
Sylvie Better be careful, I've not got fire insurance.
Lionel You going to help me then?
Sylvie What?
Lionel Get him out.
Sylvie No. I said. No. I got to do the windows.
Lionel Thought you might like to see he doesn't get hurt. Your precious little Coombes.
Sylvie He'd better not be.
Lionel Help then.
Sylvie What do you want?
Lionel Hide round there while I do the smoke. As soon as he comes out . . .
Sylvie (*moving round the side of the shed*) If he comes out.
Lionel He'll be out, don't worry.

Sylvie exits

You grab the key from the inside, slam the door, lock it, then take the key so he can't get in again. Got that?
Sylvie (*off*) Right.
Lionel Soon as you hear the door. Else he'll be straight back in again. All right?
Sylvie (*off*) Right. How will I know when he's come out? With all the smoke.
Lionel I've said, you'll hear the door open, won't you?
Sylvie (*off*) Oh, yes.
Lionel Lightning brain you've got. I'll just make my connection. Put some more on that fire, it's dying down.
Sylvie (*off*) Put the rest of your clothes on it, I should.
Lionel Get off. Now then. I'm going to pump it in from the top. There's a loose board on the roof there. Just the job. Soon have him out.

Lionel picks up the trunking and drags it off behind the shed

(*Off*) Here, hold that . . . got it? Right. Contact.

Sound of the vacuum cleaner being switched on

(*Coughing, off*) Bloody hell. Working anyway. Stand by. Give it a minute or two. Stay hidden.

The vacuum cleaner drones on

Celia comes out from the house in a housecoat. She holds the dress she was wearing in one hand and a clean cloth in the other

Celia That ridiculous woman spilt a whole jar of mayonnaise all down my—(*she breaks off*) What's going on out here? Sylvie, are you—(*she* *goes down the garden still holding her dress)* What's happening? *(She sees the piece of cardboard, picks it up and reads)* She gave me eyes, she gave me—something—ears, that's it. And humble ... *(she reads the rest in silence)* Oh, dear heaven. *(She chokes back a tear)* Dear Miles. Dear, sweet Miles. He must have pushed it under the door. Or through the ... *(she sees smoke coming from the shed and drops the wrapper)* Oh, no. It's on fire. Miles! Miles! Darling Miles ... *(she rattles the door desperately. Rather to her amazement, it flies open. She recoils from the smoke then recovers)* Miles ... *(She goes inside)* Miles.

Lionel *(off)* That was the door going. He's out.

Sylvie *(off)* What?

Lionel *(off)* He's out. Go on.

Sylvie *(off)* I can't. I'm holding this, aren't I?

Lionel *(off)* Go on. Go on. All right, I'll ...

Lionel hurries round, grabs the key from inside the door, slams and locks it from the outside

Triumph! Done it. Where's he gone? In the house?

Sylvie *(off)* I'm getting out of here, I'm choking. What did you put on this fire?

Lionel It's only rubbish. Paper, oily rags, that sort of thing. Where's he gone? I'll check he's in the house. You can switch off that machine now.

Sylvie *(off)* I'm not switching anything off. I'm not going near that smoke.

Sylvie comes round the side of the shed taking deep breaths

Cor! Suffocating.

Lionel I'll switch if off from in here then. *(He tosses her the key)* Here. Look after that. If he comes back, don't let him have it.

Lionel goes into the house

Sylvie Horrible smoke. Turns you black. Look at my hands. And that thing don't half make a din.

The shed door handle rattles briefly. Sylvie turns, hearing something above the vacuum. But as it is not repeated, she shrugs. She picks up the piece of card with the poem on it. The vacuum goes off. She stares at the card

Ears. That's what it was ... delicate ... fountain ... sweet tears ... thought and joy. *(She sniffs and drops the wrapper)* Oh, God. Any time, Mı Coombes. I'm willing to walk any time. I bought my own boots and all.

Sylvie begins to move indoors just as Toby comes out

Toby Celia, I told you not to stand too near that damn Fognorth woman, she——*(He sees Sylvie)* Ah.

Sylvie Hallo, Mr Teasdale.

Toby What's going on here?

Sylvie How do you mean?

Toby We come home early, having been thoroughly drenched by Mrs

Fognorth. I find Hepplewick dressed so far as I can gather only in a mackintosh—my mackintosh—hunting under the bed for Mr Coombes.

Sylvie That was Mrs Coombes.

Toby Rowena's here?

Sylvie She was. She set fire to Mr Hepplewick. She burnt his trousers.

Toby Remarkable woman. I take it Mr Coombes is out then, is he?

Sylvie Yes, Mr Teasdale. We locked the door so he couldn't get in again.

Toby Excellent.

Sylvie Here's the key.

Toby Thank you.

Sylvie Would it be in order for Mr Hepplewick to borrow a pair of your old trousers, Mr Teasdale?

Toby A pair of mine?

Sylvie Just to get him home.

Toby Well, I suppose so. As long as he steers clear of Mrs Coombes.

Sylvie Thank you, Mr Teasdale. I'll find him some.

Sylvie goes indoors

Toby I don't pretend to understand any of this. Still, if he's out, he's out. That's the main thing. (*He picks up the piece of cardboard that Sylvie has left and reads*) She gave me eyes, she gave me eggs. A—looks like horse and cart and de—delicious figs. This is lunacy—a hat, the fortune of suet tarts and love and thirteen jugs. Poor old Miles. Obviously gone right round the bend. Excessive solitude and over-exposure to apple crumble. The whole place smells of burnt trousers. What the hell's she been up to? If Rowena Coombes is causing men to spontaneously ignite, the county will be razed to the ground in a matter of days. How on earth did she— My God, the shed's on fire. He's set the bloody shed on fire. Hepplewick! You idiot. The whole damn shed's on fire.

Toby runs back to the house

Hepplewick! The man is a maniac . . .

Toby grabs Sylvie's bucket. With the key in his other hand, he rushes back down the garden

He can't do a thing right, can he? First the cricket pitches. Then the school boiler. And now this. (*He unlocks the shed door*) My God. (*He hurls the bucket of water inside, rather at random*) Fire! Fire! Hepplewick! Somebody . . .

He runs back indoors with the bucket for more water

(*As he goes*) Water. Water.

In a moment, Celia emerges through the smoke. Her face is black and now streaked from where she appeared to have caught the full force of the bucket. She carries the trousers. She is greatly distraught

Celia (*faintly*) Help. Help.

Toby returns with another bucket. He hurries past her

Miles ...

Toby (*without looking at her*) Celia, thank God. Where the hell have you been? Water, water. For heaven's sake, water.

Celia (*holding up the trousers*) This is all that's left of Miles. It's all that's left of him. ...

Toby throws another bucket into the shed. He rushes back past her

Toby Celia, for goodness sake, pull yourself together.

Toby goes off into the house

Celia (*hugging the trousers to her*)

> He gave me eyes, he gave me ears;
> And humble cares and delicate ...

She collapses on the grass in a faint

The Lights fade to a Black-out

To: A MIDNIGHT MASS (page 165)

OR he says:

Miles Yes. All right.

Rowena (*moved*) Oh, Miles. Dear, dear, dear Miles. (*She throws her arms around him*)

Miles Row, don't please.

Rowena What?

Miles Sort of maul me.

Rowena No, that was an embrace, Miles. People do it to each other when they love each other.

Miles Well, maybe later. I'm a bit fragile.

Rowena Sorry.

Miles Sorry.

Rowena No, fine. You let me know when you're ready for it, I'll pat you on the elbow or something.

Miles It's just I feel a bit—I need a bath, I think.

Rowena I won't argue with you there, darling.

Miles I did wash.

Rowena Yes.

Miles Celia brought me some hot water every morning and evening. Bit tricky though with that mower.

Rowena Yes. Dangerous. Are we off?

Miles Fine. Where are the kids?

Rowena Gone to the cinema.

Miles Oh. Really missed me then, haven't they?

Rowena Jasper has.

Miles Good.

Rowena I'm sure his worms are psychosomatic.

Miles Ah well, that's something to look forward to.

Rowena Oh, and darling, don't mention Hildy's condition. Not to Hildy, anyway.

Miles What condition?

Rowena Her pregnancy.

Miles Why not? Doesn't she know?

Rowena Of course she does. But she's going through this extraordinary thing of pretending she isn't. So when people tell her she is, she gets very upset.

Miles I see. What's she going to tell the baby?

Rowena Oh, she'll sort it out.

Miles She's having it with us, is she?

Rowena Naturally. She's nowhere else. Her parents have disowned her. They're very like that in Denmark.

Miles Great. Why not?

Rowena She won't say who the father is.

Miles I should ask around. She might recognize him by his racket.

Rowena Darling, I've promised.

Miles OK.

Rowena Seriously, Miles, I swear. No more.

Miles OK. Would you be terribly offended if I walked back alone?

Rowena Alone?

Miles I need to adjust slowly. When you've been away from everyone for five weeks, you need to acclimatize to people gradually. Nothing personal, Rowena, but I think you're someone I need to build up to by degrees.

Rowena Sure.

Miles See you back there then.

Rowena Right. (*She watches him for a second*) I love you, Miles.

Miles Yes. Yes. Thank you ...

Miles exits

Pause

Rowena (*staring after Miles*) God. I hope I didn't leave anything out for him to find. Terry's shoes I know I put away. It's Frank's shirt I'm not so—I don't know why they all leave their bloody clothes with me as if I was a laundry. They take them off, why can't they—(*She has a sudden horrified thought*) Ronnie's razor! Oh, well. I've only just turned over my new leaf. He can't expect miracles. (*She picks up the trousers*) Alas, poor Hepplewick. (*She looks inside the shed*) God, how on earth did he survive in here? Ugggh. I hope I'm never in a war. I couldn't bear not having a bath every morning. Anything else. If they wanted me to confess, all they'd have to do is switch off my immersion heater. (*She tosses the trousers into the shed. She sees something just inside the doorway and picks it up. It is the cardboard wrapper in which the weedkiller was once wrapped.*

It has been opened flat and something written on the inside. She closes the shed door) What's this? (*She reads*)

> She gave me eyes, she gave me ears;
> And humble cares and delicate fears;
> A heart and fountain of sweet tears;
> And love and thought and joy.

(*She drops the wrapper and sniffs*) Oh, do dry up, Rowena Coombes. You sentimental lump.

Rowena exits down the garden. A moment later, Lionel comes back from the house. He still has no trousers on. He is paying out his extension cable which is apparently plugged in in the house

Lionel (*shouting*) I still don't see why I can't borrow a pair. Only borrowing them. No harm in that, is there? Sylvie? He wouldn't mind, would he? (*He listens for a reply*) Oh, to hell with it. Now then. Get a bit of power to the cleaner, we're away. Smoke him out. That'll teach him. Had my way, I'd use dynamite. Bang! Put her in there as well with him. Red-headed tart. Burning my trousers. She hasn't heard the end of that, by a long chalk. I'll find out her phone number. Write it on the wall in the Gents by the bus station. That'll teach her.

Lionel exits behind the shed

In a second, we hear the whine of the vacuum as it is switched on and then off

(*Off*) That's working.

Lionel returns and looks in the shed window

Coombesie? Where are you? You're hiding under that table again, aren't you? Where is he? I know you're in there, Coombesie. This is your last chance to come out. You coming? (*After a pause*) No? Right. Good.

Sylvie comes out of the house. She carries a bucket of water in one hand and a very old dirty mac in the other

Sylvie Here.
Lionel What's that?
Sylvie Something to put on.
Lionel What is it?
Sylvie Cover you up. Hide the hairy matchsticks.
Lionel Watch it.
Sylvie Here.
Lionel I'm not wearing that.
Sylvie Go on.
Lionel I'll look like a flasher in that. Get me arrested.
Sylvie You'd get arrested anyway if you don't put something on. It's all right. Go on. It's his old one. He won't mind this.
Lionel (*taking the coat reluctantly*) All right. I'll be the only person wearing a mac. It's not even raining. (*He puts on the coat*) How do I look?

Sylvie Peculiar.

Lionel Said I would.

Sylvie (*laughing*) How come she burnt your trousers, then?

Lionel Never mind.

Sylvie Hot stuff, is she?

Lionel Belt up.

Sylvie Old hot pants.

Lionel I'll come and do you over in a minute.

Sylvie Better be careful, I've not got fire insurance.

Lionel You going to help me then?

Sylvie What?

Lionel Get him out.

Sylvie No. I said. No. I got to do the windows.

Lionel Thought you might like to see he doesn't get hurt. Your precious little Coombes.

Sylvie He'd better not be.

Lionel Help then.

Sylvie What do you want?

Lionel Hide round there while I do the smoke. As soon as he comes out . . .

Sylvie (*moving round the side of the shed*) If he comes out.

Lionel He'll be out, don't worry.

Sylvie exits

You grab the key from the inside, slam the door, lock it, then take the key so he can't get in again. Got that?

Sylvie (*off*) Right.

Lionel Soon as you hear the door. Else he'll be straight back in again. All right?

Sylvie (*off*) Right. How will I know when he's come out? With all the smoke.

Lionel I've said, you'll hear the door open, won't you?

Sylvie (*off*) Oh, yes.

Lionel Lightning brain you've got. I'll just make my connection. Put some more on that fire, it's dying down.

Sylvie (*off*) Put the rest of your clothes on it, I should.

Lionel Get off. Now then. I'm going to pump it in from the top. There's a loose board on the roof there. Just the job. Soon have him out.

Lionel picks up the trunking and drags it off behind the shed

(*Off*) Here, hold that . . . got it? Right. Contact.

Sound of the vacuum cleaner being switched on

(*Coughing, off*) Bloody hell. Working anyway. Stand by. Give it a minute or two. Stay hidden.

The vacuum cleaner drones on

Celia comes out from the house in a housecoat. She holds the dress she was wearing in one hand and a clean cloth in the other

Celia That ridiculous woman spilt a whole jar of mayonnaise all down my—(*She breaks off*) What's going on out here? Sylvie, are you—(*She goes down the garden still holding her dress*) What's happening? (*She sees the piece of cardboard, picks it up and reads*) She gave me eyes, she gave me—something—ears, that's it. And humble ... (*She reads the rest in silence*) Oh, dear heaven. (*She chokes back a tear*) Dear Miles. Dear, sweet Miles. He must have pushed it under the door. Or through the ... (*She sees smoke coming from the shed and drops the wrapper*) Oh, no. It's on fire. Miles! Miles! Darling Miles ... (*She rattles the door desperately. Rather to her amazement, it flies open. She recoils from the smoke, then recovers*) Miles ...

She goes inside

(*Off*) Miles.
Lionel (*off*) That was the door going. He's out.
Sylvie (*off*) What?
Lionel (*off*) He's out. Go on.
Sylvie (*off*) I can't. I'm holding this, aren't I?
Lionel (*off*) Go on. Go on. All right, I'll ...

Lionel hurries round, grabs the key from inside the door, slams and locks it from the outside

Triumph! Done it. Where's he gone? In the house?
Sylvie (*off*) I'm getting out of here, I'm choking. What did you put on this fire?
Lionel It's only rubbish. Paper, oily rags, that sort of thing. Where's he gone? I'll check he's in the house. You can switch off that machine now.
Sylvie (*off*) I'm not switching anything off. I'm not going near that smoke.

Sylvie comes round the side of the shed taking deep breaths

Cor! Suffocating.
Lionel I'll switch it off from in here then. (*He tosses her the key*) Here. Look after that. If he comes back, don't let him have it.

Lionel goes into the house

Sylvie Horrible smoke. Turns you black. Look at my hands. And that thing don't half make a din.

The shed door handle rattles briefly. Sylvie turns, hearing something above the vacuum. But as it is not repeated, she shrugs. She picks up the piece of card with the poem on it. The vacuum goes off. She stares at the card

Ears. That's what it was ... delicate ... fountain ... sweet tears ... thought and joy. (*She sniffs and drops the wrapper*) Oh, God. Any time, Mr Coombes. I'm willing to walk any time. I bought my own boots and all.

Sylvie begins to move indoors just as Toby comes out

Toby Celia, I told you not to stand too near that damn Fognorth woman, she——(*He sees Sylvie*) Ah.

Sylvie Hallo, Mr Teasdale.

Toby What's going on here?

Sylvie How do you mean?

Toby We come home early, having been thoroughly drenched by Mrs Fognorth. I find Hepplewick dressed so far as I can gather only in a mackintosh—my mackintosh—hunting under the bed for Mr Coombes.

Sylvie That was Mrs Coombes.

Toby Rowena's here?

Sylvie She was. She set fire to Mr Hepplewick. She burnt his trousers.

Toby Remarkable woman. I take it Mr Coombes is out then, is he?

Sylvie Yes, Mr Teasdale. We locked the door so he couldn't get in again.

Toby Excellent.

Sylvie Here's the key.

Toby Thank you.

Sylvie Would it be in order for Mr Hepplewick to borrow a pair of your old trousers, Mr Teasdale?

Toby A pair of mine?

Sylvie Just to get him home.

Toby Well, I suppose so. As long as he steers clear of Mrs Coombes.

Sylvie Thank you, Mr Teasdale. I'll find him some.

Sylvie goes indoors

Toby I don't pretend to understand any of this. Still, if he's out, he's out. That's the main thing. (*He picks up the piece of cardboard that Sylvie has left and reads*) She gave me eyes, she gave me eggs. A—looks like horse and cart and de—delicious figs. This is lunacy—a hat, the fortune of suet tarts and love and thirteen jugs. Poor old Miles. Obviously gone right round the bend. Excessive solitude and over-exposure to apple crumble. The whole place smells of burnt trousers. What the hell's she been up to? If Rowena Coombes is causing men to spontaneously ignite, the county will be razed to the ground in a matter of days. How on earth did she— My God, the shed's on fire. He's set the bloody shed on fire. Hepplewick! You idiot. The whole damn shed's on fire.

Toby runs back to the house

(*Off*) Hepplewick! The man is a maniac ...

Toby grabs Sylvie's bucket. With the key in his other hand, he rushes back down the garden

He can't do a thing right, can he? First the cricket pitches. Then the school boiler. And now this. (*He unlocks the shed door*) My God. (*He hurls the bucket of water inside, rather at random*) Fire! Fire! Hepplewick! Somebody ...

He runs back indoors with the bucket for more water

(*As he goes*) Water. Water.

In a moment, Celia emerges through the smoke. Her face is black and now streaked from where she appeared to have caught the full force of the bucket. She carries the trousers. She is greatly distraught

Celia (*faintly*) Help. Help.

Toby returns with another bucket. He hurries past her

Miles . . .

Toby (*without looking at her*) Celia, thank God. Where the hell have you been? Water, water. For heaven's sake, water.

Celia (*holding up the trousers*) This is all that's left of Miles. It's all that's left of him. . . .

Toby throws another bucket into the shed. He rushes back past her

Toby Celia, for goodness sake, pull yourself together.

Toby goes off into the house

Celia (*hugging the trousers to her*)

> He gave me eyes, he gave me ears;
> And humble cares and delicate . . .

She collapses on the grass in a faint

The Lights fade to a Black-out

To: A SCHOOL CELEBRATES (page 171)

A MIDNIGHT MASS

A Churchyard. This year. It is nearly midnight on Christmas Eve

The church door is closed. A gravel path leads away from it to an unseen road.

A variety of gravestones border the path

We hear church bells signifying a happy occasion

Miles is alone, pacing about in the moonlight trying to ward off the night chill

In a moment, Sylvie comes through the gate from the road. She glances at Miles, hurries up the path, then stops and turns

Sylvie Isn't it—? Yes, it is.
Miles Hallo, Sylvie.
Sylvie Mr Coombes.
Miles Hallo.
Sylvie What are you doing lurking there? Been ages.
Miles Yes.
Sylvie How are you?
Miles Very well.
Sylvie Come back then?
Miles Briefly.
Sylvie Yes.
Miles How are you?
Sylvie Fine.
Miles Good.
Sylvie Married.
Miles Ah.
Sylvie To Lionel.
Miles Really? Congratulations.
Sylvie Yes. He's well.
Miles Good.
Sylvie Still mad.
Miles Really?
Sylvie Two kids as well.
Miles Marvellous.
Sylvie They're mad, too. Like him. Still. You seen Mrs Coombes?
Miles No, I was hoping I might. I was just waiting.
Sylvie You ought to wait in the warm. Service is just about to start.
Miles Yes.
Sylvie Midnight Mass. Never miss it. Real Christmas that is, isn't it? Wouldn't be the same otherwise.

Miles No. We used to—we always used to go.
Sylvie All these commercial things. Good we still have this bit. Otherwise it would be nothing at all, would it? Christmas.
Miles No.
Sylvie Well. Good to have met you, Mr Coombes.
Miles Yes.
Sylvie Never went walking, did we?
Miles No.
Sylvie Just as well really. Don't know where that would have finished up, do we?
Miles No. Who knows? You'd have probably ended up Mrs Coombes or something.
Sylvie Never. Mrs Blisters more like, after all that walking. Bye-bye.
Miles Goodbye, Sylvie.

Sylvie goes into the church, closing the door

Meeuurr meeuurr . . . nah-nah-nah-nah . . . meeuurr . . . listen, Rowena. I'm . . . I'm not asking to come back. So don't let me lift your . . . don't let me raise any . . . not that you'd even contemplate having me . . . back. I'm sure. I've no doubt you're full of Hoggs and Arrowsmiths up to your eyebrows. Anyway. Janice and I . . . well, we're calling it a day. It was good while it lasted. Janice was a wonderful . . . marvellous . . . it was awful while it lasted. She was a foul little, two-timing creep whom I discovered in bed with her ex-husband whom she swore she never wanted to see again. . . . Why the hell does it always happen to me? So the point is, I'm making a fresh start. That's the only way to do it. Start afresh. I believe that is possible. If I didn't believe that, I'd never have come out of that damn shed when I did. Five years ago—God, it's cold.

He stops as he sees Celia coming up the path from the road

Er——
Celia (*jumping in alarm*) Oh.
Miles Hallo.
Celia (*shrilly*) I have no money so there's no point in knocking me down. I have a sharp knitting needle in my bag and I shall use it if necessary. I'm not afraid to.
Miles Celia, Celia.
Celia Who?
Miles Me, Miles.
Celia Miles?
Miles Coombes.
Celia Ciles Moombes.
Miles Miles Coombes. Remember?
Celia Miles. Good heavens. Why are you mugging?
Miles I'm not mugging, Celia. I'm just waiting.
Celia Well, it's very frightening. I wish you'd. . . . What are you doing here? I thought you'd gone for good.
Miles I thought I'd just look back briefly.

Celia To see her, I suppose? Rowena.

Miles Partly.

Celia Well, she's—she's her usual gregarious little self. As you've no doubt heard.

Miles No, I haven't—we haven't corresponded much. She was never a great letter writer.

Celia Very tricky, I should imagine, to write letters in her usual position. Perhaps for Christmas you could buy her one of those pens that write upside down. . . .

Miles Yes, well, I don't really want to hear about that, Celia. How are you?

Celia Oh. Me. Tip-top. Perfect. Toby's not too well at present but then Christmas isn't his best time. He tends to launch himself into the celebrations rather vigorously. My mother's staying with us, of course, which doesn't help. She's in bed with a migraine. So everything's very much as normal.

Miles Good.

Celia How are you?

Miles Very well.

Celia You're—living with someone, I hear.

Miles Oh, yes.

Celia She's not with you?

Miles No, she's with her—family for Christmas.

Celia Good. So glad you found someone eventually. See you again perhaps.

Miles Yes, maybe.

Celia I must get in to the service. Coming in?

Miles No.

Celia Bye-bye, then.

Miles Goodbye. Oh, Celia?

Celia Yes.

Miles Do you really have a knitting needle in your bag?

Celia Oh, yes. And pepper. And a whistle. And a razor blade.

Miles God.

Celia You can't be too careful. Not these days. Goodbye.

Miles Bye.

Celia goes into the church

Heavens. I hope she's got a first-aid kit as well. (*He paces about*) Hallo, kıds . . . no. (*He tries again*) Hallo, kids, remember me? It's your dad. No. Hi. Guess who? It's dad. Back again. Hallo, little Colin . . . hallo, big Colin. You're almost as big as I am. Hallo, Sandra. What a big girl you are. You're prettier than your mother . . . no. You're as lovely as your mother. Hallo, little—God, what's his name? Why can't I ever remember his damn name? I'm his father, I can't remember his name. What sort of father am I? Timothy, that's it. I love him, too. I just can't remember his name. (*He talks in baby voice*) Hi, Timmy. What's Father Christmas bringing my boy for his . . . God, he's nine now. Hi, Tim. Hallo, son. Young man. Oh, God, this isn't going to work.

The service inside the church starts up with a carol. Miles joins in. Suddenly from the road comes a squawk of girlish glee

Rowena (*off*) Don't you dare. Geoff, you bastard, don't do that again. I'm warning you.

Sound of another scream and a peal of laughter

All right, all right. That's it. Goodbye. See you.

Rowena comes up the path, laughing

Honestly. I don't——(*She sees Miles and stops dead*) Miles?
Miles Hallo.
Rowena Heavens. Oh, heavens. Ooo-er. Gone all weak at the knees. Hang on. Like a ghost, Miles.
Miles Sorry.
Rowena (*indicating behind her*) That was—that was——
Miles Geoff Hampton, wasn't it?
Rowena Yes. He gave me a lift.
Miles Yes.
Rowena He's a horror. Got mistletoe hanging on his driving mirror. Awful.
Miles Yes.
Rowena He was trying to spray me with this artificial snow down the back of my neck. (*She laughs*)
Miles (*laughing faintly*) Yes.
Rowena Oh, he's dreadful. I don't know why I—he's useful for lifts.
Miles Yes.

Pause

Rowena Coming to see the kids?
Miles Er——
Rowena No? They're very well. Still miss you.
Miles Do they? Honestly?
Rowena Well. Not as much as they did. I mean, after five years you can't keep crying all the time, can you? Timmy kept it up for eighteen months which I think showed great loyalty, don't you?
Miles Oh, don't start that.
Rowena Well . . .
Miles I had to get out.
Rowena Sure. How is she? Phyllis?
Miles Janice.
Rowena Janice.
Miles She's fine.
Rowena Good. Got a divorce yet, has she?
Miles No. Not yet.
Rowena Oh. I thought that was the reason you rushed ours through. So you could make an honest woman of her.
Miles Her husband's being a little difficult.
Rowena Oh, dear. (*After a pause*) I was just going to the service.
Miles Yes.

Rowena We always went. Do you remember?
Miles Yes.
Rowena Used to let Colin and Sandy stay up for it. She was only tiny.
Miles That's right.
Rowena They won't come with me any more.
Miles No?
Rowena They say it's all garbage. Everything's garbage at the moment.
Religion's garbage. Politics are garbage. Christmas is garbage. I'm
garbage. . . . Oh, well. It's a phase.
Miles Yes.
Rowena I hope it is, anyway. I've always tried to teach them to be positive. I
think that's so important. Now they sit around there like a lot of black
holes. You coming in for the service?
Miles No, I'm—I was just passing.
Rowena OK. Not even for old time's sake? No? See you then.
Miles You were absolutely right, you know, Rowena.
Rowena I was?
Miles It isn't possible. You can't start again. Not possible. You were
absolutely right.
Rowena Ah, well. We are occasionally, you know. We professional idiots.
Not as bovine as we're cow-looking. Bye.
Miles Goodbye.

Rowena goes into the church

*Miles watches as she closes the door. In a moment, he makes his way off
towards the road*

The Lights fade to a Black-out

A SCHOOL CELEBRATES

A Churchyard. This year later

The church door is closed. A gravel path leads away from it to an unseen road. A variety of gravestones border the path

We hear church bells signifying a happy occasion

As the Lights come up, the church door opens and Rowena comes out. She looks behind her to see if someone is following. Presumably they aren't as she expresses impatience and mooches about the graveyard disconsolately.

After a moment, Lionel comes out of the church, closing the door behind him

Rowena (*hearing him and turning as she speaks*) Well, thank heavens. About time. . . . Oh. (*She sees Lionel*) Sorry. I thought you were . . .
Lionel Morning, Mrs Coombes.
Rowena Good morning, Mr Hepplewick.

Silence

How's your wife?
Lionel Sylvie's very well, thank you.
Rowena Baby's due shortly, isn't it?
Lionel Any day now.
Rowena Lovely. What do you want. Boy or a girl?
Lionel I'd like a girl, I think. Then we'll have two of each.
Rowena Tidy.
Lionel Yes. (*After a pause*) How are you keeping?
Rowena Very well, thank you.
Lionel Heard you'd not been so good.
Rowena Really? Who told you that?
Lionel Oh, well. Word gets about.
Rowena Doesn't it just?
Lionel Nervous, was it? Nervous trouble.
Rowena Extremely nervous trouble.
Lionel Ah.
Rowena I kept eating light bulbs.
Lionel Did you?
Rowena Lighted ones, of course. And then I thought I was a hamster. They built me a great big wheel in the breakfast room. I ran round and round it for hours.
Lionel Did you?
Rowena Very good source of power. Nearly halved our electric bill last

winter. Or would have done. If we hadn't kept having to buy light bulbs.
Seventy-five watt ones are delicious.
Lionel Yes. Well, nice to have met you, Mrs Coombes. Don't often see you
these days, do we? (*He moves towards the gate*)
Rowena Well, I'm so busy running round my wheel.
Lionel Yes. Quite. Bye.
Rowena I say, had any more pairs of trousers burnt lately?
Lionel No, not a lot. I shouldn't think you've set fire to many either, have
you?
Rowena Not a lot, no.
Lionel Bye, then.

Lionel exits

Rowena (*standing impatiently and glancing towards the church door*) Come
on. ... (*She wanders round and reads*) "In memory of Joseph John
Hepplewick, aged seventy-five."

> This will not be the last of him you've seen.
> His poetry will linger evergreen.

(*After a pause, she considers this*) If that's the worst verse you have read,
just thank your lucky stars he's dead. Come on, Miles. Come on. I want to
go home. What are they doing in there? (*She mimicks some pompous
speaker*) "Oh, blah, blah ... fifty years of the school, blah, blah ... such a
splendid, splendid achievement. ... Our thanks are due to the following
three hundred boring old twits sitting here today. So on behalf of Celia
Teasdale's ghastly hat, may I say bravo. Three cheers for Bilbury Lodge.
Hup, rah. ...." (*She is suddenly depressed*) God, I feel so trapped. Trapped
by all these remorseless people. One new face, that's all I ask for. Before I
grow older and older and older. Hallo, Mrs Coombes. Set fire to any
more trousers lately. (*She suddenly sounds very old*) I can't even find the
buttons these days, dear ...

Miles comes out of the church

Miles Rowena, what are you doing out here?
Rowena Waiting for you.
Miles Why don't you go out of the front door the same as everyone else?
Rowena Because I'm not the same as everyone else.
Miles True.
Rowena I'm a lunatic. I'm the local village idiot. I'm allowed to go out of
wrong doors.
Miles You're not a lunatic or an idiot.
Rowena Yes, I am. Even the kids are ashamed of me.
Miles No.
Rowena They are. Whenever there's an official function, some pompous
little event like a Sports Day or a special service like today's, "Please,
Mummy, don't come. Please."
Miles Well, if you embarrass them the way you do, what do you expect?
Rowena Embarrass them?

Miles Behaving like you do.

Rowena God damn it, I'm their mother. Why are they ashamed of me?

Miles They love you very much, Row. They're just—well, they're kids. They get a little embarrassed sometimes.

Rowena Why? Why should they?

Miles Because. Because they're ordinary kids growing up normally and they're at an age when they want to be seen to be like their friends, average and normal, and so when you——

Rowena Uggh.

Miles I'm afraid they do.

Rowena After all I've done to teach them not to care. Not to be governed by boring conventional . . .

Miles Rowena, you have got to face it. The awful truth is that you have ordinary, normal, healthy kids. Now give them time and they will probably develop into hopeless eccentrics and dash around on all fours grunting. But at the moment they're going through the age when——

Rowena Well, I don't like the age they're going through. They're boring little plastic people. If I'd wanted garden gnomes instead of children, I'd have bought some . . .

Miles Don't worry. It won't be long before they start embarrassing me, I'm sure.

Rowena Like I do.

Miles I didn't say that.

Rowena You'll have to bear with me, Miles. You know what the doctors have said.

Miles Yes. They said you were perfectly balanced and normal. Unfortunately that seems to have been the worst thing that anyone could have told you. You've been trying to prove them wrong ever since.

Rowena I can feel myself growing normal, that's the trouble, Miles. Every morning now, I wake up and look at myself and say, "Oh, look. Look at that extraordinarily ordinary boring woman. Boringly going about her boring life."

Miles I don't see why it should be boring.

Rowena Well, it is. You're boring. The kids are boring. You all want your tea at teatime and your lunch at lunchtime. And they always insist on going to bed early——

Miles Because they have to get up early in the morning.

Rowena And they insist on getting up early in the morning.

Miles Because they have to go to school.

Rowena How boring.

Pause

Miles It's probably my fault.

Rowena I don't know. I don't know whose fault it is.

Miles We'd better get home.

Rowena Why?

Miles Because it's nearly time for—Oh, to hell with it. Because it's lunchtime.

Rowena Lunchtime. Yawn, yawn, yawn. (*After a slight pause*) Miles?
Miles Mm.
Rowena Can we do something new soon? Something different?
Miles Well, we're due for a holiday.
Rowena A holiday.
Miles Yes.
Rowena To Spain. Yawn, yawn, yawn.
Miles Not necessarily.
Rowena We always go to Spain.
Miles All right, we'll go where you like.
Rowena Can we?
Miles Where do you want to go?
Rowena Greenland.
Miles Oh, don't be ridiculous.
Rowena I want to go to Greenland.
Miles No, you don't.
Rowena I do.
Miles Nobody wants to go to Greenland. Except—Greenlanders.
Rowena That's why I want to go.
Miles Oh, for God's sake, come on.
Rowena I'm dying, Miles. I'm fading away.
Miles No, you're not.
Rowena I'm sinking fast.
Miles (*angrily*) Rowena, you are a forty-two-year-old woman who is no
longer as young as she used to be. You're still young but you're not as
young as you used to be. You're not twenty, there's no point in
pretending you are. The more you carry on behaving like an overgrown
schoolgirl, the more embarrassing you're going to be to everyone. To
yourself. To me, the kids. Even the bloody dog. Now for God's sake,
grow up and be your age.

Silence

Rowena (*softly*) Yes, Miles.
Miles I'm sorry.
Rowena No, you're absolutely right, Miles. Absolutely.
Miles No, I'm——

Pause

Rowena We'd better get home. Come on. (*She moves towards the road*)
Miles Rowena, I—I——
Rowena Come along, darling. I've got a lunch to cook, haven't I?

Rowena exits

Miles I'm—er—yes. Right. Lunchtime. Yes.

Miles follows Rowena off

The Lights fade to a Black-out

INTIMATE EXCHANGES is a related series of plays totalling eight scripts

This is the Eighth

LOVE IN THE MIST

preceded by *How It Began* (page 3);
A Visit from a Friend (page 5) and
Confessions in a Garden Shed (page 115)

CHARACTERS
APPEARING IN THIS SERIES OF SCENES

Celia
Miles
Sylvie
Rowena
Toby

LOVE IN THE MIST

A section of deserted clifftop. Five weeks later. It is Saturday, July 24th

The only sign of civilization is a single, solitary wooden hut. A rough footpath runs alongside the hut, winding off upwards towards the headland. It is sunny but none too warm

We hear the distant rumble of the sea far below and the sound of an occasional sheep

Miles comes chugging up the path in an anorak and walking boots. His other clothing is sensible weekend attire. He pauses, slightly puffed, and surveys the view out to sea. On looking below, he instinctively steps back. It's evidently a very long drop. Despite this minor alarm, he is a man very happy and at peace with himself

Sylvie, off, emits a moan of pain

Miles (*jovially*) Come on, Sylvie, what's the matter now?

Sylvie comes slowly and agonizingly into view, groaning with each step. She is dressed similarly to Miles

Come on.

Sylvie (*in pain*) My legs have given out.

Miles (*leaping to help her*) Here. (*He offers a hand*)

Sylvie (*taking it*) Ta.

Miles pulls her up the few remaining steps

(*Collapsing on the grass with a final grunt*) Must have a rest.

Miles Absolutely appalling. A girl of your age. Look at you. Modern youth. I don't know.

Sylvie I got cramp in my foot.

Miles That's your circulation. Bad circulation.

Sylvie Bad boots. Look at them. Horrible things. They're not even comfortable to walk in. And they're stopping all the blood to my feet. I'd have been better off in my track shoes.

Miles You can't do this sort of walking in track shoes, girl. Shred your feet to ribbons.

Sylvie Probably have anyway. I just can't feel them in these things. (*She glares at her feet*) I look awful in them. I look like my dad.

Miles Don't be ungrateful now. Your anorak looks good.

Sylvie (*unenthusiastically*) 'S all right.

Miles What do you mean—'S all right? I'll have you know these were very expensive.

Sylvie (*muttering*) Most women get fur coats, I get an anorak.
Miles Come on. Better keep moving. We don't want to stay still in this wind
for too long.
Sylvie Just a minute. I still want my breath.
Miles I don't know. (*He wanders away slightly, investigating their surround-
ings further*) You'd better be fitter than this when we start the big one.
Sylvie Yes. I'm having second thoughts about that and all.
Miles Oh no, no backing out.
Sylvie You want to talk all the way round?
Miles Yes.
Sylvie England?
Miles That's the idea.
Sylvie Bloody hell.
Miles And Scotland and Wales.
Sylvie I think you're going on your own.
Miles Come on. First little ten minute walk and you want to give up.
Sylvie Well . . .
Miles Just look around. Go on, look around you. Look at this view.

Without moving, Sylvie glances round

You see any people? You see any houses? You see any factory chimneys
chucking out smoke? Any cars? Any motorways? Any charabanc loads of
trippers?
Sylvie No.
Miles You see what I mean? We're totally alone. Extraordinary really in a
country this size it's still possible to feel this isolated, alone.
Sylvie You can be that at home.
Miles What?
Sylvie Alone. You don't have to come all this way. Try sitting in our house
on Saturday evenings.
Miles Yes, that's—very philosophic.
Sylvie It's true as well. (*She starts undoing her bootlaces*)
Miles But there's a difference surely. At home, possibly you're lonely but
here you can't be lonely, can you? Because there's me. Can you?
Sylvie (*engrossed in her task*) No.
Miles I mean, here we're alone but not lonely. Are we?
Sylvie No.
Miles So. (*After a pause*) Different.
Sylvie Yes. (*After a pause*) Probably.
Miles What are you doing?
Sylvie Getting these off.
Miles Your feet'll freeze.
Sylvie I want to make sure I still got some.
Miles Well, hurry up. We've got to get back for tea. The hotel does a very
good tea.
Sylvie Does it?
Miles According to the guide. Specially recommended.
Sylvie We should have had our supper there last night.

Miles No, no. Not dinner. Lunch and dinner to be avoided, apparently, so it says. Breakfasts are fine. Ours was very good this morning—well, mine was. But their teas are the highspot.

Sylvie So we won't be eating there tonight?

Miles I think we might regret it. That book's not often wrong.

Sylvie Go back to that other place then?

Miles Probably. It's the only one within reasonable distance. Do you mind going back there?

Sylvie No.

Miles Very good, I thought. Very good indeed. Mine was. (*He senses she's not that happy*) I'll look up and see if there's anywhere else when we get back to the hotel if you like.

Sylvie No.

Miles But I don't want to drive too far. Otherwise I can't drink. And I do like a glass of wine.

Sylvie (*scornfully*) A glass.

Miles What?

Sylvie You had more than a glass last night.

Miles Well.

Sylvie You had most of the bottle.

Miles Only because you didn't want it.

Sylvie I didn't like it.

Miles There you are.

Sylvie You could have left it. Every drop.

Miles I wasn't leaving a claret like that. I don't drink those every day. It's a pity you didn't like it.

Sylvie It was a bit sour really.

Miles It could have been a little cool, I suppose.

Sylvie (*wistfully*) I'd have liked champagne.

Miles Yes, darling, but I did look very carefully and there was not a decent vintage champagne on their list, I do promise you. And there's no point at all in taking a chance. Not with champagne, there really isn't.

Sylvie I thought we might have had champagne cocktails.

Miles Yes, we will. We will. How are your feet?

Sylvie Numb.

Miles (*wandering round the hut*) I wonder what this is.

Sylvie It's a hut.

Miles (*mildly irritated*) Yes, I know it's a hut. I can see it's a hut. I'm just wondering what it's for. (*He looks in the window but apparently can see nothing*) Ah, I know. I think I know what this is. It's a refuge. What they call a refuge. Walkers, climbers. If they get stranded, you see, they can use this. Saved many a life these places have when the weather closes in. Snow, sleet, fog—suddenly a human being's very vulnerable. You see a place like this and you're grateful to step inside and—(*He tries the door*) Ah. This one appears to be locked. Yes. Probably because it's summer. They're not needed that much in the summer. Keeps out the vandals. I mean, you've got blankets—all sorts of things in there—(*He tries to look in the window*)—I think there are anyway. How are you doing?

Sylvie I'm getting quite hungry. All that talk of food.

Miles You should have got up for breakfast. Wonderful breakfast.

Sylvie It was too early.

Miles Early? They serve till half past nine. That's hardly early, is it? What time do you normally get up?

Sylvie Seven.

Miles Well, then.

Sylvie I'm on holiday. Two days holiday. I'm having a lie-in. I thought I might have got my breakfast in bed. I thought they did that in hotels.

Miles Yes, but this isn't that sort of hotel. It's an inn. It's more of a good old-fashioned inn. There's only about three of them running it. Him and his wife and that—that rather rude chap.

Sylvie I nearly clocked him one.

Miles Yes.

Sylvie He winked at me, you know.

Miles Did he?

Sylvie When he was showing us the room, he winked. Made me feel all dirty.

Miles Right, we'll see about that. We'll see.

Pause

Sylvie I thought we'd have a bathroom as well.

Miles Well, we haven't. They don't have them. Bathrooms attached. I asked. There's one right next door.

Sylvie (*dubiously*) Well. You don't know who else has been in there, do you?

Miles Don't be ridiculous. You had a bath this morning, didn't you?

Sylvie No, I didn't.

Miles I thought you were going to.

Sylvie I was. Only people kept rattling the door handle trying to get in. Made me nervous. I couldn't concentrate.

Miles So you didn't get one?

Sylvie No. I had a stand-up wash at the basin.

Miles Ah.

Sylvie Half at a time.

Miles Ah.

Sylvie Like I have to at home.

Pause

Miles Ship out there, you see?

Sylvie Oh, yes.

Miles Some lone trawler laden with fish back from the high seas doing its daily battle with the elements.

Sylvie It's an oil rig.

Miles What?

Sylvie It's not a boat. It's an oil rig.

Miles Is it? (*He looks again*) Oh, yes.

Sylvie I told you you needed new glasses.

Miles I do not need new glasses.

Sylvie Yesterday coming here, we went round and round that roundabout because you couldn't see the signs. Four times.

Miles It was extremely badly signposted.

Sylvie Cursing and swearing.

Miles How was anyone expected to see that sign?

Sylvie I saw it.

Miles Well, you're—you weren't driving. If you're driving you have to concentrate on the road. You can't risk accidents looking at signposts.

Sylvie We had time to get out and read them the speed you were driving.

Miles Oh no, now . . .

Sylvie Thought we'd never get here.

Miles I'm not breaking legal speed limits, I'm sorry. We got here in one piece. That's the main thing.

Sylvie Yes.

Miles And I promise you we'll get back in one piece.

Sylvie Yes.

Miles Now if you want to go joy-riding in bright red two-seat open-topped suicide wagons doing a hundred and twenty in the outside lane, don't come to me. You want to take your life in your hands every time you get in a car. . . . (*After a pause*) I used to have one of those. Little MG. I was absolutely lethal. Liability. Danger to everyone on the road. Thank God I saw sense before I killed myself. (*He muses*)

Silence

Sylvie It's a pity we haven't got a double bed though.

Miles Yes. That is a shame, I must say. Still, we overcame it.

Sylvie Yes.

Miles They don't—er—they don't alawys have them in hotels these days. They're dying out apparently. Double beds. So I read. Sadly. Still, we improvised, we improvised.

Sylvie Lot of hard work though, wasn't it?

Miles Well.

Sylvie Moving all the tables and the lamps and then pushing them together. Then stripping them off and then laying the mattresses the other way and then re-making them. Then putting the tables and the lamps back again. Took hours.

Miles Yes.

Sylvie You were knackered before we got started.

Miles Now, now, that isn't true. Unfair.

Sylvie That and all the wine. You kept slipping over in your socks.

Miles It was after midnight, we couldn't make too much noise.

Sylvie We made enough. That bloke winked at me again this morning. I think he sleeps up above us.

Miles Never mind. It may have been complicated but it worked. And it was worth it, wasn't it?

Sylvie Oh, yes.

Miles Well, wasn't it?

Sylvie (*smiling at him*) Yes, it was worth it.

Miles Well, then.

Sylvie I don't know that it was worth putting everything back again this morning though.

Miles It didn't take a minute.

Sylvie Now we've got to do it all again tonight, haven't we?

Miles We could hardly have left the room in that state. I mean, if they'd seen it in that state the whole lot of them would have started winking.

Sylvie Just makes it a bit less—what do you say—spontaneous, doesn't it?

Miles Well, I don't know that it does any harm to be a little bit calculating occasionally in these sort of matters. All this wham, bam business. It's all right when you're ... Experience tends to point to other approaches.

Sylvie Anyway, they saw the bed anyway.

Miles Who did?

Sylvie She did. Mrs Landlord. While you were having breakfast. She just banged in and saw me.

Miles What were you doing?

Sylvie I was in the bed.

Miles You're sure she saw you?

Sylvie Yes, she spoke to me.

Miles What did she say?

Sylvie Well she just sort of stood there and said, "Oh". Like that. "Oh". Then she said, "Well, I'll have to see about this. I'll have to see." Then she went out again.

Miles Have to see about what?

Sylvie I don't know.

Miles You didn't tell me this before.

Sylvie I forgot. All that bathroom business put it out of my mind.

Miles I see.

Sylvie It's all right, isn't it? She can't do anything to us, can she?

Miles No. Of course it's all right. I should think. Yes. They can't prosecute people for pushing the furniture around, can they? Rubbish. (*He looks out to sea*) Look at that sea. Look at it. Grey, merciless.

Sylvie Cold.

Miles Yes. Ready to go on then, are you? I think we could just about reach that point there before it's time to turn round.

Sylvie (*getting to her feet*) This looks like one of those builders' huts.

Miles I was hoping we'd get a bit further. Never mind.

Sylvie The sort they have on building sites.

Miles Come on.

Sylvie If we go to that same place tonight for supper——

Miles Dinner, yes.

Sylvie Can I wear my evening dress again?

Miles Yes—er—yes. You can do.

Sylvie Only I haven't got another one.

Miles Don't worry. No, don't worry.

Sylvie I wouldn't want people to say, oh, it's her again. Her with one dress.

Miles Well, actually, Sylvie, you could ring the changes if you wanted to by—er—by wearing something more casual. I mean, that dress is quite formal.

Sylvie (*anxiously*) Was it wrong?

Miles No. No, it's very nice—it's just more the sort of dress you'd expect to see at a Hunt Ball, say, or a very formal dinner party.

Sylvie I got it from the Oxfam shop.

Miles Oh, did you?

Sylvie Mrs Coombes—your wife sold it to me.

Miles Did she?

Sylvie So the dress isn't right then?

Miles Well, if we're being very honest, not for that type of restaurant. It's more a bistro really.

Sylvie (*glumly*) Right. I'll wear my jeans then.

Miles They'll do fine. Fine.

Sylvie They're all I've got. Not the same, is it, though. Going out to dinner in jeans. I mean, you don't really feel you're going out, do you? Might as well stay at home really. Was the hat all right?

Miles Yes, the hat was—the hat was splendid.

Sylvie It's an evening turban.

Miles Is that what it was.

Sylvie I like it.

Miles My wife sold you that, too, did she?

Sylvie Yes. She said they're right back in.

Miles Bit ironic really, isn't it? My wife equipping you with a wardrobe in order for you to go away for a weekend with her husband.

Sylvie Oh, she didn't know it was for this.

Miles I wouldn't bet on it.

Sylvie I just said I was going away for the weekend, somewhere special and might need to dress up, that's all.

Miles In that case she did know.

Sylvie She's a very nice person, isn't she, Mrs Coombes?

Miles Yes. Yes, she's very nice. Yes.

Sylvie Lively and vivacious and always laughing.

Miles Yes, she laughs quite a lot.

Sylvie I think I'd like to be like her when I get to her age.

Miles Well, I wouldn't get too like her, Sylvie, otherwise there'd be no point in my going away with you, would there? Might as well stop at home as you're fond of putting it.

Sylvie She has a lot of fun, I bet.

Miles Now come on, we really must get moving.

Sylvie Hey.

Miles What?

Sylvie Come on then.

Miles What?

Sylvie Want to kiss me?

Miles Er—Yes, of course.

Sylvie (*leaning seductively against the hut*) Come on then.

Miles kisses her somewhat perfunctorily

That wasn't much.

Miles Well, it's cold, Sylvie. The wind's frozen up my face. I can hardly move my mouth.

Sylvie Pete Bartlett kisses better than that.

Miles Who the hell's Pete Bartlett?

Sylvie Oh, he's horrible. He comes up and he tries to kiss you. And he's slobbering, you know—like a great big St Bernard. He goes—(*she demonstrates*)—blurrrp . . . blurrrp . . . blurrrrp.

Miles jumps back

Miles Yes, well, don't do it on me.

Sylvie It's horrible, isn't it? Blurrp . . . blurrp. Imagine that coming at you.

Miles Yes, don't do it. It's horrible.

Sylvie It is. You kiss quite well though.

Miles Thank you.

Sylvie When your face is working properly. Give us a warm then. (*She clings to him*)

Miles hugs Sylvie to him

Oh, I love you.

Miles Yes.

Sylvie You love me?

Miles Yes.

Sylvie I really love you.

They hug

Hey, it's disappeared.

Miles What has?

Sylvie That oil rig. Someone must have nicked it. It's gone, look.

Miles Oh, yes. So it has. (*Expertly*) They sometimes move them, you know. These oil platforms. Move on, drill somewhere else.

Sylvie Really?

Miles Oh, yes.

Sylvie You know a lot of things.

Miles Well, I've been—I've read a bit.

Sylvie I haven't. Wish I had sometimes. I've never read nothing.

Miles Well, you've still time for heaven's sake. Start now. You're still . . . you've still got plenty of time.

Sylvie (*giggling*) Funny that bloke this morning, wasn't he?

Miles Who?

Sylvie The one in the bar.

Miles (*smiling faintly*) Oh yes.

Sylvie Hope your daughter's not under age, sir. I like that.

Miles Yes.

Sylvie I had to laugh.

Miles Yes. I know you did.

Pause

Sylvie It's the mist.

Miles What is?

Sylvie That oil rig hasn't moved. It's the mist. Look, coming in.

Miles Oh, yes. That's a sea mist, that is.

Sylvie You had the wrong glasses on again, didn't you? (*She pulls him by the hand*) Come on, then.

Miles Mm?

Sylvie You don't want to do any more walking, do you?

Miles Well, I thought we might walk as far as the——

Sylvie Let's go in the shed.

Miles Eh?

Sylvie Get our boots off again. Have a bit of fun in the shed.

Miles Oh, we don't—not in the shed.

Sylvie 'S all right.

Miles (*pulling back from her*) Oh no, Sylvie, it's all——

Sylvie We won't have to move the beds first anyway.

Miles It's locked.

Sylvie Bust it open then.

Miles Certainly not, that's—that's vandalism.

Sylvie You're scared.

Miles No, I'm not.

Sylvie Yes, you are. You're scared to kick in that shed in case you get caught.

Miles No, that is not the reason. I simply believe that that shed is the property of someone else—who sees fit and is—indeed perfectly justified—in locking his property and I respect the right of an—individual to lock his shed. As indeed I hope he would respect my right to lock my shed. In fact, one could say in fact, that that's the crux of the whole business. If, as the socialists claim, it is the right of every individual to own a shed, then it is the Tories' claim that he has every right to lock it.

Sylvie Depends if he's got anything in there.

Miles Oh well, that's the other lot.

Sylvie (*pushing open the door*) It's open anyway. It was just stuck.

Miles Ah, well. Bang goes another political theory.

Sylvie Come on. (*She draws him into the hut*)

Miles We still shouldn't, you know.

Sylvie It wasn't even locked. They don't mind us being in here obviously.

Miles Yes, but you see it's intended for emergencies.

Sylvie This is an emergency. I can't wait till teatime. Come on.

Miles Yes, well, we mustn't disturb things. There'll be blankets in here, first aid and—oh . . .

They both look round at the completely empty hut, save for one old oil drum

Sylvie Empty.

Miles Yes. Vandals. Typical. Stolen everything. Look at it. Completely bare. Supposed to be fully equipped this hut. I think there's even meant to be an emergency phone. They've stolen that. Now what's going to happen? The next time some lone walker is injured, lost, trapped by snow—nothing here for him. By this sort of action they've actually endangered human life. I wonder if they realize that. No, they don't give a damn. Not a damn. Typical of this bloody modern society. Just rip it up. If it isn't yours, destroy it. (*He kicks the oil drum*)

Sylvie All right, all right, all right.

Miles Well . . .

Sylvie All right. Whoa, boy, whoa. Sit down here. (*She sits him on the oil drum*) I'll just close the door.

Miles (*looking at his watch rather nervously*) We don't want to miss tea.

Sylvie You won't miss a thing, I promise you. Here. (*She kneels down in front of him*)

Miles What are you doing now?

Sylvie I'm going to take your boots off.

Miles Is this necessary? I'd rather you didn't.

Sylvie You tell me another way to get you out of your trousers I'm willing to try. (*She starts unlacing one of his boots*) Here we go.

Miles I don't think your sisters would approve of this.

Sylvie My sister's at school. She won't know.

Miles I meant, the sisters. As in sisterhood of women.

Sylvie Oh, that lot.

Miles I don't think they'd approve of you undoing a man's boots for him.

Sylvie Bugger them. You can only afford to be rude about men either if you can get them without trying or else because you don't like them anyway. People like us in between, we're glad for what we can get our hands on. I'll suck your bootlace if you like.

Miles Sylvie . . .

Sylvie Up you get then.

Miles Look, no. Listen, Sylvie, I'm sorry. No. I'm not going to be able to— to go through with this. Not in this shed, I'm sorry.

Sylvie Why not?

Miles It's just——

Sylvie Sheds make you impotent, do they?

Miles This one does a bit, yes. I'm sorry, it's just that men—oh, to hell with it—men of my age, well, some of us, well, we need a bit of—comfort with our sex, frankly. We can't just bang about in a shed like we used to. Not any more. I'm sure you'll find exceptions. You'll probably come across an ex-Marine drill sergeant of sixty-five who'd be happy to have it away on the roof but average men, and I'm afraid in this respect I am an average man, we need a bed. Or even two beds side by side. And sheets—and— general recuperative facilities for afterwards.

Sylvie (*coolly*) Right then.

Miles I hope you understand. You're not hurt, are you?

Sylvie No. You can put your bloody boots back on yourself. I'm not going to.

Miles You are hurt, I can see that. Terribly hurt.

Sylvie I'm not hurt. I'm frustrated.

Miles I'm sorry. It's not you, Sylvie. It's me.

Sylvie I know it's you.

Miles Good. So long as that's clear.

Sylvie You need a whole bottle of wine and two whiskies before you can face me, don't you?

Miles No, no, that's not true. Oh dear. (*He starts putting on his boots*)

Silence

Sylvie (*helpfully*) I'm on the pill.

Miles I know you are. (*After a pause*) What are you thinking?

Sylvie I'm going to go and join those liberationists now. Come and kick your shed door down during the night.

Pause

Miles We'll have a great evening, I promise you. I'll buy you some champagne.

Sylvie Be two of us falling over then, won't there?

Miles (*angrily*) It was a polished wood floor and I had my socks on. It was a perfectly natural, understandable thing to do for me to fall over.

Sylvie Well, I should keep your boots on tonight then since you're so coy about taking them off.

Miles I think you're being deliberately insensitive.

Sylvie No, I'm not, you poor old sod.

Miles looks despairing

Sorry. (*After a slight pause*) You're probably right. There's a horrible smell in here anyway, isn't there?

Miles Yes, there is.

Sylvie Mucky little vandals and all, weren't they?

Miles Yes, we'll get going. Just a second. (*He finishes doing up his boots*)

Sylvie (*looking out of the window*) You can't see the sea at all now. Mist's come right up to the cliff. Happened really quickly that did.

Miles Ah, yes. They do, they do. These sea mists, they move very quickly.

Sylvie Like oil rigs.

Miles All right, all right.

Sylvie (*thoughtfully*) I hope my mum's all right.

Miles Your mum?

Sylvie Yes. Mrs Bateman from next door was going to look in and my sister's here tonight and she can stay till tomorrow, till Sunday night and by that time, I'll nearly be back. So she won't be on her own very much. She should be all right.

Miles She can get about all right?

Sylvie Oh, yes. She has to with the little ones. No, it's only if she has one of her bad do's.

Miles That's unlikely, isn't it?

Sylvie Oh, yes. They're not that frequent. Anyway, if there's any bother, they'll get in touch.

Miles Get in touch?

Sylvie Yes.

Miles Where?

Sylvie At the hotel.

Miles You gave them the hotel number?

Sylvie Yes, of course I did. Couldn't go without telling them where I was, could I?

Miles Ah.

Sylvie What's wrong with that?

Miles Well, when this Mrs What's-'er-name rings up, if she has to, who's she going to ask for?

Sylvie Me.

Miles What name?

Sylvie Sylvie Bell. (*Realizing*) Oh.

Miles Let's just hope she doesn't ring.

Sylvie She probably won't.

Miles I mean, apart from anything else, they won't know who the hell she's talking about.

Sylvie (*agitatedly*) Well, it's not my fault. I'm not used to all this, am I? I mean, what name was I supposed to give her? Oh, Mrs Bateman, I'm going away and I'm changing my name to Mrs Higginbottom.

Miles It doesn't matter. It's too late now. They're all winking at you anyway, what the hell.

Sylvie What do they know me as at the hotel, then?

Miles Since you're with me signed in under my name, Mrs Coombes, presumably.

Sylvie (*aghast*) Mrs Coombes. Oh, God.

Miles Yes.

Sylvie (*quite shocked*) That's your wife's name, isn't it?

Miles Yes.

Pause

Miles moves to the door

Sylvie I didn't mean to take her name.

Miles That's OK, she's pretty generous with it. Anyway, it's mine. I only lent it to her.

Sylvie It's a really terrible smell in here, isn't it?

Miles It is. Come on.

Sylvie (*as they step out*) I didn't realize it when we came in because I had my mind on other—oh . . .

Miles Oh, hell.

While they have been in the hut the fog has grown quite thick

Sylvie You can't see a thing, can you?

Miles It's OK, OK. No problem.

Sylvie You can't even see the cliff.

Miles No, that's over there. We're all right. All we have to do is head straight back down there, see? If we keep away from the cliff there'll be no problem. Just a second . . .

He fumbles in his pocket and produces a small child's compass

Sylvie What's that?

Miles It's a compass. It belongs to the kids, actually, but I borrowed it. Thought it might be handy. Also, I wanted to get used to using one before we started on the big walk. This'll really come in handy when we're staggering around the Hebrides. Now—(*He consults the compass*)—the hotel will be, let me see, north-east. Maybe nor' nor' east.

As Miles consults it, Sylvie moves round to look

Hang on, don't move around too much.

Sylvie Sorry.

Miles So that way'll be north. So we want to be heading that way.

Sylvie moves again

Hang on, don't keep moving, Sylvie.

Sylvie I'm sorry.

Miles No, you see, my darling, every time you move about like that, then the needle follows you. So then I've no idea which direction magnetic north is. I keep getting north from a different direction. . . . It shouldn't do that, should it? Stand a little bit further away, would you? Well clear.

Sylvie (*backing away from Miles*) Over here.

Miles That's better. That's better. Bit further. (*He shouts*) No, not too far, that's the cliff!

Sylvie Oh.

Miles Hang on, the damn thing's pointing at me now. Why the hell's it pointing at me? Look, I'm moving round, the thing's pointing at me. (*He moves round in circles, agitatedly trying to avoid the compass needle*)

Sylvie I think it's this way.

Miles (*ignoring her*) Wait a minute. I'll put it down. I think what we're doing is, we're both creating a magnetic field. That's what we're doing.

Sylvie I didn't know people were magnetic.

Miles sets the compass down and steps back

Miles (*squinting to see it*) Oh, yes . . . ah, yes . . . there now. As I move away, you see, it's settling. I'm pretty sure now it's pointing true magnetic north, you see. Except now we can't see the damn thing, can we?

Sylvie We best just leave it there for the next person.

Miles (*snatching it up impatiently*) Oh, to hell with it. This way. Come on. Give us your hand.

Sylvie takes Miles's hand. They begin to move carefully off in roughly the direction they came

(*As they go*) Yes, you remember we took this path when we first forked off that cart track so if we can get back on the cart track, we turn right and that should take us on to that B road. . . . Come on . . .!

They exit

Miles's voice fades away into the fog. A silence. The mist grows thicker. An unseen sheep bleats nearby. After quite some time, Miles's voice is heard again approaching from the other direction

Miles Now if my guess is right . . . it's another twenty-five, thirty yards to the fork and then we should be on the cart track. Yes, you see, here's another of these huts. They must position them every half mile or so along the coast just to . . .

They stare at the hut

This is the same one, isn't it?

Sylvie It could be. (*She opens the door, sniffs inside and swiftly closes it again*) Yes, it's the same one.

Miles Yes. I had a feeling it was. Oh, hell. (*He takes out his compass again and looks at it*)

Sylvie Is it still pointing at you?

Miles (*stuffing it back in his pocket*) Yes. I don't know how Captain Cook ever found his way round, I'm sure.

Sylvie I think it's that way, you know. That way.

Miles I don't think it is, you know.

Sylvie Definitely it is. Come on.

Miles Now, wait.

Sylvie We——

Miles Sylvie, listen a moment. Now listen. Can you hear anything?

Sylvie (*listening*) No.

Miles Listen again.

Sylvie (*listening*) All I can hear is the sea.

Miles Exactly. The sea. Now we are only a few yards, if you will remember correctly, from that cliff which is a sheer couple of hundred feet drop.

Sylvie Right.

Miles Now we have no way of telling which direction that cliff is.

Sylvie It's over there.

Miles We have no real way of telling.

Sylvie (*moving*) I'm telling you, it's over here.

Miles (*sharply*) Sylvie, for God's sake, don't move around.

Sylvie We've got to move around. I want to get back.

Miles Now listen to me. Don't get excited. Now I've read about this. It's very clearly stated what you do in these circumstances. You stay put. You do not, repeat, do not run around in fog like this. Because that's the easiest way in the world to have a serious accident. You saw what happened to us just now? You can lose all sense of direction in a fog like this. Your senses become totally confused. We'll have to stay put.

Sylvie How long for?

Miles Till it lifts. They never last long, these sea mists. Quarter of an hour and they just evaporate. Then we'll be back in bright sunshine, you'll see.

Sylvie It's getting thicker.

Miles Now, please, trust me. We'd better sit in the hut and wait for it to clear.

Sylvie I'm not sitting in there.

Miles We'll have to.

Sylvie It stinks in there.

Miles Sylvie, it is getting colder and colder out here. We're not dressed for this sort of weather. You haven't even got your sweater on.

Sylvie We'll die in there.

Miles We'll die out here. Haven't you read about it? People are found regularly. People like you who thought they knew better than the experts. They're found lying in little huddled frozen bundles of anorak. Their body temperatures——

Sylvie All right, we'll go in there then.

Miles (*going inside the hut*) Good. Thank you.

Sylvie (*following him*) Anything for a bit of peace. I'm going to leave the door a bit open to get some air in. Phew.

Miles We'll get used to it. (*After a slight pause*) Probably.

Sylvie What are we going to do while we're waiting then?

Miles Not much we can do, is there?

Sylvie The only thing we could have done you don't want to do.

Miles It's hardly the moment, is it?

Sylvie At least we'd have died happy. A great holiday, I must say. Fogbound in a smelly old shed.

Miles All right, it won't be for long.

Sylvie I must remember to send my friends a postcard. Wish you were here. Wherever we are.

A scratching sound is heard behind the shed

Miles (*hearing something*) Just a minute.

Sylvie What?

Miles I heard something.

Sylvie What?

Miles Somebody moving. Somebody's round the back of the hut.

Sylvie It's the vandals back again.

Miles Ssh. (*He listens*)

Sylvie They forgot to break the windows.

Miles (*sharply*) Ssh. (*He says quietly*) Wait here. I'm going out to investigate. Stay here.

Sylvie Here?

Miles Yes, absolutely quietly.

Sylvie I'm not staying in here.

Miles Ssh.

Miles opens the door a little more and creeps out. He picks up a rather ineffectual-looking stick and starts to make his way very slowly round to the back of the hut.

After a moment, Sylvie comes out of the hut and follows Miles at a distance

Miles reaches the back of the hut. He strains his eyes to see into the fog. Suddenly, very close to him, a sheep bleats loudly. Miles, startled, hurls his stick at it and retreats hastily

Miles (*hurrying past Sylvie and pushing her aside*) Oh, my God it's a—it's a thing. It's a big—it's a black-faced woolly thing. It's a thing.

Sylvie (*following him into the hut*) It's all right. It's a sheep.

Miles (*slamming the door*) I don't know what it was, Sylvie. It was black with wool. It was a thing.

Sylvie It was a sheep.

Miles A what?

Sylvie A sheep. It was a sheep.

Miles Was it?

Sylvie Yes.

Miles It didn't look like a sheep to me.

Sylvie Definitely.

Miles It looked a bit big for a sheep.

Sylvie They are quite big.

Miles Are they?

Sylvie Close up they are.

Miles Yes, maybe you're right. I usually only see them from train windows. They look fairly harmless from there.

Sylvie They're harmless.

Miles You're sure it was a sheep?

Sylvie Yes, it went baa.

Miles Did it? I didn't wait to hear the baa, I just saw the face.

Sylvie Bit jumpy, aren't you?

Miles Well, surprised, that's all.

A silence. Sylvie giggles. Miles is not so amused

Sylvie (*laughing*) Black-faced woolly thing.

Miles stares out of the window

I'm opening this door again.

Miles Well, don't let it in here.

Sylvie It won't come in here. It's too smelly in here. It's got more sense.

Miles If we're not back before dark, they'll report us missing at the hotel. Probably come out looking for us.

Sylvie That bloke'll be winking his head off.

Silence. Sylvie kicks the oil drum

It's wonderful, this place. (*She kicks the oil drum*) When I get married I think I'll come back here for my honeymoon. (*She kicks the oil drum. Silence. She kicks again*) This where you came for yours, was it?

Miles Look, for the love of Mike, Sylvie, don't keep on.

Sylvie All right.

Miles (*angrily*) Well, you've done nothing but moan since we got here. You moaned about the journey, you moaned about my driving, you've complained about the hotel, the bed, the bathroom, the restaurant, the wine, the walk, the shed. This was all done for you, you know. All for you, every bit of it. I think the least you might do is pretend you're having a good time.

Sylvie What was done for me?

Miles Everything. Absolutely everything.

Sylvie It was not, I beg your pardon.

Miles Oh, yes it was.

Sylvie I beg your pardon but it wasn't.

Miles It was.

Sylvie I'm sorry, I beg your pardon. I didn't ask to come here. I didn't ask to spend a weekend shifting beds about and walking around in damn great boots. I wanted to go to a proper hotel.

Miles That is a proper hotel.

Sylvie No, it isn't, so there. Because I know about proper hotels as it happens. Because my Aunty Enid used to work in a proper hotel. In proper hotels, you get your own bathroom. And you get free face tissues and soap that's wrapped up in special paper with a gold seal so no one's used it before. And you have new towels every day, not like here, and you just sling them on the floor when you've finished with them. And you get a shower cap that's wrapped up in cellophane too. And a shoe-cleaning kit. And a notice that says "Do Not Disturb" so people don't come busting in and a radio by the bed and a colour television. And they come and make your bed properly too and don't just stand there saying, "Oh, yes, we'll have to see about this," and winking at you. And they have a hall porter and cocktail bars and powder rooms and pianos playing in the lounge. And most of all, you get your breakfast served in bloody bed whenever you want it. That's what I call a hotel so there. (*She pauses breathless*)

Miles I'm not rising to that. I'm simply not rising to that.

Sylvie And if I go to the trouble to wear my evening dress and my evening turban, I expect to be taken out somewhere decent as well, just while I'm complaining.

Miles What are you talking about?

Sylvie That place you took us.

Miles What was wrong with that? That was decent.

Sylvie I didn't think so. A lot of bricks and candles and no tablecloths. Looked as if it hadn't been finished off properly.

Miles It cost enough.

Sylvie Scruffy lot of people with beards and women with dirty hair. If I go out, I want a bit of high life. I can——

Sylvie }
Miles } (*together*) { —get all that at home.

Miles Well, great, I suggest you go home then. Because you're a pain in the arse here.

Sylvie Right, I will. (*She is now quite upset*) You wouldn't even buy me a vodka martini, would you?

Miles No, I wouldn't because I knew you wouldn't like it.

Sylvie I'd never had one, had I?

Miles I bought you a snowball.

Sylvie (*tearful*) I've had snowballs. I have snowballs when I go out with Tom, Dick and Pete Bartlett. I wanted something else. I wanted something special. That's what this was all supposed to be about. Special.

That's why I came because it was going to be special. And it's all like the same as—ordinary.

Miles (*gently*) Yes, well, I'm afraid it invariably is, Sylvie, I'm sorry to say. We spend our lives looking forward to things. They very rarely turn out quite as they should.

Sylvie Well . . .

Silence

Miles Still, it was worth a try, wasn't it? I'll—we'll drive back first thing tomorrow.

Sylvie (*sadly*) Yes.

Miles If you can bear another night.

Sylvie Yes.

Miles We needn't bother moving the beds together so you needn't——

Sylvie Oh, don't get like that.

Miles Like what?

Sylvie All sorry for yourself. It was my stupid fault for building it all up.

Silence

Miles Oh, dear. It appears that all the most dramatic moments in my life are destined to occur in sheds. Maybe fate's trying to tell me something.

Sylvie Come on, I'm not staying here.

Miles Where are you going?

Sylvie If we sit here much longer we'll pick the rest of us to bits then there'll be nothing left at all. Let's try and keep something to remember otherwise it's been a complete waste of time.

Miles You can't walk in this.

Sylvie (*going out*) I'm going to.

Miles Sylvie, please, you'll get lost.

Sylvie Better than being suffocated. You coming?

Miles No, I'm not and neither are——

Sylvie Bye-bye, then. See you back there.

Sylvie exits

Miles (*running to the door of the hut*) Sylvie! (*He calls into the fog*) Sylvie, you're going the wrong way. (*He peers hopelessly into the fog*) Sylvie? (*He mutters*) She'll be back in a minute wandering round in circles if she doesn't die of exposure. (*He shouts*) Then what am I going to tell your mother, Sylvie? (*He mutters*) Sorry, Mrs Bell. Took your daughter away to seduce her. I'm afraid she froze to death. Here's her anorak. Terribly sorry. One of those things. You win some, you lose some. (*He yells*) Sylvie, where the hell are you? (*He snatches out his compass*) Oh, this damn thing. Will you stop pointing at me? (*He hurls it down, then says more calmly*) Sylvie. Come on, now. Follow my voice, Sylvie. Just come to my voice, Sylvie. She's fallen over the cliff, that's what's happened to her. Sylvie. Or eaten by sheep. That was never a sheep. Sylvie. Sheep are small and friendly. That thing was ferocious. It snarled. Sylvie.

Rowena (*off, very distantly*) Hallo.

Miles Sylvie? Was that someone? Sylvie.
Rowena (*off, distant*) Hallo.
Miles It was. Come on, Sylvie, over here. Sylvie.
Rowena (*off, distant*) Miles.
Miles Sylvie.
Rowena Miles.
Miles That's it, Sylvie. Good girl.
Rowena Miles.
Miles This way, Sylvie.
Rowena (*off, closer*) Miles.
Miles Rowena?
Rowena Miles.
Miles Rowena.

Rowena emerges from the fog

Rowena Miles. Oh, there you are.
Miles Yes.
Rowena Thank heavens for that. God, this is thick.
Miles What are——? How did you get here?
Rowena Well now. Phew. Just a sec. Get my breath. A saga indeed.
Miles Yes, I thought it might be.
Rowena I'm not snooping on you, darling, I'm really not. You must believe me. I'm all for this, you know that. You and what's-her-name. Absolutely super. The thing is there is a rather distraught Mrs Bateman who's been looking after what's-her-name's mother, it appears.
Miles Sylvie's mother.
Rowena Yes. And she tried to phone what's-her-name at the number of the hotel she'd given her. Only of course they'd never heard of what's-her-name. So then the distraught but enterprising Mrs Bateman phones me and says how do we get hold of you both? So I said, well, I'll phone the hotel. Only by that time you were out. So. Chapter Four. I persuade good old Terry Hogg to turn out on his Saturday afternoon off and drive over here to find you. And then, Chapter Five, the hotel said—or rather a little man who kept winking at me said—you'd both gone for a walk in this direction. So we drove along very slowly in the fog which was just as well because we nearly hit something which we thought at first was a sheep. Only it turned out to be what's-her-name. So she's in the car with Hogg and I'm here. Rescue service, sir.
Miles And I take it the reason you're here is that Sylvie's mum's had a turn, is that it?
Rowena According to Mrs Bateman. She was quite hysterical on the phone like a very, very passionate episode of *The Archers*. You coming?
Miles Is the road very near?
Rowena It's about fifty yards over the hill. Why? (*She notices the hut*) What's this place?
Miles It's an emergency hut for walkers if they get stranded.
Rowena Oh, jolly useful. (*She sticks her head inside and recoils immediately*) Ugh. What on earth have you been doing in there?

Miles I haven't been doing anything in there.

Rowena Quite revolting. (*She closes the door*) Are you sure this is a rescue hut?

Miles Yes. What else could it be?

Rowena I think it's part of the roadworks, you know, darling.

Miles Roadworks?

Rowena Yes, there's a huge construction job at the bottom of the hill. I think they're building a motorway.

Miles Oh. Are they?

Rowena Come on. We've got to run her back, you see, to her mum. I mean, we'll drop you off at the hotel so you can drive her back if you'd rather.

Miles Yes.

Rowena Does that mean yes or no? Come on. Oh, did you approve of the evening dress?

Miles Mm?

Rowena I thought she looked absolutely knock-out. I mean, if she actually managed to stand up straight—she'd be a real stunner. Can't you try and persuade her, darling? To hold things in a bit.

Miles Yes, I will.

Rowena Oh, and the hat. That was me. That was sheer inspiration. Her boots weren't me, I promise.

Miles No, they were me.

Rowena Come on, darling. Terry wants to get back, too. (*She starts to go*) Is it good value that hotel? I think I might come out here sometime, if you recommend it. If I can brave all that winking. Darling, they're waiting. (*She stands impatiently*)

EITHER he says:

Miles OK. OK. (*He starts to follow her*)

Rowena You don't look very bright. Has she been giving you a bad time?

Miles Not really. I think I've been giving her a bad time actually.

Rowena I don't believe that. You've never given anyone a bad time. You want to run her home or not?

Miles No, you take her. I'll follow up in mine. I'll have to check us out.

Rowena Oh, that'll be dreary for you. Driving home alone. I'll tell you what. T. Hogg can take her and I'll drive with you, if you like.

Miles OK. You're sure that's——?

Rowena You'll need someone to navigate for you. I'll jog alongside the car reading the road signs for you.

Miles Oh no, not if we're going to have jokes all the way back, please.

Rowena Whoops. Now let me take your arm, can I, over this?

Miles There you are then.

Rowena When you get to our age, dear, you need a little support, you see. Not as sprightly as we were.

Miles No, that's true enough.

Rowena and Miles exit slowly

Rowena (*prattling away into the fog*) When I was a gel, you know, I used to take these tussocks in a single bound—whoops, careful, darling. I was like a gel possessed, I can tell you. . . . Of course, my stays slowed me down a little but nonetheless. . . . (*Her voice fades away into the fog*)

The Lights fade to a Black-out

To: A WEDDING (page 199)

OR he says:

Miles Yes. I—I think I'd rather walk back, if you don't mind.

Rowena Walk?

Miles Yes. I'd like a bit of a think. I'll go this way.

Rowena That way?

Miles I'll see you back home.

Rowena What am I going to tell what's-her-name?

Miles Tell her I'm walking back the other way. You won't mind running her home, will you?

Rowena No. Do I take it that's the end of a beautiful friendship between you two?

Miles Oh, I don't know. I don't think we ever got to be friends. Not enough in common for that. Cheerio then.

Rowena Do be careful. I think it's the sea that way, darling.

Miles No, it's not. Sea's over there. Path's this way. See you.

He disappears into the fog

Rowena Bye-bye. (*She calls*) I'll check in the fridge when I get back. If we've got anything to eat, I'll try and fix us something for——

From the fog we hear a sudden cry from Miles as he steps off the cliff

Miles? Miles? (*In alarm*) Darling.

Rowena stands very worried as the Lights fade to a Black-out

To: A SIMPLE CEREMONY (page 205)

A WEDDING

A Church. This year later

The church door is closed. A gravel path leads away from it to an unseen road.
A variety of gravestones border the path

We hear church bells signifying a wedding, followed by some pre-wedding
organ music from within the church

The church door opens and Sylvie, in full bridal regalia comes out and walks
halfway down the path to see if anyone is coming. Obviously there is not. She
looks up at the church clock and scowls with annoyance

Sylvie (*looking back towards the road*) Where is he? (*She moves back to the*
church, looks inside and speaks to someone) I'm coming. Well, I can't, can
I? I don't know. How do I know . . .? Yes, I know . . . all right. (*She*
mutters) I don't care if you have got another one, you'll have to wait,
won't you? Not my fault.

Miles enters hurriedly from the road. He has on his dark wedding suit

Miles (*breathlessly*) Sylvie, I'm so sorry. I just don't know what to say. I'm
so, so sorry.
Sylvie 'S all right. You're here anyway.
Miles I'm sorry. I was on time, everything just went wrong.
Sylvie I'll tell him we're ready now. Wait a sec.

Sylvie goes in to the church

Miles It wasn't my fault, it really wasn't. I—oh. . . . (*He breathes deeply*) I
don't know how I got here as it was.

Sylvie comes out of the church

Sylvie Well, that's marvellous, isn't it? Now we're ready and he's not.
Thirty people sitting in there and he's not ready.
Miles Who?
Sylvie The vicar. Old Fognorth's gone off to make a phone call now.
Miles That's a bit much. Right in the middle of your service?
Sylvie He says he's going to try and put the other lot off. Otherwise they're
going to arrive in the middle of ours.
Miles Oh, this is my fault, isn't it, it's my fault.
Sylvie No, it'll be him. He's disorganized about everything. He's always
double booking. Christenings in the middle of funerals. Double weddings.
Stupid old trout.
Miles You're looking very lovely, Sylvie.

Sylvie I feel daft in all this.

Miles No, it's very romantic. You look beautiful, really.

Sylvie (*embarrassed*) Waste of money. I only did it for my mum.

Miles Pity she can't be here.

Sylvie Yes, well. She saw me anyway.

Miles Did she?

Sylvie Yes, I went up the hospital yesterday. They let me put it all on to show her.

Miles Really?

Sylvie Yes, I felt really daft. Parading up and down women's surgical in my full get up. They all loved it, mind. Couple of them started crying. So did my mum.

Miles (*looking into the church*) Well, they all seem happy enough in there listening to the music.

Sylvie Driving them all up the wall, I should think. He's been round four times, the organist.

Miles Who's your bridesmaid in there? She's very pretty. Is she a friend of yours?

Sylvie (*smiling*) No. You know her.

Miles Do I?

Sylvie That's Rachel. My sister. You know, Tubsy.

Miles Good heavens, is it really? (*He looks in again*) So it is. Not Tubsy now.

Sylvie No way.

Miles Very attractive.

Sylvie Yes. All that running round paid off, didn't it? (*After a pause*) I wish he'd hurry up. My stomach keeps turning over.

Miles You'll be fine.

Sylvie As long as it goes all right, you see. The trouble is I've had to organize it all myself practically. If anything goes wrong, it'll be my fault. Now I've checked the best man—Pete Bartlett. He's got the ring because I phoned him before he left home. The flowers are there. I checked. And those cars had better be there afterwards or I'll want to know why. It's all been left to me, you see. If I'd left it to him. . . . Great start, isn't it? Haven't even married him yet and I find out he's useless. Last chance to get out, I suppose.

Miles (*half joking*) Go on, run for it then, you'd better be quick.

Sylvie No. I don't think I could do that. Not to Lionel Hepplewick. He'd just fall apart.

Miles Well, so long as you know what you're taking on, Sylvie.

Sylvie Oh, I know what I'm taking on all right. I'm taking on what I always knew I was going to take on from the day I first went to school. From the minute I first—grew up. I had a few little dreams of other things but I knew what I was really going to take on.

Miles This all sounds very sad, Sylvie.

Sylvie No, it's not meant to be sad. It's going to be very rewarding. I'm sure it is. No great surprises I don't suppose. I'll have kids—several, I hope. And I pray they'll all come out normal. And I'll probably be too busy to

think about much else. I'll see Lionel's taken care of, of course. I'll be a
very good Mrs Hepplewick. I'll make damn sure I am.

Miles Remember, what was it, five years ago when you were Mrs Coombes?

Sylvie No, I was never Mrs Coombes.

Miles For a night you were.

Sylvie No.

Miles That was a bit of a dream really, wasn't it?

Sylvie Yes.

Miles You ever—do you ever look back on that?

Sylvie No.

Miles Ah. I'm afraid I do. (*A pause, then he smiles*) It really was quite
amusing, some of it, wasn't it? What about the hut, do you remember the
hut?

Sylvie No.

Miles Oh, you must remember the hut.

Sylvie No.

Miles And the sheep.

Sylvie I don't remember anything. (*She looks back into the church*) I'm
going to go in there and start shouting in a minute.

Miles Do you want me to hurry him up?

Sylvie No, you're doing enough.

Miles Nonsense, I'm doing nothing.

Sylvie You're putting yourself out for me. That's enough.

Miles I'm happy to do it for you, Sylvie, you know I am.

Sylvie I'm sorry I had to ask you. It was just difficult, you know, finding
someone to give you away. I mean, you're the only man I know well
enough who's old enough.

Miles Ah. (*After a slight pause*) Do you love Lionel?

Sylvie Course I do. What a question. It's not a marriage of convenience,
you know.

Miles No, of course not.

Sylvie He's a good man.

Miles I'm sure. I'm sorry.

Sylvie (*turning back to the church*) Right. I think I'm going to go and sort
that vicar out now. I've had enough of this.

Miles Now, Sylvie, don't do anything rash. Don't spoil your day.

Sylvie You stay there. I'll be back. It's my wedding. I've paid for it. It's my
fight.

Miles OK. OK. (*He backs away*)

Sylvie goes into the church

Miles wanders round the churchyard, waiting

> She gave me eyes, she gave me ears
> And humble cares and delicate fears.
> A heart the fountain of sweet tears
> And——

meeuurrh—nah. . . . Ladies and gentlemen, I feel a great pleasure . . . I feel greatly pleasant . . . I feel pleasant. No. It was a very pleasant pleasure for me when Sylvie asked me to give her away. I have known Sylvie considerably . . . for some considerable years and indeed, perhaps, feel more qualified perhaps, than perhaps I should to do this very pleasant duty. No, this pleasurable duty. I've got an awful lot of pleasurables in here. Why do I have to do these damn things? I hate them so much. Er— ladies and gentlemen . . .

Rowena comes out of the church

Rowena Where are you going, darling? You're not off, are you?

Miles No, I'm waiting. I'm just waiting.

Rowena We're all waiting. I do think that Fognorth's a dunce, I really do. I mean, fancy holding us all up like this. I think I'm going to write anonymously to the Bishop or something. It's not fair on Sylvie. She's in there as white as a sheet.

Miles She is as white as a sheet. No, it's my fault. I'm to blame. I was fifteen minutes late at least.

Rowena But why?

Miles Because I got home from the office, I thought in masses of time to change. . . .

Rowena But I laid everything out for you.

Miles No, you didn't, darling.

Rowena Yes, I did, darling. I laid your suit on the bed.

Miles No, darling, I'm afraid that wasn't my suit. I don't know whose it was but it wasn't mine. It's some chap with very short arms, a big chest and fond of Polo Mints because his pockets were full of them.

Rowena Lord, I know whose that is.

Miles My suit I found in the back of the kids' wardrobe. That took fifteen minutes. These shoes were in Timothy's toy box and they had Lego wheels sellotaped to them.

Rowena Oh, they were Timothy's racer. I made them for him. You didn't break them up?

Miles Of course I broke them up. I wanted my shoes.

Rowena Oh dear, they took me hours to make.

Miles I'm as fond of the kids as you are but I draw the line at having to roller skate down that aisle just in order to please Timmy.

Rowena Have you got everything? Have you got the ring?

Miles No.

Rowena Why not?

Miles Because I don't need a ring.

Rowena Oh, no, of course you're on the other side.

Miles Yes.

Rowena I keep thinking you're best man. I forget.

Miles No.

Rowena You're dad.

Miles No, I'm not.

Rowena Well. She obviously has pretty fond memories of your little escapade all those—what was it—five years ago, was it?

Miles Yes.

Rowena She must remember you fondly because she wouldn't have asked you to give her away. It's a great honour.

Miles I'm the only man she knows of the right age.

Rowena Nonsense.

Miles It's true. She told me.

Rowena Well, don't believe it.

Miles She doesn't even remember.

Rowena Oh yes, she does.

Miles Not a thing. She's forgotten all about it.

Rowena I'd be awfully surprised if she had. I really would. I speak from a great deal of experience, Miles, and I must say whatever else, you're not a man one forgets that quickly. If ever. I don't know what there was between you. You were certainly the most incongruous couple I ever saw, I must admit. But I'm willing to bet you anything you like that she'll remember you for the rest of her life.

Miles Why should she?

Rowena Because one does, darling. One always does whether one wants to or not, damn it. (*She looks back to the church*) Oh, they're ready, come on.

Miles (*smoothing his hair*) Oh, hooray.

Rowena They're all waving furiously, come on.

Miles Do I look OK?

Rowena Marvellous. You look absolutely radiant.

Miles Thank you. Right?

Rowena Right. Off you go then. (*Gently*) Go and give her away.

Miles Yes.

Miles smiles and goes into the church. Rowena hesitates for a second and then follows him, closing the door

The Lights fade to a Black-out

A SIMPLE CEREMONY

A Churchyard. This year

The church door is closed. A gravel path leads away from it to an unseen road. A variety of gravestones border the path

We hear church bells signifying a happy occasion

As the lights come up, Toby, a rather red-faced man in his early forties, is midway through a speech. He is addressing a group of unseen people a little distance from him and out of sight of us in the direction of the road. He is standing in a corner of the churchyard in front of a small, low, new-looking toolshed. This is fairly undistinguished except that above the door it has a bronze plaque screwed into the woodwork. This, at present, is covered by a simple drape. Beside Toby and listening intently to his speech is Rowena, rather drawn and pale, dressed as for some small formal ceremony

Toby (*in mid flight*) ... perhaps I ought to explain to some of you who've come along here this afternoon the reason for this ceremony. It was decided some months ago that it was high time we did something, those of us who knew him and loved him, to commemorate the memory of our old friend Miles Coombes who died so tragically and prematurely five years ago as a result of a climbing accident. The Governors of the school decided in consultation with myself as Headmaster that a bronze plaque with some simple inscription would probably be most fitting in the circumstances. Fitting to commemorate the memory of our friend and, of course, one time Chairman of the Board of Governors. We approached Miles's widow, Rowena, and I'm happy to say she agreed with us. But where should we put it? Well, according to Rowena and this is something I must confess I didn't know about Miles, although I was probably his greatest friend, according to Rowena—and I'll have to take her word on this—Miles was a man particularly drawn to sheds. He was, I suppose, to coin a phrase a bit of a shedophile. Or maybe, with his close connections to the world of teaching, even a shedagogue. No, seriously, as I say, I was surprised but Rowena, as his wife, must surely be the best judge. Now, by a very fortunate coincidence, it so happened that our vicar, The Reverend Fognorth, was in the very act of replacing the existing churchyard toolshed. A happy coincidence indeed for what more fitting place for this plaque could there be than in the churchyard itself. So there we have it. We've got the plaque, we've got the shed and we also have Mrs Hogg, Rowena, here today to unveil it for us. Thank you.

Toby steps back and applauds Rowena as she steps forward

Rowena (*rather nervously*) My husband will tell you—my present husband
that is, Terry, of course—will tell you that I'm a woman of few words.
The trouble is I do tend to say these words rather a lot. But they're usually
the same few words.

Toby laughs politely

(*Smiling gratefully*) In this instance, I have extremely few. Miles was
someone extremely special and extremely dear. There are some people
when you love them, it's very easy to tell them so. There are others whom
one never manages to say it to at all. Not properly. Even though you love
them just as much. I'm afraid, so far as I was concerned, Miles was one of
those people. Which is a pity because I think, rather ironically, he was one
of those people who most needed to be told. Anyway, too late now. So
this shed is for Miles. It would have been nice to have given him a
cathedral or something, I suppose, but Miles was never very grand and
I'm sure wherever he is that a shed will suit him down to the ground.
Miles's shed. (*She unveils the plaque*)

Toby leads the applause

Toby (*to the assembled audience*) Thank you all very much for coming.
(*Quietly, to Rowena as people disperse*) This is an extraordinarily bizarre
idea, Rowena, it really is. I mean, why a shed?
Rowena It's lovely. It's a lovely shed.
Toby I mean, I was going to have the thing screwed on the cricket pavilion.
Much more his mark. He wasn't a gardener, was he?
Rowena Miles? Heavens no.
Toby Well, what's all this shed business about then?
Rowena Oh, nothing really.
Toby Nothing?
Rowena Nothing at all.
Toby You're all right, are you?
Rowena Perfectly.
Toby You don't look so good, you know. Very pale.
Rowena (*joking it off*) Strain, you know, darling, nervous strain.
Toby Well, take care of yourself.
Rowena I still miss him, you know, Toby. Isn't that awful? It's five years
since he died. You'd think I'd have got over it by now. But I still mope.
Terry gets furious of course, whenever I mention him. He refused point
blank to come today. Just stamped out.
Toby (*tentatively*) He's—er—he's treating you all right, is he? Is he?
Rowena Terry? Why do you ask?
Toby Well, it's just we've had one or two worries about him from a couple
of sources at the school. It appears he might have been—mistreating the
kids.
Rowena Oh, God.
Toby I don't mean just kicking some little blighter in the bum for being lazy
but—er—quite vindictive stuff. I thought I'd better warn you. It could all

blow up. Only if it turns out to be true, of course. Probably isn't. I mean, some of these kids are the most fearful liars.

Rowena No. They probably aren't lying.

Toby Has he with you?

Rowena Toby, you sort things out from your side. All right? Anything I did, unlike the children, I did with my eyes open, quite voluntarily. I've only myself to blame. Now then I must away, back to the family. I'll bring the kids up here to see Daddy's shed tomorrow. They'll be very thrilled.

She opens the shed door and goes inside for a second

(*From within*) Yes, it's lovely. I shall probably come up and just come in here occasionally and think of him.

She comes out

Thank you very much for arranging this, Toby, bless you. (*She moves away*) I'll see you on Tuesday for the thing in the afternoon. The exhibition.

Rowena exits down the path to the road

Toby (*watching her go*) Right. (*He stands watching her for a moment*) I hope to God she's all right. She gets nuttier and nuttier. (*He approaches the plaque and reads it*) "This shed has been erected on this site in memory of Miles Percival Coombes, a friend and governor of Bilbury Lodge School. A heart the fountain of sweet tears and love and thought and joy." That's rather nice. Wordsworth, I think. Well, if somebody'd dedicated a shed to me after I'd died, I think I'd come back and haunt them. Still, he was a bit mad as well. Probably did like sheds for all I know.

He is about to close the door when Sylvie, pregnant and sensibly dressed appears from the road

Oh, hallo, Mrs Hepplewick. How are you?

Sylvie Very well, thank you, Mr Teasdale.

Toby Family all well, are they?

Sylvie Yes, thank you, Mr Teasdale.

Pause

Sylvie stares at the shed

Toby Came up for the dedication, did you?

Sylvie I was passing. Thought I'd see what was going on.

Toby Well, as you see. All a bit crazy, I'm afraid. A little bit mad. But then they're that sort of family.

Sylvie Yes.

Toby Of course, you knew them quite well.

Sylvie Yes, I did.

Toby Yes.

Sylvie Some time ago.

Toby Yes. (*After a pause*) How's the new baby? When's that due?

Sylvie Not till March.
Toby And this'll be ...
Sylvie My third.
Toby He's certainly keeping you busy.
Sylvie Yes, he's keeping me busy. (*She opens the door of the shed*) May I?
Toby Yes, of course. Nothing much in there. I think they're moving their
stuff in on Monday. The—er—Church ground staff. Do you understand
what all this shed business is about?

Sylvie does not reply

I don't. (*After a pause*) Extraordinary.
Sylvie I think it's just her little joke. His wife's. She's full of little jokes, that
one.
Toby I'm afraid I don't see it.
Sylvie I don't think it's meant for you.
Toby Well, who the hell is it meant for?
Sylvie (*finishing her examination*) Yes, that's lovely. Thank you very much.

Toby stares at her mystified

Could you tell me, is it left unlocked, do you know?
Toby Well, I've no idea. In the daytime I should think when they're
working it should be. Probably lock it at night.
Sylvie Oh, that's all right. I might just—come up and sit in it for a while.
Now and again.
Toby (*his eyes narrowing*) Oh, yes.
Sylvie Just for old time's sake.
Toby Yes. Jolly good.
Sylvie I might even put my boots on, you never know.
Toby Yes, I should if I were you, yes.
Sylvie Goodbye, then.
Toby Yes. Goodbye, Mrs ... Hepple—Hepplewick. Regards to your
husband.
Sylvie (*moving off*) Yes.
Toby (*calling after her*) I say?
Sylvie Yes?
Toby Do you think there are likely to be any more of you?
Sylvie What?
Toby Women. Wanting to come and sit in it. I mean, I'm sure it'll be all
right. It's just I think I ought to warn the vicar. I mean, only if there's
going to be a lot of you.
Sylvie No, I doubt if there'll be any more of us.
Toby Right. Fine. As long as I know.
Sylvie (*after a moment's thought*) No, there definitely won't be any more.
Good afternoon, Mr Teasdale.
Toby Afternoon, Mrs ...

Sylvie exits to the road

*Toby looks inside the shed again to see if there's anything he's missed. He
emerges and shakes his head*

Quite extraordinary ...

He locks the shed and walks away, still shaking his head

The Lights fade to a Black-out

FURNITURE AND PROPERTY LIST

A Cricket Match

HOW IT BEGAN and A VISIT FROM A FRIEND

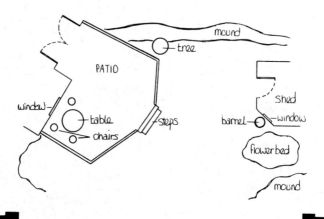

On stage: Table. *On it*: John Player cigarettes, lighter, ashtray, cup and saucer ι
Swing set on the tree
Shed door closed
Patio doors open
Trees set across to house
Dustbin (padded)
In shed: Half a shovel, box of weedkiller, wheelbarrow without a wheel
and an old gin bottle

Off stage: 2 mugs of coffee **(Celia)**
Several old paint tins **(Sylvie)**

Personal: **Miles:** diary

DINNER ON THE PATIO

Strike: Ashtray, cigarettes, lighter, cup and saucer

Set: Patio table. *On it:* 4 glasses, 4 place mats, 4 napkins, 4 sets of cutlery,
candle in a glass bowl, matches and a bottle

4 white chairs, 1 at each place
Windows set ajar
Curtains open
Window box set

Off stage: Glass of sherry **(Miles)**
Glass of sherry, wine bottle and corkscrew **(Celia)**
4 glass dishes of salad on a tray **(Celia)**
Lady's coat **(Celia)**
Tea trolley. *On top tier:* 2 plates, oven gloves, ladle, casserole
On bottom tier: Pudding bowls, cream jug, dessert

A CRICKET MATCH

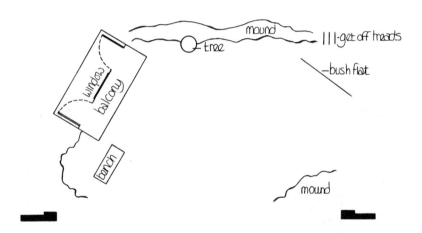

Strike: All

Set: Bench
Canvas chair
Tin score numbers
7 bottle tops
Boundary rope
3 flags
In the pavilion: 1 scoreboard set upside down, 1 team bag

Off stage: Cricket bag. Inside: cricket outfit, batting gloves, bat, batting pads, thigh
pads **(Miles)**
3 cricket balls
Blood-stained sports shirt **(Toby)**

Personal: **Miles:** watch

Toby: Piece of paper in pocket, pocket full of bottle tops
Reg: cricket pads, cricket bat
Celia: bag containing a cardigan
Rowena: Large (male) brimmed hat with feathers, Miles's watch

A SENTIMENTAL JOURNEY

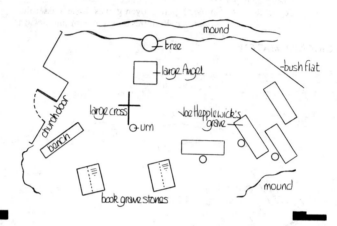

Strike: All

Set: Bench
              Several gravestones
              Large cross
              Large angel
              Urn
              Joe Hepplewick gravestone

A 50TH CELEBRATION

Stage plan as for A SENTIMENTAL JOURNEY

A Game of Golf

HOW IT BEGAN, A VISIT FROM A FRIEND and DINNER ON THE PATIO as
previously set

A GAME OF GOLF

Strike: All

Set: Hole with moveable flag
              Golf bunker
              Mattress (*off*)
              Box of sand (*off*)

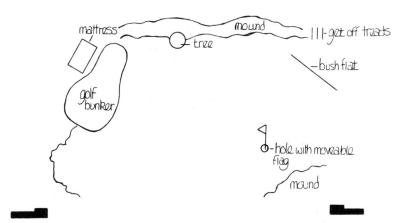

Off stage: Golf bag with dummy bottom holding a number of golf balls **(Miles)**
               Golf driver, golf bag with clubs **(Irene)**
               Bag of golf clubs, 1 iron, crumpled map of the golf course **(Toby)**
               Number of golf balls **(Rowena)**

Personal: **Toby:** golf card, pencil

EASTER GREETINGS

Stage plan as for A SENTIMENTAL JOURNEY

Off stage: Bunch of daffodils **(Celia)**

Personal: **Miles:** watch

A TRIUMPH OF FRIENDSHIP

Stage plan as for A SENTIMENTAL JOURNEY

A One Man Protest

HOW IT BEGAN and A VISIT FROM A FRIEND as previously set

CONFESSIONS IN A GARDEN SHED

Stage plan as for HOW IT BEGAN except the shed is far more centrally placed so that
the interior is visible and the dustbins are downstage, in view

Set: In shed: Shovel, 2 hoes, wheelbarrow without a wheel and a sack and
         shovel set on top, mower, stepladder, deckchair, tennis racquet, shears,
         broom head, gardening gloves, vice, chisel, shell tin, small watering can,
         yellow watering can, blow torch, flower pot with hat on top, bucket with
         cassette and football inside, large watering can, 2 buckets with a hoe
         and sickle set inside, fork, wooden box with sickle, chest expander and

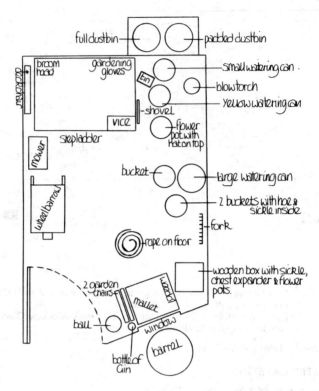

Interior of shed

> flower pots, box of weedkiller, mallet, old gin bottle, 2 garden chairs and a ball, a rope, paint tins, tyre, carpet, carpet sweeper, Dettol tin, shooting stick, old fertilizer bag filled with straw
> Dustbins (1 padded)
> Barrel set against shed
> Garden fence attached
> Gate set open

Off stage: Some rubbish, including some old bottles and a book **(Sylvie)**
More rubbish **(Sylvie)**

Personal: **Miles:** watch
Celia: raincoat, bag of shopping

A ONE MAN PROTEST

Stage plan as for How It Began with the addition of 2 chairs by the patio table

Set: Newspaper (The *Guardian*)
Undrunk cup of tea
Cigarettes
Lighter

Off stage: Empty, dirty plate on a tray **(Celia)**
Pudding dish of apple crumble and a spoon **(Celia)**
Cup of coffee **(Celia)**
2 lengths of flexible trunking from a vacuum cleaner **(Lionel)**
Drum of extension cable, wide, heavy duty adhesive tape **(Lionel)**
Lionel's burnt trousers **(Lionel)**
Bucket of water, old, dirty mac **(Sylvie)**
Housecoat, Celia's dress, clean cloth **(Celia)**

In shed: Cardboard wrapper **(Rowena)**

Personal: **Lionel:** piece of paper in pocket
Rowena: watch

A MIDNIGHT MASS

Stage plan as for A SENTIMENTAL JOURNEY

Strike: All

Set: Bench
Several gravestones
Large cross
Large angel
Urn

A SCHOOL CELEBRATES

Stage plan as for A SENTIMENTAL JOURNEY

Strike: All

Set: Bench
Several gravestones
Large cross
Large angel
Urn
Joe Hepplewick gravestone

Love In The Mist

HOW IT BEGAN, A VISIT FROM A FRIEND and CONFESSIONS IN A GARDEN SHED as previously set

LOVE IN THE MIST

Strike: All

Set: Shed. In it: oil drum
Twigs
Stick
Broken fence

Off stage: Dry ice machine
Smoke gun

Personal: **Miles:** walking boots, anorak, watch, child's compass
Sylvie: walking boots, anorak

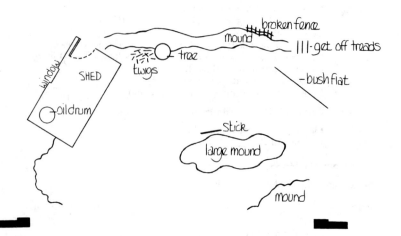

A WEDDING

Stage plan as for A Sentimental Journey

Strike: All

Set: Bench
            Several gravestones
            Large cross
            Large angel
            Urn

Personal: **Sylvie:** full bridal outfit
            Miles: dark wedding suit

A SIMPLE CEREMONY

Stage plan as for A Sentimental Journey but with the addition of a new tool shed by
  the church

Strike: All except the shed. Move shed usc and attach a bronze plaque above the
            door and cover with a simple drape

Set: Bench
            Several gravestones
            Large cross
            Large angel
            Urn

Personal: **Sylvie:** maternity dress

LIGHTING PLOT

A Cricket Match

To open: Full general lighting

Cue 1	**Miles** disappears from view behind the hut *The lights fade to Black-out*	(Page 14)
Cue 2	As scene DINNER ON THE PATIO opens *Full general lighting*	(Page 16)
Cue 3	**Celia:** "Before you start eating the table." *Lighting gradually subdued, particularly in garden area*	(Page 22)
Cue 4	**Miles:** "Oh, hell." *Garden area now in near darkness*	(Page 31)
Cue 5	**Celia:** "Eat your chicken." *The Lights fade to Black-out*	(Page 38)
Cue 6	As scene A CRICKET MATCH opens *Full general lighting*	(Page 43)
Cue 7	**Celia:** "Hope he'll be all right." *Lights dimmed slightly*	(Page 57)
Cue 8	**Miles:** "I've got a few things to say to him as well." *Lights dimmed further for a storm*	(Page 60)
Either *Cue* 9	As **Celia** and **Miles** exit *The Lights fade to Black-out*	(Page 66)
Cue 10	As scene A SENTIMENTAL JOURNEY opens *Full general lighting*	(Page 69)
Cue 11	As **Miles** exits *Black-out*	(Page 73)
Or *Cue* 9	As **Rowena** and **Miles** exit *The Lights fade to Black-out*	(Page 67)
Cue 10	As scene A 50TH CELEBRATION opens *Full general lighting*	(Page 75)
Cue 11	As **Miles** goes back into the church *The Lights fade to Black-out*	(Page 78)

A Game of Golf

To open: Full general lighting

Cue 1 to *Cue* 5 As above

Cue 6	As scene A GAME OF GOLF opens *Full general lighting*	(Page 81)

Either

Cue 7	**Miles** (*off*): "Oh, dearest life, joys sweet, oh, sweetest love …" *Black-out*	(Page 102)
Cue 8	As scene EASTER GREETINGS opens *Full general lighting*	(Page 105)
Cue 9	As **Rowena** exits *The Lights fade to Black-out*	(Page 108)

Or

Cue 7	**Irene:** "Do you hear that, Coombes? Red-handed." *Black-out*	(Page 104)
Cue 8	As scene A TRIUMPH OF FRIENDSHIP opens *Full general lighting*	(Page 109)
Cue 9	As **Celia** goes around the side of the church *The Lights fade to Black-out*	(Page 112)

A One Man Protest

To open: Full general lighting

Cue 1	As before	(Page 115)
Cue 2	As scene CONFESSIONS IN A GARDEN SHED opens *Full general lighting. Interior of shed lit*	(Page 115)
Cue 3	**Miles:** "Damn nearly. So are you." *Lights dimmed slightly*	(Page 118)
Cue 4	**Miles:** "Does that seem unreasonable?" *Lights dimmed further for a storm*	(Page 118)
Cue 5	**Rowena:** "I'll leave you in peace." *Lights increased gradually to full general lighting*	(Page 122)
Cue 6	**Miles:** "I'm never coming out, do you hear me? Never again." *Black-out*	(Page 133)
Cue 7	As scene A ONE MAN PROTEST opens *Full general lighting*	(Page 135)
Cue 8	**Celia** collapses on the grass in a faint *Black-out*	(Page 157)

Either

Cue 9	As scene A MIDNIGHT MASS opens *Moonlight effect lighting*	(Page 165)
Cue 10	As **Miles** exits *The Lights fade to Black-out*	(Page 169)

Or

Cue 9	As scene A SCHOOL CELEBRATES opens *Full general lighting*	(Page 171)

Cue 10	As **Miles** follows **Rowena** off *Black-out*	(Page 174)

Love in the Mist

To open: Full general lighting

Cue 1 to *Cue* 5 As in A ONE MAN PROTEST

Cue 6	**Celia** shakes her head and goes inside *The Lights fade to Black-out*	(Page 133)
Cue 7	As scene LOVE IN THE MIST opens *Full general Lighting*	(Page 177)
Cue 8	**Sylvie:** "... who else has been in there, do you?" *Lights dimmed slightly*	(Page 180)
Cue 9	**Sylvie:** "Come on." *Lights dimmed further*	(Page 185)
Cue 10	**Sylvie:** "Mucky little vandals and all, weren't they?" *Lights dimmed for mist effect*	(Page 187)
Either *Cue* 11	As **Rowena** and **Miles** exit slowly *The Lights fade to Black-out*	(Page 197)
Cue 12	As scene A WEDDING opens *Full general lighting*	(Page 199)
Cue 13	As **Rowena** exits *The Lights fade to Black-out*	(Page 203)
Or *Cue* 11	**Rowena** stands very worried *The Lights fade to Black-out*	(Page 197)
Cue 12	As scene A SIMPLE CEREMONY opens *Full general lighting*	(Page 205)
Cue 13	**Toby** locks the shed and walks away, still shaking his head *The Lights fade to Black-out*	(Page 209)

EFFECTS PLOT

A Cricket Match

Or
Cue 15   On opening of scene A 50TH CELEBRATION   (Page 75)
           Sound of church bells signifying a happy occasion, followed by
           the sound of singing

A Game of Golf

Cue 1 to *Cue* 4 As above

Cue 5   On opening of scene A GAME OF GOLF   (Page 81)
           Sound of birds singing. Pause. The birds cautiously restart
           singing

Either
Cue 6   On opening of scene EASTER GREETINGS   (Page 105)
           Sound of church bells signifying a happy occasion

Cue 7   **Miles:** "What the hell."   (Page 107)
           Sound of clock chiming

Or
Cue 6   On opening of scene A TRIUMPH OF FRIENDSHIP   (Page 109)
           Sound of church bells signifying a happy occasion, followed by
           the sound of a church service just finishing

Cue 7   **Miles:** "Well."   (Page 111)
           Sound of clock chiming

A One Man Protest

Cue 1 to *Cue* 3 As before

Cue 4   On opening of scene CONFESSIONS IN A GARDEN SHED   (Page 115)
           Sound of birds singing

Cue 5   **Rowena:** "I'm saying nothing. So there." *Pause*   (Page 118)
           Sound of rain pattering on a roof

Cue 6   **Rowena:** ". . . There's something in the shed . . ."   (Page 122)
           Rain stops

Cue 7   On opening of scene A ONE MAN PROTEST   (Page 135)
           Sound of birds singing

Cue 8   **Lionel** exits   (Page 153)
           Whine of vacuum cleaner as it is switched on and off

Cue 9   **Lionel:** "Right. Contact."   Page 154)
           Whine of vacuum cleaner being switched on

Cue 10   **Celia:** "She gave me eyes, she gave me—"   (Page 155)
           Smoke machine on

Cue 11   **Lionel:** "Triumph! Done it."   (Page 155)
           Smoke machine off

Cue 12   **Sylvie** picks up the piece of card   (Page 155)
           Vacuum cleaner off

Repeat Cues 8–12 for pp. 159–161

Either
Cue 13   On opening of scene A MIDNIGHT MASS   (Page 165)
          Sound of church bells signifying a happy occasion

Cue 14   **Miles:** "Oh, God, this isn't going to work."   (Page 168)
          Sound of church service starting with a carol

Or
Cue 13   On opening of scene A SCHOOL CELEBRATES   (Page 171)
          Sound of church bells signifying a happy occasion

Love in the Mist

Cue 1 to *Cue* 6 As in A ONE MAN PROTEST

Cue 7   On opening of scene LOVE IN THE MIST   (Page 177)
          Sound of the distant rumble of the sea and the bleat of an
          occasional sheep

Cue 8   **Sylvie:** "At the hotel."   (Page 188)
          Start the dry ice machine for the fog

Cue 9   Silence. The mist grows thicker   (Page 189)
          Sound of a sheep bleating. Mist increases

Cue 10   **Miles** strains his eyes to see into the fog   (Page 191)
          Loud sound of a sheep bleating

Either
Cue 11   On opening of scene A WEDDING   (Page 199)
          Sound of church bells signifying a wedding, followed by some
          pre-wedding organ music

Or
Cue 11   On opening of scene A SIMPLE CEREMONY   (Page 205)
          Sound of church bells signifying a happy occasion

Cue 12   **Rowena** unveils the plaque   (Page 206)
          Sound of applause

MADE AND PRINTED IN GREAT BRITAIN BY
LATIMER TREND & COMPANY LTD PLYMOUTH
MADE IN ENGLAND